Isaac Smith Homans, Robert Mushet

The coin book

Comprising a history of coinage

Isaac Smith Homans, Robert Mushet

The coin book
Comprising a history of coinage

ISBN/EAN: 9783337221898

Printed in Europe, USA, Canada, Australia, Japan

Cover: Foto ©Andreas Hilbeck / pixelio.de

More available books at **www.hansebooks.com**

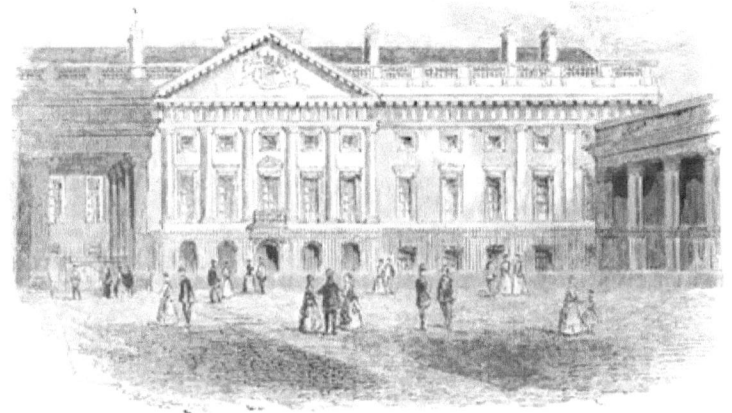

THE ROYAL MINT, LONDON.—Erected 1807–1813.

THE UNITED STATES MINT, PHILADELPHIA.—Erected 1829–30.

THE

COIN BOOK,

COMPRISING

A History of Coinage; A Synopsis of the Mint Laws of the United States; Statistics of the Coinage from 1792 to 1870; List of Current Gold and Silver Coins, and their Custom House Values; A Dictionary of all Coins known in Ancient and Modern Times, with their Values; The Gold and Silver Product of each State to 1870; List of Works on Coinage; The Daily Price of Gold from 1862 to 1871.

WITH ENGRAVINGS OF THE PRINCIPAL COINS.

———

PHILADELPHIA:
J. B. LIPPINCOTT & CO.
1873.

CONTENTS.

ENGRAVINGS.

Fac similes of the leading Gold and Silver Coins of
the UNITED STATES, FRANCE, GREAT BRITAIN,
MEXICO, PRUSSIA, RUSSIA,
and SPAIN.

A HISTORY OF COINAGE.

A HISTORY OF COINAGE IN GREAT BRITAIN,

With Preliminary Remarks on the Coins and Moneys of Account in Ancient and Modern Times.

BY ROBERT MUSHET,

OF THE ROYAL MINT, LONDON.

(From the Encyclopedia Britannica.)

MONEY is a measure of value and medium of exchange: coinage is the art of fabricating money.

So soon as nations emerge from a state of barbarism, when simple barter no longer suffices to meet their wants, they will invent some common or conventional measure of value by which to exchange their products and carry on their commerce. In the rude ages of society, cattle are said to have been the common medium of commerce; and among the patriarchs of old they were the measure of man's wealth and greatness. The armor of DIOMEDE, says HOMER, cost only nine oxen; but that of GLAUCUS cost a hundred oxen. In some countries, in former times, salt was the measure of value and instrument of exchange; and in others shells formed the circulating medium. But as the necessities of nations multiply, and their commercial transactions extend, they soon discover the inadequacy of these means, and will search for something of a more steady and durable character, which shall serve both as a circulating medium, as well as a medium of exchange with other countries trading with them. From a very early period metals, as possessing that character in a high degree, were chosen to perform these important functions. They are not only less perishable than other articles, but they can, without loss, be divided into any number of parts, and be united again by fusion: they can be hammered or rolled into plates, and moulded into any shape: and occupying less bulk than other articles, they are easily transported from place to place.

" Different metals (says ADAM SMITH) have been made use of by different nations for this purpose. Iron was the common instrument of commerce among the ancient SPARTANS, copper among the ancient ROMANS, and gold and silver among all rich and commercial nations. Those metals seem originally to have been made use of for this purpose in rude bars, without any stamp or coinage. Thus we are told by PLINY, upon the authority of TIMÆUS, an ancient historian, that, till the time of SERVIUS TULLIUS (550 B. C.), the ROMANS had no coined money, but made use of unstamped bars of copper, to purchase whatever they had occasion for. These rude bars, therefore, performed at this time the function of money."

Before the invention of coined money, the precious metals were exchanged by weight only; but as many obvious inconveniences attended that custom, as an initiatory step pieces of metal rudely shaped were stamped with their weight; and then by degrees the art of coining money was introduced, intended not only to indicate by the stamp of the sovereign authority the weight, but also the fineness of the coin. So long as copper and iron performed the functions of money and measure of value, probably the weight only was the test of value; but with regard to gold and silver, another element enters into their appreciation of as much consequence as the weight itself. The quality or fineness of these metals, by which the value is determined, can only be discovered by the laborious process of assay; and therefore (as ADAM SMITH remarks), before the institution of coined money, unless this tedious and difficult operation were undertaken, people must always have been liable to the grossest frauds and impositions; and instead of a pound weight of pure silver, might receive, in exchange for their goods, an adulterated composition of the coarsest and cheapest materials. To guard the public against such frauds, to facilitate exchanges, and thereby encourage industry and commerce, mints were established, in which pieces of metal of determinate weight and fineness were stamped by public authority, in order to declare the quantity and uniform goodness of the money so stamped, that it should pass from hand to hand without doubt or suspicion.

In early times these coins, or pieces of metal, constituted or denoted weights of different denominations; or, in other words, they expressed the weight or quantity of metal contained in them, as in the ROMAN *as* or *pondo*, which, when money was first coined at ROME, signified a pound weight of good copper, consisting of twelve ounces, as in our troy pound. So the ENGLISH pound sterling originally expressed not a coin exchangeable into 20 shillings, but simply a pound weight of silver of sterling fineness. The FRENCH *livre* likewise contained, in the reign of CHARLEMAGNE, a pound weight of silver of a determinate quality. And on the authority of ADAM SMITH, the Scots' money-pound contained, from the time of ALEXANDER I. to that of ROBERT BRUCE (1306), a pound of silver of the same weight and fineness with the ENGLISH pound sterling. ENGLISH, FRENCH, and SCOTS pennies, too, contained all of them originally a real pennyweight of silver, or 240th of a pound. The shilling also seems originally to have been the denomination of a weight, and not of a coin of conventional value.

As the transition from mere barter (by which one product of labor is exchanged for another), to the use of metals as instruments of commerce, indicates an advance in civilization; so the transition from the latter to the fabrication of coined money, however rude and inartificial at first, marks another progressive step in culture and refinement; while the various designs impressed on the coin, and the mode of manufacture, testify in nice degrees the slow advancement of society in art, taste, and ingenuity.

An inquiry, therefore, into the coinage of a country like GREAT BRITAIN, from the earliest times, possesses an interest apart from the subject itself as a mere antiquarian research, because it throws an indirect ray of light on the social condition of the people from age to age, and enables us to note the progressive steps of their improvement in taste, refinement, and mechanical invention, as well as to ascertain their comparative wealth and social comfort, indicated by the value of the necessary articles of life. The subject partakes not, indeed, of the true dignity and importance of history; but, in a less ambitious channel of research, it is not without utility and instruction.

In order to illustrate the necessary connection that exists between the social and political condition of a nation and its coinage, we need only to refer to the rude ill-fashioned coins of our semi-barbarous ancestors, and contrast them with the elegant and highly-finished specimens of the present day. The forge and hammer, and other manual appliances, are now superseded by mechanical contrivances of the highest order, which, with artistical design and beauty, co-operate to embellish and impart elegance to the coin of the realm. If this description be true of the external features of our currency, it is equally true with respect to the uniformity of its fineness; of more importance than even taste and beauty. The somewhat mysterious and alchemical ordeal of trying "by fire, by water, by touch, by weight, or by all or any of them," has found a less empirical and more certain substitute in the scientific art of assaying the precious metals.

Another pre-eminent advantage we have acquired by means of those mechanical contrivances referred to, is the vast rapidity with which money can now be coined and issued to the public—an element in the comparison of ancient and modern times of great significance to a commercial country, like GREAT BRITAIN, in which the currency is liable to be disturbed by external causes, and in which the public exigencies are as uncertain as they are urgent and imperious.

It is not too much to assert, therefore, that in a view of the coinage of GREAT BRITAIN we possess within certain limits a faithful record of the progress of its civilization. The view is of necessity a contracted one, but not the less true and authentic. Like the history of the customs, habits, and modes of life of a nation, it fills but a subordinate part, and aims no higher; nevertheless a knowledge of it is not only useful but indispensable. The coinage of a country speaks with unerring accuracy and truth; and so long as coins are extant to bear witness to barbarity or refinement, rudeness or taste, ugliness or beauty, clumsiness or elegance, we cannot, as in some other historical researches, be perverted by prejudice or deceived by ignorance. It is truthful, because it bears the impress of truth, and stands as a kind of living memorial of past generations. A rude, shapeless coin, with an effigy resembling the unformed scrawl of a child, is as certain a proof of the low state of civilization in art and mechanism as analogous imperfections would be in painting or sculpture; while a beautiful and elegant and well-finished coin speaks convincingly of corresponding ideas and tastes in the nation. And when such evidences of refinement prevail among the people, the state and excellence of the coinage will always afford a subject of pleasure and congratulation. In GREAT BRITAIN our coins have not certainly attained the highest degree of excellence, though for some time they appeared gradually approaching it; and we would fain hope that in future the step may be progressive rather than retrograde; though as a commercial nation we are too apt to be indifferent to such claims on our admiration as objects of taste call forth, however jealous we may be of the fineness of the coinage. It is indeed too frequently the tendency of modern ideas of economy, applied to public works, to give little encouragement to whatever concerns art and enterprise.

Though we have in this cursory manner pointed out some of the uses to which a history of the coinage may be made subservient, our design is to give only a brief outline of the subject, accompanied by a detailed description of the various operations and processes concerned in the fabrication of money, as well as some account of the recent changes introduced into the constitution and management of the Royal Mint.

Money in ancient times.

On the first landing of JULIUS CÆSAR (54 B. C.) on the shores of BRITAIN, he describes the inhabitants as a race just emerging from barbarism, and their money could not therefore be of a high order. Their use of money was circumscribed by their simple wants and limited commerce; and, according to him, it consisted of rude pieces of brass and iron rings, regulated to a certain weight, which probably were in use strung together, as the Chinese do at this day with their inferior money. He makes no allusion to coins or money of gold or silver, and it may be inferred none existed; for although foreign coins at one period circulated freely in BRITAIN, it is improbable amongst such a people as the ancient Britons that such should have been the case. Both STRABO and TACITUS, indeed, speak of the gold and silver of BRITAIN, as if indigenous to the soil; but as gold has not been discovered in any considerable quantity since that period, and as silver is not found except in combination with lead, we may conclude these writers received their information from mere hearsay or tradition. It is not probable that a people emerging from barbarism, without art or science, should have imported gold for the purpose of coinage; nor can we give them credit for that degree of skill and ingenuity necessary to separate the silver from the lead in their mines. So far from this being probable, we are informed that even the brass of which their chief money consisted was imported from abroad, though the soil was rich in copper; and that of iron they produced but a small quantity, being devoid of skill and enterprise.

TACITUS says, "BRITAIN produces gold, silver, and other metals to reward its conquerors:" but in refutation of this, Dr. HENRY, as well as others, remark, that if the BRITONS had any gold or silver amongst them, either coined or uncoined, when they were first invaded by the ROMANS, it was certainly unknown to their invaders, which it is not likely to have been if they came in quest of treasure, as SUETONIUS avers, who says that not the gold but the pearls of Britain, famous then, were the chief incitement to CÆSAR'S invasion. Writers on such subjects often deal in hyperbole, attributable to want of accurate information with regard to the countries they described. Thus, according to DIODORUS SICULUS, even GAUL was famous for the abundance of its gold, and the GAULS for their skill and dexterity in discovering, refining, and working that metal. We cannot believe the gold to have been the produce of their own mines, though it may have been common among them. Their coins are represented to be of pure gold, without any alloy of baser metals; and not only their coins, but their rings, chains, and other trinkets, were made of gold equally fine.

The first attempt of the ancient BRITONS to coin money, though not accurately ascertained, may be referred to a period subsequent to CÆSAR'S second invasion (53 B. C.); and we may suppose the appearance of ROMAN coins amongst them prompted them to imitation, however rude and unlike. As their coins consisted of gold and silver, as well as inferior metals, indicating, therefore, a rapid stride in refinement and civilization, some have, not without plausibility, conjectured them to be of foreign origin, imported in the way of commerce; because the initial letters stamped on them appear to have some reference to the names of certain Gaulish princes, mentioned by CÆSAR or TACITUS. Dr. HENRY observes on this curious subject—"It is not unreasonable to suppose that some of the GAULS, retiring from their country to avoid the ROMAN yoke, and settling in BRITAIN, which was still free after the retreat of CÆSAR, brought with them the art of coining money, in the same taste in which it was practised in GAUL, immediately before the conquest of that country by the ROMANS; when a new and more beautiful manner was introduced. This conjecture is confirmed by the remarkable resemblance of these coins to those of the ancient GAULS." But RUDING, who is always a truthful and generally an accurate guide in such curious researches, takes exception to this, and remarks, that "if we proceed to examine the coins themselves, they furnish no proofs to justify their appropriation to any country. The far greater part of them are without any legend; and on the rest are to be found only initial letters, or at most single syllables, which, by the ingenuity of antiquarians, have been compelled to express any meaning they have thought fit to adopt." It is singular, however, that a nation without any known mines of gold or silver, and without any commerce worthy of the name, whose inhabitants were exceedingly poor, and with whom the value of money was great, should have indulged in such a token of refinement as a gold currency. Yet certain it is, that a considerable number of the coins of CUNOBELINE have been preserved, containing his name, sometimes in full, sometimes abbreviated, with the name of the capital of his kingdom—CAMALODUNUM (COLCHESTER),—and so far we cannot question their appropriation to an ancient British king. The dominions of this petty monarch extended from the coasts of NORFOLK, SUFFOLK, and ESSEX, westward across the island to the banks of the SEVERN; and he is supposed to have reigned during the times of AUGUSTUS, TIBERIUS, and CALIGULA (26 B. C. to 40 A. D.). Possessing the wisdom to appreciate the refinement and civility of the ROMANS, this monarch seems to have introduced considerable improvement into his coins, forming them in a measure on the model of the ROMAN money. "On some of these coins," says RUDING, "the name of the monarch is given with a Latin termination, and the devices which are impressed upon others are evident imitations of the coins of AUGUSTUS CÆSAR. All the letters are plainly ROMAN. But it is in outward appearance alone that these coins agree with the ROMAN money of that period in which CUNOBELINE is generally supposed to have reigned, for in weight they are widely different. The cause of this variation from the prototype in so important a point cannot now be ascertained; but it seems to justify a suspicion that the weights were regulated in conformity with other British money then current: and in confirmation of this suspicion, it may be observed that some of the coins which bear CUNOBELINE and CAMALODUNUM resemble in type those which are usually attributed to earlier British kings."

But the improvements introduced by this monarch were destined to be of short duration; because a few years after his death, BRITAIN having again been subjected to the ROMAN dominion under CLAU-

DIUS (A. D. 43), and by his severity reduced to a mere province of the ROMAN empire, the native mints ceased to coin British money; and, agreeably to the ROMAN policy, an edict was issued to the effect that all money current should bear the imperial stamp.

Though the ROMAN money, which must have been abundant, continued to circulate in BRITAIN after the inroad of the SAXONS, about the middle of the fifth century, mints were subsequently established in various places, regulated by laws which the SAXON conquerors brought from the CONTINENT, and which differed in many particulars from those of the ROMANS. Some have indeed doubted whether these people, at their invasion of BRITAIN, possessed any knowledge of the art of coining money—supporting their opinions on the authority of TACITUS; but the best authorities on the history of our coinage controvert this hypothesis by the better testimony of the coins themselves. "Sceattæ," says RUDING of the SAXON coins so called, "are known of the early kings of KENT, some of which must have been struck within the sixth century; and there are others so similar to them in type, as to justify their appropriation to the same people, but which, from their symbols, were evidently coined before their conversion to Christianity, and were, therefore, probably brought with them from the CONTINENT." This distinguishing mark—the cross—is also wanting on the sceattæ of ETHELBERT I., king of KENT (A. D. 568), in whose reign the conversion of the SAXONS from paganism by the monk St. AUGUSTIN commenced.

Of the internal constitution of the heptarchic mints no records remain; but if we may judge by specimens of coins extant, the taste and mechanical skill of the SAXONS were scarcely superior, if at all, to those of the ancient BRITONS. Unlike these, they disdained to follow the ROMAN models (of which many beautiful specimens must have been preserved), but pursued a rude and barbarous method of their own; and hence their coins are found to differ in form, type, and weight, from those current amongst them at the same time. They are of equal weight and fineness with the later ANGLO-SAXON pennies. The coiners, or moneyers, as they are called, stamped their names upon the money; but the custom of adding the place of mintage was of rare occurrence, and almost solely confined to the ecclesiastical coins of CANTERBURY.

When the heptarchy was dissolved, and its different petty kingdoms united under one rule, the mints were regulated by laws framed in the WITTENAGEMOTE, or great council of the nation; and besides the royal establishments, the mints of YORK and CANTERBURY enjoyed the privilege of coining money; but it is conjectured, with much probability, that the dies were supplied by the crown, and that the sovereign participated to a certain extent in the profit.

The most ancient coins known to have existed amongst the ANGLO-SAXONS were the sceattæ, supposed to be the first coined by them in BRITAIN. They are of very rude and clumsy workmanship, while their weights vary from 7½ to 20 grains and upwards. By

the laws of Athelstan (924–940), the value of this coin is stated to
be such, that 30,000 of them equal L.120, and it was therefore less
valuable than a penny by a 25th part. Besides these, there appears
to have been also another coin of inferior denomination, worth a
quarter of a penny, but of what metal it was composed we are
ignorant.

The penny was the next coin made of which we have any knowledge. The word appears, says Ruding, in the laws of Ina, king
of the West Saxons, about the year 688, and is in a manner, therefore, consecrated by its antiquity. Its probable origin is derived
from *pendo*, to weigh; and if that etymology be admitted, it will
appear probable, observes the same authority, that "the penny was
not known to the Saxons before their arrival in Britain, but was
adopted, together with its name, at the same time that mÿnet, from
moneta, was introduced." The penny may be considered, therefore,
the ancient unit of our currency.

Of that coin, 240 are supposed to have been fabricated out of a
pound weight of silver, giving thus 24 grains to each, and making
the pound consist of 5760 grains, as at present. Hence the origin
of our *pennyweight*, equal to 24 grains, and the 240th part of a
pound. Twenty pennies to the ounce seem to have been also the
weight of the Norman coins of that denomination. "The legal
weight of the penny," Clarke observes, "continued through the
whole period of the Saxon government. It was always the 240th
part of the pound. Their laws, from the first mention of it to the
last, give it this uniform valuation." Nevertheless, there is evidence
to show that, at different periods, if not during the same period,
there were two pound weights in use, one as above, and another consisting of only 5400 grains troy, called the Tower pound.

There was likewise a halfpenny coined in silver, and probably a
farthing, or quarterpenny of the same metal; which will not appear
surprising if we consider the great value of money in those ages
and consequent low price of the necessaries of life. Besides these
subdivisions of the penny, there seems to have been also another
piece equivalent to the third part of that coin, which continued in
use as late as the reign of Henry I. (A. D. 1100). "But," says
Ruding, "even so small a coin as one-fourth of a penny could not
be sufficiently minute to answer the common purposes of exchange,
at a time when most of the necessary articles of life were to be purchased at prices so far beneath what is now considered to be their
value; when, for instance, in the reign of Athelstan, an ox was
sold for thirty pennies, and a sheep for one shilling."

Accordingly, the Anglo-Saxons coined inferior money of brass,
called *styces*, two of which were equal to one farthing. They had
also other moneys, or denominations of money, the exact nature of
which cannot now be determined; but of the sceattæ, the penny,
the halfpenny, the farthing, and styca (all undoubted coins) specimens remain, except the farthing. The mancus, the mark, the
thrisma, the ora, and other denominations in Saxon, Danish, and

NORMAN times, were probably like talents and shekels, weights of
current money, and not coins. In truth, the origin of all coin
denominations in early times were weights; for originally the precious metals passed by weight in commerce; and when for conve-
nience pieces of metal came to be stamped, these pieces were well
known weights of the country where they were coined. The smaller
coins were regular subdivisions of the greater, made into so many
for each pound.

The SAXON shilling differed from the NORMAN shilling of 12 pence
in value, six of them making only 30 SAXON pennies, or a mancus.

The Pound	Was a denomination of money only, and not a coin, and signified as many coins as were made out of a pound of metal = 5,400 grains troy.
The Mark	The same; an ANGLO-DANISH denomination, ⅔ds of a pound = 8 oz. = 3,600 grs.
The Mancus	The same; a weight equal to 30 pennies = 6 shillings.
The Ora	The same; DANISH subdivision of the mark, ⅓th or one ounce = 450 grs.
The Thrisma	Three SAXON pennies; not a coin.
The Shilling	Five pennies = 112½ grs.; do.
The Sceattæ, Penny, Halling, Feorthling, Styca	Real coins.

240 Pennies = 1 Pound	5 Pennies	= 1 large Shilling.
160 .. = 1 Mark	4 ..	= 1 lesser do.
30 .. = 1 Mancus	3 ..	= 1 Thrisma.
20 .. = 1 Ora	20 Sceattæ	= 1 Shilling = 5½ grs. troy.

We can discover no satisfactory evidence of the SAXONS having
coined money in gold; and if coins of that metal circulated amongst
them (as appears to have been the case), the inference is, they
came from abroad; as, for example, *bezants*, which sometimes occur
in ANGLO-SAXON transactions, deriving their appellation from BYZAN-
TIUM or CONSTANTINOPLE, and so of others. "During the existence
of the ANGLO-SAXON and Anglo-Danish government," says RUDING,
"there is reason to believe no other metals besides silver and brass
were coined in their mints." The use of the latter metal seems to
have been rejected by the ANGLO-NORMAN monarchs, and silver
became the sole material of coinage for a long established period,
until gold was introduced by HENRY III.

Ancient mode of coining.

Our knowledge of the mode of coining money in early times is
extremely imperfect; but all agree that it was rude and inartificial,
and so appears to have continued for many centuries. Neither the
ANGLO-SAXONS nor ANGLO-NORMANS were famous for their skill or
inventive powers. To both we are beholden for many excellent
laws, but not for those mechanical arts and contrivances which so

much now contribute to the wealth and glory of ENGLAND. And, therefore, it cannot but be esteemed a remarkable fact, that a nation which, above all others on the face of the earth, is distinguished for mechanical invention, and pre-eminent for those arts which elevate a kingdom in the scale of civilization—remarkable for its restless activity, enterprise, and adaptation of natural laws to useful purposes in almost every branch of science—should, in its infancy and even for ages after, have displayed none of these national characteristics. On the contrary, it seems to have been wholly indebted to the CONTINENT for those advantages. And when improved machines were introduced into ENGLAND for the coinage of money, the nation was slow in adopting them. Like our hand-loom weavers, the people opposed any invention that seemed to militate against the interests of manual labor, while at the same time they had little aptitude to turn the inventions of others to their own advantage.

The metal brought to the mints for coinage was, after being tried, reduced to sterling or standard by alloy when too fine, and refined if too low in quality; but by what means the latter operation was performed we remain in ignorance. The metal so melted was cast into small bars, and these were flattened by a hammer; and out of these fillets or plates, square pieces were cut of nearly equal weight, and then rounded at the forge. These were stamped simply by fixing a die in a block of wood, while another was used as a punch, and repeatedly struck with a hammer till it received the required impression. Money fabricated in this rude manner was necessarily imperfect, from the difficulty of always placing the two dies exactly over each other when the blank piece was between them, as well as from the improbability of a man being able to strike a blow with such force and precision as to make all parts of the impression equally perfect.

Even in the reign of EDWARD I. (1272–1307), it is recorded in the Red Book of the Exchequer, that the new money then coined was made in the following manner: first, the metal was cast from the metal-pot into long bars, which were cut with shears into square pieces of as exact a weight as possible, and these were with the tongs and hammer forged into a round shape; after which they were blanched, that is, made white by annealing and boiling, and afterwards stamped or impressed with a hammer to make them perfect money.

From this unskilful and imperfect process, scarcely any improvement seems to have found its way into ENGLAND until the introduction of the machines called the *mill* and *screw*, applied first to the coinage of FRANCE about the middle of the sixteenth century. The coining-press or mill was of FRENCH origin, the invention of which is generally ascribed to one ANTOINE BRUCHER, an engraver, who in 1553 first tried it in the palace of HENRY II., for the stamping of counters. It continued in use till 1585, when it was laid aside on account of its being found more expensive than the hammer coinage, and so remained until the year 1623, when BRIOT, a French artist, unable to persuade the government to adopt it again, came over to ENGLAND, where it was immediately put in practice at the mint, under the direction of BRIOT himself, who was appointed chief engraver. It was, however, abandoned for the reason assigned, until one BLONDEAU, forty years after, persuaded CHARLES II. to introduce it again into the mint, with some other mechanical improvements of his own invention; and eventually it created a revolution both in the manner of coining and in the appearance of the coins themselves. For the great change which then took place in the form and impression of the new money struck by this invention, gave it a decided superiority over the old coinage.

The *mill* and *screw* are generally conceived to be synonymous with the coining-press as one machine; but it is not improbable that two distinct machines were comprehended in that expression; the screw or mechanical power employed in giving the impression to the coins, and the mill or mechanism driven by horse-power, by which the metal was rolled instead of being hammered into plates. The introduction of a mere coining-machine would have been of little use without a corresponding improvement in other processes, and quite incompatible with the slow and clumsy mode of forging the metal formerly in use. The inference is in some degree corroborated by the reputed costliness of using the machine; for a coining-press will cost little more than the labor of working it. Before the introduction of steam-power, human labor was employed in driving the coining-presses; but probably animal labor was used in driving the rolling-mill, and hence the expense must have been considerable, if not compensated by the extent of the coinage.

Sterling, etc.

In the fabrication of money from the precious metals, it is a fundamental law that some particular standard should be adopted as regards the composition of the metal; and this was called by our SAXON ancestors *sterling.* The origin of the word, which has remained so many ages in familiar use, is involved in some obscurity; but it is generally understood to have expressed what we now call the *standard* of our silver currency, for it was never applied to coins made of the more precious metal, gold. While by custom and habitude we speak of pounds sterling, our SAXON and NORMAN ancestors signified by these words pounds in weight of coin of sterling silver. On this curious subject, it is remarked by RUDING, that in ENGLAND, and all over the continent of EUROPE, it designated the standard quality of our silver money; and it is a striking circumstance in the history of our coinage, that the fineness of the silver coins, which was expressed by that word, has preserved its integrity unbroken from the reign of HENRY II. (at the lowest calculation), down to the present time— a period of more than 600 years. This standard consists of 11 ounces 2 pennyweights of fine silver and 18 pennyweights alloy to the pound troy, or 18·222 dwts. Dr. HENRY, in his *History of* GREAT BRITAIN, says that the standard of ANGLO-SAXON money consisted at one time of 9 parts of silver and 1 of copper; but that must apply to a very early period, as there can be no doubt of the great antiquity of the *sterling*. If, to perfect the proposed decimal system of coinage, the standard were altered or reduced to $\frac{9}{10}$ths as respects silver, the coincidence would be singular.

Sterling silver remained in high repute all over the CONTINENT, because it was superior to any other currency; and even in ENGLAND the words conveyed for centuries the ideas of goodness and purity. And we may remark here that the gold coins of ENGLAND, from the reign of HENRY III., when they were generally introduced, to the reign of HENRY VIII., who debased their purity, were made of fine gold. This is a remarkable circumstance, because as gold in its native state is rarely discovered so pure, the existence for a long period of a coinage fabricated of that metal in a state of purity necessarily implies the knowledge of the art of refining, which must have been practised at a very early period. PLINY, indeed, says that in his time gold was refined by mercury, which mingled with it, but rejected all alloy, and the gold was freed from the mercury by squeezing both in skins, in which operation the mercury ran through and left the gold in a pure state. Some of the GREEK gold coins were also of great purity, as those of PHILIP OF MACEDON, and his son ALEXANDER THE GREAT, rivalled by those of the other princes and cities which immediately followed. Those of the successors of ALEXANDER in EGYPT were 23 carats 3 grains fine, and 1 carat grain alloy, which we give on the authority of JACOB in his book on the "Precious Metals." PINKERTON, on the authority of a FRENCH writer, informs us that the goldsmiths of PARIS, in assaying some gold coins of VESPASIAN, found in them no more than a 788th part of alloy. But though the GREEK and ROMAN coins attained so high a standard, their silver coins were not so pure. Those of the GREEKS were inferior to ours; and also the ROMAN of the earliest period, though slightly.

During the reign of HENRY VIII., the currency of both gold and silver was greatly debased and corrupted, as compared with that of former reigns. He fabricated coins of what was called crown gold, 22 carats fine, which was eventually adopted as the standard of our gold currency. Some of his silver money was so much depreciated as to contain no more than a third part of fine silver. But notwithstanding this nefarious and dishonorable proceeding on the part of the crown, the true, ancient, and venerable standard or sterling was always regarded by the people with a degree of affection and reverence somewhat similar to that which on great occasions they expressed in favor of their ancient laws and charters. So soon, therefore, as Queen ELIZABETH was firmly fixed on her throne, she listened to the reasonable demands and just representations of the country, and restored the ancient standard of our silver coin, which happily has remained untouched to this day.

The following table will show the variations of the standard from EDWARD I. to the reign of ELIZABETH. From the most authentic documents, it appears the standard remained uniformly the same through the long extended period from EDWARD I., and perhaps before, to the 34th year of HENRY VIII., when the proportion fell to 10 ounces of fine silver, and 2 ounces of alloy to the pound weight troy.

	Fine Silver.		Alloy.		Fine silver p lb.
	Oz.	Dwts.	Oz.	Dwts.	Dwts.
From EDWARD I. to HENRY VIII.	11	2	..	18	222
34th year HENRY VIII..........	10	..	2	..	200
36th...........................	6	..	6	..	120
37th...........................	4	..	8	..	80
1st EDWARD VI.................	4	..	8	..	80
3d.............................	6	..	6	..	120
4th............................	3	..	9	..	60
6th.....	11	1	..	19	221
MARY, and PHILIP and MARY....	11	1	..	19	221
ELIZABETH.....................	11	2	..	18	222
VICTORIA......................	11	2	..	18	222

In the earliest times, the silver coins were equal in weight and in tale; that is, each penny was a pennyweight of silver, or 24 grains. Such was, indeed, the theory; for the coins in reality rarely reached to the counterpoise of a pennyweight. The intention was frustrated either by the great imperfection of manufacture, or, as RUDING maintains, from design—as the irregularity was too nearly general to be attributable to accident. But may this discrepancy not in part be explained by supposing that at one period the pound contained only 5400 grains, which would give only $22\frac{1}{2}$ grains to the penny instead of 24 grains? No doubt also the profit of the *shere*, or remedy on the coin for errors of fabrication, sometimes offered too strong a temptation to our monarchs who looked to the coinage of money as a considerable source of revenue; while, on the other hand, the dishonest propensities of the moneyers, and the evil habit of clipping the coin, increased the evil. In consequence of the diminution of weight, arising from one or all of these sources, any considerable payment in coin required to be made by weight, and the deficiency made good. Exchanges were also instituted to change light money for that of full weight; and it was no uncommon artifice of our kings of old to call in the coins, in order that they might have the profit of the shere: and at such times the coins were taken by weight and not by tale, inflicting, therefore, great loss on the possessor.

It is observed by RUDING, that the professed standard weight of 24 grains continued for more than 200 years from the NORMAN conquest, that is, until the 28th year of EDWARD I. (A. D. 1300). From that time until the 43d of ELIZABETH, a period of full 300 years, the legal weight of the coins was progressively diminished; and yet notwithstanding the variations in the price of bullion which have taken place since the conclusion of her reign, the weight continued stationary for more than 200 years—that is, until the 55th year of the reign of GEORGE III. (1815).

We have already incidentally remarked, that anciently what we now denominate a pound in currency was in reality a pound weight of sterling silver; and if that assertion be correct, then it follows that silver relatively to gold is three times cheaper than it was in former times. A pound of silver was worth then 240 pennies, or say 20 shillings: now the market value is about 60 shillings, or 720 pence, and the mint price 66 shillings. In researches of this nature it is difficult, laborious, and often impossible to obtain full and accurate information of such particulars from existing records; but evidence of the interesting fact may be deduced from inferential or collateral testimony. For example, we have on record, so late as the reign of EDWARD III. (1327), that the pound of silver was coined at the rate of 25 shillings; and a pound of gold at the rate of only L.15; whereas in the reign of CHARLES II. (1660–1685) silver was coined at 62 shillings, and gold at L.44, 10s. If we assume the relative value of gold and silver to be as 15 to 1; then in the reign of HENRY I. (1100–1135) it was 9 to 1 only; and therefore nine pounds of silver should be esteemed the equivalent in exchange for one pound of gold. But in the calculation allowance ought to be made for the difference in the fineness of gold at the two periods.

Privilege of coining.

The privilege of coining money has always been claimed as a prerogative of the executive power, which was guarded with extreme jealousy. "The legitimation of money," says Sir MATTHEW HALE, "and the giving it its denominated value, is justly reckoned *in jura majestatis*, and in ENGLAND it is one special part of the king's prerogative." And RUDING observes, "As to the impression of the coins, the stamping thereof is the unquestionable prerogative of the crown, and it was in very few instances communicated to those persons on whom the privilege was conferred; for, in general, the dies were sent either from the Exchequer, or from the master of the mint in the Tower." The privilege implied that the authority of the crown was necessary to give legal currency to the coin; and although BLACKSTONE thinks it did not extend to the debasement of the coin to the injury of the people, no one can doubt that the power was not always legitimately exercised. In truth, it is only in the case of a depreciated currency that the king's proclamation is necessary to give legal circulation to the coin of the realm; and as a protection to his subjects, the tender is limited within narrow bounds.

In early SAXON and NORMAN times, royal establishments existed in almost every town of any importance for the coinage of the king's money. During the reign of ETHELRED, who died in 1017, it is said that no less than 38 mints were in various places employed for this purpose. The reason is not difficult to perceive. The communication between different parts of the country was extremely imperfect and hazardous, and it became necessary to institute mints and exchanges in provincial towns for the purpose of supplying the neighboring districts with money to carry on their commerce; but as communication was rendered easier, these subordinate mints and exchanges by degrees fell into disuse, till at length they all became concentrated in the metropolis, where one establishment has been found adequate for the supply of the whole kingdom.

After the NORMAN conquest, the number of mints was greatly reduced, so that in the reign of HENRY VI., who died 1461, the only mints in ENGLAND were at BRISTOL, CANTERBURY, COVENTRY, DURHAM, LONDON, NORWICH, OXFORD, and YORK; but in the reign of HENRY VII. (1485–1509), they were further limited to CANTERBURY, DURHAM, YORK, and LONDON. It is supposed by some, that in the time of ELIZABETH, when the currency was purified and improved, all the coins of the realm were struck in LONDON only, as no traces of other mints are to be found from that period; but it remains on record that in the reign of WILLIAM III. (1689–1702), when a great recoinage of silver took place, several local mints were employed along with the one in the metropolis in order speedily to complete that vast undertaking.

ATHELSTAN is said to have been the first monarch who enacted any regulations for the government of the various mints. In his laws, promulgated about the year 928, it is provided that one sort of coin only should be current throughout the kingdom; and he granted to various towns by name a number of coiners or moneyers proportionate to their size and consequence, and to all boroughs of inferior ranks one moneyer each. The provincial mints were under the control of that within the Tower of LONDON, from which, as paramount, the dies were issued, and for which the moneyers paid a regular fee upon every alteration of the coins. They seem also to have paid an annual rent (we presume for the use of the premises), which in the city of LONDON amounted to L.75—a very considerable sum at that time. The rents of the other mints, however, were much lower than this.

The chief use of the exchanges appointed in various places was to increase the facility of distributing the coins made at the mints, to change new money for old, to receive the coins when called in by the monarch when light, clipped, or defective, and for the purpose of purchasing bullion for the supply of the mints; for it appears our monarchs claimed the exclusive right of purchasing bullion, and appointed officers (to whom they delegated that branch of the prerogative), called *custodes cambii*, and *custodes monetæ*. It was the duty of these functionaries not only to exchange the current coins, but also to receive wrought plate and foreign coins according to their fineness; and as the exportation of the coins of the realm was prohibited, they furnished persons going out of the kingdom with foreign money in exchange for ENGLISH, and also supplied merchants and strangers coming into the kingdom with ENGLISH coins in exchange for foreign.

From these sources, and from the coinage of money, the crown derived a considerable revenue, which from time to time it sought to augment by means not the most scrupulous or honorable.

Ancient constitution of the mints.

The constitution of the mints in the earliest times of BRITISH histo   and the regulations applied to the coinage, are questions of antiquarian research, which will be deemed more curious than profitable. The materials for such an inquiry are extremely meagre and incomplete; for, according to RUDING, both the ANGLO-SAXON laws and DOMESDAY-BOOK are silent on the subject. They frequently mention the moneyers, but make no allusion to any other officers of the mint; though it is reasonable to suppose that the crown, whose prerogative it was to coin money, must have had some jurisdiction over those who were employed in the practical operations. It may be inferred that each mint was supervised by a head or mint-master, whether of the mint-proper or the exchange, who, receiving a certain rate on the coinage, paid those under him; while the moneyers, on the other hand, out of their allowance, paid the laborers under them. This may not have been the case at the earliest period of our history, but the custom may certainly be traced back to very remote times.

On the early SAXON coins are found, besides the names of the monarchs, those of other persons who are with great probability conjectured to be the moneyers, and not the mint-masters; because, on the later ANGLO-SAXON money the names of those officers frequently occur, with the addition of their title of office; and this fact, coupled with the silence of ancient records, has led RUDING to conclude that they were the only persons employed in the ANGLO-SAXON and early ANGLO-NORMAN mints. He thinks, too, this opinion is corroborated by the circumstance, that in the reign of HENRY I. (1100–1135), when the money was so much corrupted as to call for a sentence of most exemplary severity on the offenders, the punishment is said to have been inflicted upon moneyers only, without the least mention of any other officer. This was also the case on a similar occasion in the reign of HENRY II. (1154–1189). But if it be true that the moneyers were required to stamp their names on the coins as a token of their responsibility, and as an attestation of the integrity of the coin, the punishment of any other persons might not have been necessary. RUDING remarks on this subject, that "It should seem that the *reeve* had in the ANGLO-SAXON times some kind of connection with the mint or jurisdiction over it; for in the laws of CNUT it is provided, that if any person accused of false coinage should plead that he did it by license of the reeve, that officer should clear himself by the triple ordeal. If he failed to do this, he was to suffer the same punishment as the falsifier himself; which, in the same chapter of the law, is said to be the loss of that hand by which the crime was committed—without any redemption either by gold or silver. As it would scarcely be possible for the reeve to prove the falsity of such an accusation, it seems probable that his situation with respect to the mint was such as to make it his duty to super-intend the operations of it, and to prevent all clandestine practices." The same authority further observes, that after the NORMAN conquest the officers of the mint appear to have been in some degree under the jurisdiction of the court of exchequer, as they were ad-mitted to their respective stations in that court, and took before the barons the customary oath of office.

Mr. RUDING is unable to determine the exact period when it became necessary to place some superintending authority in the mint to prevent the bad practices of the moneyers; but adds, it is prob-able such an officer, if the *gerefa* or reeve were not a presiding func-tionary, was appointed between the twenty-sixth year of HENRY II. (1180), when the moneyers alone were punished for the adulteration of the money, and the third year of RICHARD I. (1192), when HENRY DE CORNHILL accounted for the profits of the cambium of all ENG-LAND, except WINCHESTER. This, however, appears to be con-jectural; for this the first warden of the mint was most probably appointed to collect the revenue arising from the seignorage charged upon the coinage of bullion, although the duties might also extend to the fabrication of the coins, with the view of preventing the mas-ter or the moneyers from taking any undue advantage of the crown or the public by the debasement of the currency.

In the reign of EDWARD I., about 1279, it appears all the mints in ENGLAND became consolidated under one master, TOURNEMIRE of MARSEILLES, who became personally responsible for the entire coin-age. Between him and the king an agreement, somewhat analogous to the future mint indentures, was entered into, by which an allow-ance was secured to him to cover all the charges of coinage. In this we have the germ of that system of contracts or agreements by which the mint was afterwards carried on.

But, according to RUDING and others, the mint did not attain its full constitution of superior officers until the eighteenth year of EDWARD II., *i. e.*, at the beginning of the fourteenth century; when an officer under the title of comptroller first appears, who delivered in his account distinct from those of the warden and master, as theirs likewise were from each other. "Thus they operated as mutual checks, and no fraud could be practised without the criminal con-currence of all those three persons." One of the peculiar duties required of the comptroller was, annually to make out a roll, called usually the comptrolment-roll, containing an account of all the gold and silver coined, and to deliver it on oath before one of the barons of the exchequer. It was always written on parchment, and formed a permanent record of the coinages of the mint.

The office of king's assayer constituted another check of even greater importance; for to this officer was confided the assaying of

2

all the bullion, after it had been melted for coinage, as well as the coin itself, and hence he became responsible to the king for the purity of the whole coinage. Persons exercising those functions are found on record in the reign of HENRY III. (1216–1272), but it is probable some such officer existed from the earliest period of the fabrication of money, although we are unable to define the precise date of his appointment. In after times the office, by degrees, acquired more consequence and authority, as no coin could be issued to the public without the sanction of the king's assay-master; and therefore, as RUDING remarks, he became "the sole guardian of the purity of many millions of money." And it may be added that, in modern times at least, the responsible duty has always been discharged with honor and fidelity, and to the great advantage of the public.

This ancient and honorable office was swept away, with the old constitution of the mint, in 1851.

Besides these, there was another officer of some importance in ancient times, who bore the title of *cuneator*, or keeper of the dies; and which still exists under the quaint name of "clerk of the irons." This office is supposed to have been hereditary; and the person executing its duties is said to have appointed the engravers of the dies, who were thus under his immediate cognizance and authority. He took charge of the dies as they were struck, accounted for them, and supplied the various local mints with dies. By right of office he claimed the broken dies as his perquisite.

Moneyers.

The moneyers were persons strictly employed in the fabrication of the coin; but in what manner they were paid, and what degree of rank they anciently held, are subjects open to dispute. It cannot be doubted, however, that as regards the operative branches of the mints, they were persons of some importance, though not necessarily of high rank. In times when mechanical knowledge was rare, and skill in any art deemed a mystery, such endowments were greatly valued, and gave importance to the possessor. After a careful analysis, RUDING is disposed neither to place them in the rank of superior officers nor of common workmen. They were probably employed under a superintending head, on the part of the crown; enjoying, at the same time, peculiar rights and privileges of their own. Without being exactly a corporate body, that is, having a charter of incorporation from the crown, as a company of mechanics they may have possessed some of that exclusive spirit which characterized the trades of LONDON. Theirs was a craft and mystery, which would naturally assume some of the consequence of other crafts. On various occasions they appear to have acted as a recognized body, and their petitions and remonstrances were listened to by the monarch as if they had rank and power separate from the general officers of the mint. This will appear quite natural and consistent to those who are conversant with the customs and usages in ancient times. Nothing can be more absurd than to measure those simple and primitive ages by the standard of modern society; and to conclude that the moneyers were only common workmen because they worked with their own hands, subjecting themselves to servile duties unbecoming officers of the mint, must only betray ignorance of history, and of the mode of life in former ages.

We have already observed, that they stamped their names on the coins as a mark of responsibility—a custom which prevailed at a very early period in this island; for, according to RUDING, they are found upon the money of EGBERT, king of KENT (827), which is the second in point of antiquity in the ANGLO-SAXON series, and must be dated about the middle of the seventh century. They were usually stamped on the reverse of the coin, but in some few instances they are found on the obverse, whilst the name of the monarch is removed to the other side. They amounted sometimes to 300 or 400; and it appears seven or eight moneyers were attached to each mint, employing laborers under them, when the exigencies of the case required it. In ancient times, it is said, they were compelled to march with the VICOMES when he went with the army, and were severely fined on refusal; and whenever the king came to a place where a mint existed, they were obliged to coin as much money as he pleased out of his silver. Hence they were sometimes called king's moneyers and are so entitled in a writ of HENRY III. And when one of them died, the king had a certain sum for a relief; and if he died intestate, his property devolved to the king. They paid a certain annual rent to the king, and also a kind of fine upon any renewal of the money for the dies, which were sent from the mint in the Tower. In some cases they had houses allowed to them rent free. And amongst their peculiar privileges, they appear to have been exempt from local taxation; for HENRY III., in the writ already alluded to, commands the mayor of LONDON not to disturb them by exacting tallages contrary to their privileges. On the other hand, on pain of disfranchisement and imprisonment, they were required not to distribute any coin till delivered into the office of receipt and assayed; they were enjoined to work whenever required; they were punished for false coinage, etc. According to SIR MATTHEW HALE, it was deemed treason if they made the coins too light, or not of the legal fineness.

The moneyers of modern times arrogated corporate rights and privileges, and a vested right therefore in the coinage of the country; but RUDING justly remarks, that they never were a corporate body exclusive of the other officers of the mint; for it seems in the reign of EDWARD I. the privileges which belonged to the moneyers alone extended to all the officers of the mint; and after various confirmations of succeeding monarchs they were afterwards granted and secured to them as a corporate body in the first year of Queen ELIZABETH. Nevertheless they were a very ancient body, as we have shown, and they enjoyed not corporate but prescriptive rights of a peculiar kind, which have now been abolished, along with other rights and privileges, by an act of the legislature.

It has been contended that the names marked on the coins were not those of the moneyers, so called, but of the minter, monetarius, or mint-master, who with his journeymen under him conducted the whole operation; but such a conclusion is contrary to the truth, and directly opposed to the evidence of history as well as the authority of the best writers. The number of such is sufficient of itself to disprove the assumption.

Seignorage.

Connected with the subject of coinage is the seignorage, or profits of coinage, which appear at one time to have formed no inconsiderable part of the revenues of the crown; and which were often levied without regard to principles of justice and equity, or the interests of the people. The seignorage was not always a regular, much less a moderate rate, but depended on the caprice, the avarice, or the necessities of the sovereign. And accordingly, under one pretext or another, the coin was frequently called in and renewed, merely to augment this pecuniary advantage. "The profits of the seignorage," says Lord LIVERPOOL, in his *Letter to the King*, " was so much considered by our monarchs as a certain branch of their revenue, that they were occasionally granted, whole or in part, either to corporate bodies for their advantage, or for defraying certain charges expressed in the grant itself. They were sometimes granted to individuals by way of pension," etc.

The seignorage was not properly a money charge for coining, but arose from a certain deduction made from the bullion coined, and comprehended—1st, the charge for defraying the expenses of coinage (included in a rate allowed to the master of the mint); and, 2dly, the sovereign's profit by virtue of his prerogative. RUDING supposes the former of these to have been almost coeval with the invention of coined money. But it is probable this deduction did not long remain limited to that simple charge, as the monarch by increasing it discovered a facile and profitable mode of enhancing his revenue. In the earliest mint account that is met with, says RUDING, namely, one of the 6th year of HENRY III. (1222), the profit on the coinage is stated to have been 6d. in the pound. This appears from the entries under that year of bullion coined in the mint at CANTERBURY, where the profit upon L.3898 is stated to have been L.97, 9s. 2d., which is exactly sixpence in the pound. Of that sum the king had L.60, 18s. 3½d., and the archbishop L.36, 10s. 10½d.; and the whole sum of L.97, 9s. 2d. is stated to be the amount of *exitus lucri*, that is, we presume, the clear profit, after all the expenses were deducted. And this agrees with the seignorage taken in the 28th year of EDWARD I., amounting to 1s. 2¼d. upon every pound, out of which the master of the mint had 5½d. for all expenses, and there remained 9d. clear profit to the king. But as this latter date is about 78 years subsequent to the former, it is not improbable that the seignorage had been raised during that time in the proportion of nine to six.

The profit of the *shere*, or the remedy, as now it is called, was also sometimes considerable. This was strictly an allowance made for unavoidable imperfections in the fabrication of the coin, as regards weight only, which from time to time was made instrumental to the illegal gain of the king and wardens of the mint. But as there is the same chance of an increase as of a decrease in the lawful weight, it is manifest no considerable profit could be derived from this source unless by a uniform and systematic coinage of the money under the weight, though perhaps within the remedy. Some idea of the extent of such profits may be formed from the confession of Sir WILLIAM SHARINGTON, who, in the reign of EDWARD VI. (1547–1553), was vice-treasurer of the mint at BRISTOL. He says, "that in three years he profited by the *shere* more than L.4000, answering to the king for the say and sheare 12d., and taking the profit of the rest to himself."

It is remarked, however, by SNELLING, in his *Silver Coinage*, that "it does not appear that our princes made any considerable advantage of this, until Queen ELIZABETH, in her fourteenth year (1572), allowed LONISON the master only eighteenpence, instead of fourteenpence farthing, in every pound, to bear all expenses; which obliged him to avail himself of the remedy, amounting to sixpence farthing in the pound, as appeared by the report of the commissioners appointed to examine into this affair; after which the queen empowered him, by commission, dated December 31st, in her twenty-first year (1579), to coin silver at 11 oz. 1 dwt. in fineness, and 60s. 3d. in the pound weight, which were delivered by tale, taking thus half the remedy, which amounted to about 6¼d. as before." It seems, however, that LONISON took a still further advantage, and *shered* the silver at sixty shillings and fivepence or sixpence, and the gold at L.36, 8s., and after at L.36, 3. 6d., while he paid to the queen's subjects only 60s., or L.36, by tale, by which means the public paid eleven shillings instead of four shillings for gold; and two shillings and sixpence instead of one shilling and sixpence for silver.

Toward the latter end of her reign, and during the first seventeen years of JAMES I. (1603–1620), the money was again paid out by tale, and therefore the profit of the shere came to the crown, which before belonged to the merchant. The latter monarch by a proclamation made a reduction on the seignorage levied on the coin.

At the great re-coinage of silver in the reign of WILLIAM III. (1689–1702) the money is said to have been *shorn* at something more than L.3, 2s. 3d. per lb., and made current at L.3, 2s.; thus allowing 3d. per lb. weight for the profit of the shere, or rather more than eight shillings in every hundred pounds of money.

With respect to times and usages more modern, RUDING observes, that "in the present mode of conducting the coinage, very nearly the whole advantage of the shere is given to him who brings bullion to the mint; for the coins are by the increased skill and attention of the moneyers found greatly within the remedies allowed. Thus it will appear, from a reference to the account of a trial of the pyx in 1799, that when the remedy allowed has been 1 lb. 3 oz. 18 dwts., the actual deficiency has amounted to no more than 1 dwt. 15 grs. If the whole advantage of the shore had been taken, it would have produced from the coinage of about five years, which was then tried, nearly L.80,000." As silver is coined exclusively by the crown, any profit of this kind goes to the benefit of the public; but with regard to gold, the importer receives the advantage, if any. For it should be observed that the remark of RUDING, on the increased skill and attention of the moneyers, is as applicable now as then to the coinage of the realm, while at the same time the remedies have suffered considerable diminution, so that the chances of gain and loss must be esteemed nearly equal.

There is, however, another more certain source of profit to the importer of gold into the mint for coinage, not alluded to by writers on the subject, and that is the increment on the assay, or on the fineness of the metal, which to that extent augments the standard weight, and consequently the value of his bullion. The assay report which accompanies the gold, and by which its market value is computed, does not according to usage come closer than one-eighth of a carat grain, or $7\frac{1}{2}$ grains per lb. troy; but when the importer carries his gold to be coined, another assay is made at the mint, much finer and more delicate than the trade-assay, in order to attain the exact standard, and he receives any benefit arising from fractional parts; in a word, he has delivered to him a greater weight of coined money than his bullion represented by the assay on which he purchased it. On an average, this profit is supposed to be equivalent to about one sixteenth of a carat grain $= 3\frac{3}{4}$ troy grs., or nearly 8d. per lb. weight. By a return made by the Bank of England, this gain, or increase of bullion, is estimated to have amounted to the large sum of L.59,262, 16s. 6d. on L.48,659,648 coined between 1816 and 1837.

By an act of CHARLES II. (1678) the seignorage formerly levied on the coin of the realm was entirely abolished; and it was ordained that whoever brought sterling silver, or crown or standard gold to the mint, should receive in exchange an equal weight of the current coin. And for the encouragement of coinage the king undertook to bear all the expenses, so that the importer received standard weight for standard, and sterling for sterling in coin, "without any defalcation, diminution, or charge for the assaying, coinage, or waste in coinage;" and to defray these charges the monarch was authorized to raise certain duties upon wines, spirits, etc., as, in the words of the act, "it cannot be reasonably expected that the expense, waste, and charge of assaying, melting down, and coinage, be borne by your Majesty.

1st *James II.*, *cap.* 7.

This important act was revived and continued by JAMES II. (1685) as a great benefit to the country, lest "this kingdom be deprived for the future of so great a good as it hath thereby for these years last past enjoyed;" and also by WILLIAM III., in whose reign (.689–1702) several acts were passed to improve the coinage, and punish those guilty of clipping the coin. In the reign of GEORGE III., at the instance of Lord LIVERPOOL, a seignorage was again put upon silver, and so much of the act of CHARLES II. as related to coining silver brought to the mint without charge was repealed, as well as a former act of GEORGE III., which required sixty-two shillings to be coined out of every lb. troy of silver.

14th George III., cap. 42.

By the act 56th GEORGE III. (1816), cap. 68, it was enacted that the pound of silver should be coined into 66 shillings, "of which 62 shillings per lb. shall be delivered to the importer, and 4 shillings retained for assaying, loss, and coinage;" and any surplus, after defraying these charges, was ordered to be carried to the consolidated fund. It was further enacted that old silver coin of the realm brought to the mint may be exchanged for its full nominal value in new silver coin; but in effect this act destroyed all temptation on the part of the public to coin silver, and consequently that branch of the coinage now devolves on the crown.

At the same time that the silver currency was depreciated (though coined of the legal standard of fineness), the legal tender was reduced from L.25 to 40 shillings, and so remains to this day. Formerly, gold and silver respectively were tenders to any amount; but, as the act declares, "great inconvenience having arisen from both these precious metals being concurrently the standard measure of value, and equivalent of property," gold coin was declared to be hereafter the only legal tender and measure of value.

7th William IV., cap. 9 (1837).

The amount realized by the seignorage was formerly retained by the master of the mint to defray the expenses of coinage, agreeably to the act, and the surplus paid to the public account; but by a subsequent act of WILLIAM IV. (1837), to regulate the financial arrangement of the mint, the seignorage was required to be paid into the bank to the credit of the consolidated fund, and the charges of the mint to be brought annually before parliament.

When the market price of silver is 5s. per ounce, the seignorage is equivalent to precisely ten per cent. (the cost of coinage being about 2 per cent.), and hence there is a very large apparent profit to the crown; but as the government is subject to the renewal of the silver currency, and to the great loss accruing from the wear of the coin, and consequent diminution of the weight, the gain from this source eventually cannot be considerable.

The following table will succinctly afford a view of the seignorage on gold and silver from as early a period as can be obtained:

TABLE TO SHOW THE SEIGNORAGE ON THE COINAGE, FROM THE REIGN OF EDWARD III. TO THE REIGN OF VICTORIA; AND THE VARIATIONS IN THE VALUE OF GOLD AND SILVER.

REIGN.	One lb. of Gold coined into	Seignorage of the Crown.	Allowance to Master of Mint.	One lb. of Silver coined into	Seignorage of the Crown.	Allowance to Master of Mint.
	£ s. d.	£ s. d.	£ s. d.	£ s. d.	£ s. d.	£ s. d.
30th Edward III....	15 0 0	0 6 8	0 1 2	1 5 0	0 0 9¼	0 0 6¼
Henry VI......	22 10 0	0 13 0	0 2 6	1 10 0	0 2 0	0 0 7
Henry VIII....	22 10 0	0 2 6	0 1 10	2 5 0	0 1 0	0 0 10
34th Do. ...	28 16 0	1 4 0	0 3 4	2 8 0	0 8 0	0 2 4
36th Do. ..	30 0 0	2 10 0	....	4 16 0	2 0 0	....
37th Do. ...	30 0 0	5 2 0	....	...	...	....
Edward VI ...	34 0 0	1 0 0	....	7 4 0	4 4 0	....
6th Do.	36 0 0	0 2 9	....	11 8 0	8 8 0	....
19th Elizabeth ..	36 0 0	2 7 0	0 1 6	3 0 0	0 1 6	....
25th Do. ..	36 0 0	0 6 0	0 4 9	3 0 0	0 1 10	....
27th Do.	33 0 0	0 7 0	0 5 9	...	..	....
43rd Do.	33 10 0	0 10 0	0 5 9	3 2 0	0 2 0	....
James I......	40 10 0	1 10 0	0 6 5	3 2 9	0 2 6	....
10th Do.	44 10 0	2 5 0	0 6 0	....	....	....
17th Do.	44 10 0	1 1 0	0 6 0	....	...	....
Charles I	41 0 0	1 1 5	0 6 5	3 2 0	0 2 0	....
1650 Commonwealth	41 0 0	0 15 0	0 2 5	....	....	....
Charles II ...	44 10 0	Nil.	0 2 5	3 2 0	....	....
George I...	46 14 6	Do.	....	3 6 0	0 4 0	....
Victoria......	46 14 6	Do.	....	3 6 0	0 4 0	....

As a collateral branch of the subject, it is of some interest to inquire how bullion was supplied to the mint to be coined into money.

Supply of bullion.

As we have seen, STRABO and TACITUS speak confidently of ancient BRITAIN having produced abundantly gold, silver, and other precious metals, the reputation of which afforded an incitement to conquest; while SUETONIUS ascribes to the pearls of BRITAIN the temptation as well as reward to JULIUS CÆSAR to visit the wild, barbarous, and inhospitable regions of the north. Probably both assertions are equally without foundation, originating in the fabulous character given to distant and unknown countries.

So far from the BRITONS being skillful in mining (who could not so much as clothe themselves with any art higher than barbarians), it is said that the brass or copper out of which their rude money was fabricated came from abroad, and that of iron they produced an inconsiderable quantity, though both iron and copper abound in ENGLAND and WALES.

It appears that from an early period silver was found in BRITAIN, which probably was extracted from the lead mines; for it is asserted that the art or process of separating silver from lead was discovered and practised in times very remote. But on this head our researches have not brought to light accurate information, and perhaps the inquiry would be deemed more curious than profitable.

In the reign of EDWARD I. (1272–1307), silver was discovered in DEVONSHIRE, probably combined with lead; and as there existed a great scarcity of bullion, the laws enacted with regard to mines were exceedingly strict in requiring the silver to be brought to the mints for coinage; and of the produce of the mines, the king claimed ½d, while the other ⅔ds were granted to the owner of the soil. At this period a considerable amount of foreign bullion appears to have been purchased for the mint, according to the account of WILLIAM DE WYMONDHAM, warden of the mint. The scarcity of the precious metals seems to have induced all manner of fraud to be perpetrated by those who worked in metals; and accordingly an act of EDWARD I. commands that all vessels of gold shall be assayed, touched, and marked, and that "none shall from henceforth make or cause to be made any manner of vessel, jewel, or any other thing of gold or silver, except it be of good and true alloy, that is to say, gold of a certain touch, and silver of the sterling alloy, and that none work worse silver than money. And that no manner of vessel of silver depart out of the hands of the workers until it be assaied by the wardens of the craft; and further that it be marked with the leopard's head. And that they work no worse gold than of the touch of PARIS." By the laws of EDWARD III. (1327–1377), goldsmiths are forbidden to melt sterling farthings or halfpennies to make into vessels; none are permitted without the king's license to convey gold or silver forth of the realm; no false money or counterfeit sterling is allowed to be brought into the kingdom to defraud the people; and to encourage coinage, "all people of what realm or dominion they be, may safely bring to the exchanges, and to no place else, bullion, silver in plate, vessel of silver, and all manner of money of silver of what value soever it be, and there receive good and convenient exchange." By another act it is rendered unlawful to exchange money, or derive any profit therefrom, except the king's exchangers; and "it is accorded, that the money of gold and silver, which now runneth, shall not be impaired in weight nor in alloy; but as soon as a good way may be found, the same be put in the ancient state as in the sterling." And it is required, that the moneyers and other wardens and ministers of the money shall receive plate of gold and silver by the weight, and in the same manner shall deliver the money when it shall be made.

In consequence of the great scarcity prevailing of halfpence and farthings of silver, it is enacted by a law of HENRY IV. (1399–1413), that a third part of the silver "brought to the bullion" be coined into these denominations, and goldsmiths and others are forbidden to melt them. And it is ordained by the same monarch, "that none from henceforth shall use to multiply gold or silver, nor use the craft of multiplication; and if any the same do, that he incur the pain of felony in this case."

Henry V.

A singular law of HENRY V. (1413–1422), ordains that every foreign merchant buying wool in ENGLAND to carry it abroad, shall bring to the master of the mint for every sack one ounce of bullion of gold, and for every three pieces of tin an ounce of gold, or the value in bullion of silver, upon pain of forfeiture. And that no English gold shall be received in payment but by the king's weight; a great part of the gold current being of light weight, and of inferior quality; and to remedy this great evil, the king offers pardon to all his lieges who shall bring the same to the mint to be made into new money.

Henry VI.

In the reign of HENRY VI. (1422-1461), it is enacted to the intent that more bullion be brought to the mint and coined, that the master of the mint "keep his alloy in the making of white money according to the form of his indenture." And he is required to strike, from time to time, half nobles, *farthings* of gold, groats, half groats, pence, halfpence, and farthings, for the ease of the people, according to the tenure of the indenture betwixt the king and him."

These and other laws up to the time of ELIZABETH (1558), were passed with the view of encouraging coinage, intimidating false coiners and clippers of coin, and securing bullion for the mint; but their operation must, to a great extent, have been ineffectual; for as respects coining, the inducement was such that no merchant would have taken his bullion to the mint except by compulsion, as he was not only subjected to all the charges of coinage, but likewise had to pay the king's seignorage—his gold or silver being returned to him in coined money, less these onerous exactions. The profit must, therefore, have been uncertain; but, probably from finding no ready market for his precious ware, and the laws being stringent against exportation of coin and bullion, he had no alternative but to take it to the mint. As the population and wealth of the country increased, there appears to have been difficulty in supplying the country with money, and hence the crown from time to time was induced to remit or diminish both the seignorage and the mint charge.

James I.

In the reign of JAMES I. (1603-1625), the lead mines of WALES were discovered by Sir HUGH MIDDLETON, and the silver from that source was coined into money.

With regard to gold, of which probably very little existed in ENGLAND in former times, it is said that none was coined until the reign of EDWARD III. (1327), when the first entry of its being brought for coinage remains on record. But we may more strictly date the coinage of that metal from the reign of HENRY III. (1216). As we previously observed, the gold of that period was coined at 24 carats fine, or pure gold, and so continued at that standard till the eighteenth year of EDWARD III. (1345), when it fell to 23 carats 3½ grs. and ½ carat grain of alloy; caused, no doubt, by the extreme difficulty, if not impossibility, of obtaining gold, by refining or otherwise, of a quality so superior; for it may be inferred that whatever may have been the process of refining pursued in those times, by fire or by water, there existed some method of purifying gold as well as silver, though no authentic knowledge of it has descended to us.

The high standard referred to, not exceeded by any other coins known, continued to prevail till the reign of HENRY VIII. (1509), who, to augment his revenue, corrupted the whole currency, and reduced some of his gold coin as low as 20 carats fine. He likewise coined crowns of gold of the standard of 22 carats fine, which subsequently took the name of crown gold, and which, in the reign of CHARLES II. (1660–1685), was made by law the sole standard of gold in ENGLAND, and so continues to this day. We find that money of both qualities circulated in ENGLAND till the reign of the latter monarch.

The difficulty referred to in supplying the mint with bullion now no longer exists, while the various expedients adopted to induce it to come to the mint are no longer necessary. When silver coin is required by the public, the master of the mint orders a supply of bullion, in bars or foreign coin, to be purchased in the market, which he pays for by a draft on the BANK OF ENGLAND. When gold coin is called for, the bank, on the contrary, sends bullion to the mint for coinage, and supplies the public exigencies; for it may be remarked that since the merchant was enabled by law to receive at the bank the fixed rate of L.3, 17s. 9d. an ounce standard for his bullion, the temptation to employ the mint ceased; because, as the mint price for gold is L.3, 17s. 10½d. an ounce, the difference was found scarcely sufficient to cover the loss of interest on capital.

Premium on Gold and Silver.

In modern times the market value of gold and silver has remained almost stationary for some years, and consequently the relative proportion of one metal to the other has scarcely varied. This fact proves that the supply and demand have been uniform; but now we have some evidence of disturbing causes, in the recent marvelous discoveries of gold in CALIFORNIA and AUSTRALIA, which may eventually destroy the equilibrium; and as the discovery of AMERICA and its treasures of silver gradually altered the relative proportions of the precious metals, so may recent discoveries in course of time effect a similar change. Remarkable, indeed, would it be, if the causes referred to were eventually to reduce the proportion of 15 to 1, the average of modern times, to 9 to 1, the proportion calculated by good authorities to have existed in the reign of HENRY I. The following table shows the approximate relative value from the reign of that monarch to that of VICTORIA; and it may be deduced from it, that the rise in the value of gold from the accession of JAMES I. to CHARLES II. was equal to 32 per cent.; and from CHARLES II. to GEORGE III.—a period of 135 years—no less than 39¾ per cent.

Relative proportion of Silver to Gold, from the reign of Henry I.
(1100) to the reign of Victoria (1837).

REIGN.	Years.	Proportion of Silver to Gold.		Standard of Gold.	
Henry I.	1100–1135	.. 9	to 1	24 carats.	
Henry III.	1216–1272	.. 10	.. 1	..	
Edward III.	1327–1377	.. 12	.. 1	23	3½
Henry VI.	1422–1461	.. 10	.. 1	..	
Edward IV.	1461–1483	.. 11 151·955	.. 1	..	
Henry VIII.	1509–1543	.. 11 59·220	.. 1	22	..
34th Do.	1543	.. 10 10·23	.. 1	..	
36th Do.	1545	.. 6 9·11	.. 1	..	
37th Do.	1546	.. 5	.. 1	..	
3d Edward VI.	1550	.. 5 5·33	.. 1	..	
4th Do.	1551	.. 4 788·955	.. 1	..	
5th Do.	1552	.. 2 394·955	.. 1	..	
6th Do.	1553 {	.. 11 117·955	.. 1	23	3½
		.. 11 1·10	.. 1	22	..
Elizabeth.	1558	.. 11	.. 1	..	
43d Do.	1601	.. 10	.. 1	..	
James I.	1603–1625	.. 12	.. 1	..	
Charles II.	1660–1685	.. 14 331·682	.. 1	..	
William and Mary.	1689–1702	.. 15	.. 1	..	
George I.	1714–1727	.. 15	.. 1	..	
56th George III.	1760–1820	.. 14 288·1000	.. 1	..	
Victoria.	1837	.. 15	.. 1	..	

Materials of Money.

Among the ANGLO-SAXONS, silver and brass formed the material of money coined by them, though foreign gold circulated to a limited extent; but, says RUDING, "the use of the latter appears to have been rejected by the ANGLO-NORMAN monarchs, and silver became the sole material of coinage for a long-extended period, until the more precious metal, gold, was introduced into the mint by HENRY III. (1216). The penny was consequently the lowest coin until the reign of EDWARD I. (1272), and afterwards farthings were coined in silver, and so continued as long as the increased value of silver allowed, but at length their size of necessity so much diminished, that the making of them ceased in the reign of EDWARD VI. (1547). Gold and silver, therefore, formed the only coins during several centuries, to the great inconvenience of the people, who required for their ordinary purchases money of a lower denomination; and it has been conjectured that some kind of metallic tokens circulated, as a substitute; for it is not possible a nation could carry on the daily transactions of life without some medium of exchange proportionate to the low value of all the necessaries of life.

We find that JAMES I. (1607–1625), to remedy this evil, caused tokens of brass and copper to be struck as a substitute for the farthing, but at a value so much inferior to the rate at which they were issued, that they rapidly sunk into contempt.

CHARLES II. (1665-1672), among other great improvements, has the merit awarded to him of introducing a new coinage of copper, which was issued under certain limitations. In the year 1684 it appears some coins were also fabricated of tin; and JAMES II. coined others of gun-metal and pewter.

Recoinage of Silver.

After the changes effected in the mint in the reign of CHARLES II. (1660-1685), by the adoption of improved mechanical contrivances—which caused a revolution in the various processes of coinage, and a change in the duties of the moneyers and others engaged in the mint, as well as a great reduction in the rate per pound paid to the master of the mint, and to the moneyers, by reason of the rapidity and economy resulting from the new machinery—we have no great event to record till the reign of WILLIAM III. (1689-1702), when a great recoinage of silver took place, and when some important laws were enacted for the improvement and regulation of the currency. Notwithstanding the recoinage of the money of the commonwealth under CHARLES II., and the act for the encouragement of coinage, the silver money at that period appears to have been greatly depreciated; partly by base money circulating with the silver, but chiefly by a great loss of weight caused by the dishonest practice of clipping and defacing the coin of the realm. The extent of the evil may be estimated by the fact, that no less a sum than L.7,000,000 sterling was coined in silver, the expenses of which were defrayed out of certain duties levied for that purpose. This undertaking being beyond the capacity of the mint in London, other establishments were instituted or revived, so that the coinage should keep pace with the money brought in to be exchanged. "The king," says HUME, "ordered mints to be erected in YORK, BRISTOL, EXETER, and CHESTER, for the purpose of the recoinage, which was executed with unexpected success; so that in less than a year, the currency of ENGLAND, which had been the worst, became the best, coin in EUROPE."

The state of the coin had previously become a national grievance, so intolerable, that it could not escape the attention of parliament; and accordingly a committee of the commons' house was appointed to deliberate on the state of the nation with respect to the currency. A recoinage was strenuously recommended by Mr. MONTAGUE, who acted on this occasion by the advice of Sir ISAAC NEWTON (1700-1710); but vehement opposition was made to that proposal by a large section of the house and of the people. "Another question arose," says HUME, "whether the new coin in its different denominations should retain the original weight and purity of the old, or the established standard be raised in value. The famous LOCKE engaged in this dispute, against Mr. LOWNDES, who proposed that the standard should be raised. The arguments of Mr. LOCKE were so convincing, that the committee resolved the established standard should be preserved with respect to weight and fineness. They likewise resolved, that the loss accruing to the revenue from clipped money should be borne by the public." To meet this, a tax on glass windows was subsequently raised to the amount of L.1,200,000.

In order to facilitate and hasten the exchange of coin, a reward of 5 per cent. was offered to all who should bring in either milled or broad unclipped money, to be applied in exchange of the clipped money throughout the kingdom. A reward of 3d. an ounce was also offered to all persons who should bring wrought plate to the mint to be coined.

A bill was likewise brought in for taking off the obligation and encouragement for coining guineas for a certain period. "Upon which," says HUME, "the commons proceeded to lower the value of this coin; a task in which they met with great opposition from some members, who alleged that it would foment the popular disturbances. At length, however, the majority agreed that a guinea should be lowered from 30s. to 28s., and afterwards to 26s. Eventually a clause was inserted in the bill for encouraging people to bring plate to the mint, settling the price of a guinea at 22s.; and it naturally sunk to its original value of 20s. 6d."

In the great controversy on the restoration of the currency at that time, Mr. LOWNDES, who differed from Mr. LOCKE, wished to execute the coinage at a rate per ounce conformable to the market price of silver, so that the new currency, we apprehend, should form the standard of value; overlooking the fact, that the market price exceeding the mint price arose from the deficiency in the weight of those coins by which silver was bought and sold. "Mr. LOCKE," says a writer on the subject, "with that acuteness for which he was so justly esteemed, contended that if 5s. 2d. of the coin weighed an ounce, that would necessarily be the market price of silver; and that its high price arose from 6s. 4d. of the then currency containing no more than an ounce of standard silver. Consequently, if the coinage were executed at a higher rate than the standard of the 46th of ELIZABETH, or 5s. 2d. an ounce, it would be done at the expense of that justice and integrity between the government and the people which no government would sanction that regarded the rights of personal property. Mr. LOCKE's arguments were so decidedly just, and so convincing, that the government carried the whole nation with them in the measure, though it was heavily felt, owing to the exhausted state of the country, after the long and expensive war it had been involved in."

Despite LOCKE's arguments, and the policy founded upon them, soon after the great coinage was completed the market price exceeded the mint price of silver; the consequence of which was the rapid disappearance of the new coins, which found their way to the melting-pot, and were sold in bars in the market. Hence before the year

1717 the greater portion of the recoinage had disappeared from circulation, to the detriment of the realm.

Sir Isaac Newton, in September, 1717, delivered in his report on the subject to the Lords of the Treasury, in which he gives it as his opinion that gold was considerably overrated in the mint with respect to silver; and in consequence of this report, the guinea was by proclamation declared current at 21s. This reduction helped the relative proportion of gold to silver to approximate nearer to those of the market prices; and as the avowed intention of Newton's report was to give that rise in value to the silver coin which would protect it from being melted down, it appears to have answered its purpose, but only in degree. For "though the recommendation in Sir Isaac Newton's report," says the above authority, "was carried into effect by making the guinea current at 21s., yet it did not restore silver to its function as the standard of our money, and this because the current value was not made lower. Sir Isaac Newton seemed aware of this himself, and recommended that 10d. or 12d. should be taken from the guinea, instead of 6d. This, however, was not done; and as the rate of 21s. to the guinea, the proportion of standard gold to silver at the mint, was as 15·07 to 1, the proportion of the market (as we find by the prices of gold and silver) was about 14·50 to 1—which constitutes a difference of about 3 per cent., gold being still thus much rated above its value to silver; and consequently not only was no silver coined, but the good and heavy coins were still melted for the higher price they brought in the state of bullion."

No other legislative measure having been taken than the one referred to, and the market proportion of gold to silver having seldom afforded any encouragement to the public to coin silver, we can have no difficulty in assigning a satisfactory reason for the degraded state of our silver currency during the last century, and up to 1815.

Recoinage of Gold, 1774.

In the year 1774 (George III.) and onwards, there was a general recoinage of the gold currency, which forms another prominent feature in the history of the mint. The professed object of this undertaking was the reformation of the currency, by withdrawing the light and defective coins then in circulation; but the real motive was to prevent, if possible, the new and heavy coins issued from the mint being melted down and sold as bullion. For, by reference to the prices paid by the Bank of England for gold, it appears that 80s. an ounce was the market value, while, at the same time, £..4 of the gold coin then circulating would not weigh more than one ounce. The holders of bank-notes demanded in payment new and heavy coins, which were immediately turned into bullion, and sold at the rate of 80s. an ounce; and this being done on an extensive scale, the bank was compelled to have annually a large coinage of gold to meet the demand. To remedy this inconvenience, the recoinage was undertaken and completed, and it had the effect anticipated; for the price of gold since that period has rarely ever exceeded, but has generally been under the mint price. In truth, as the price at which the bank purchases gold is fixed by act of parliament, and as the bank is compelled to buy all gold tendered to it at the price of 77s. 9d. an ounce standard, some naturally enough question the fact that we have any market price for gold bullion in ENGLAND. There cannot be a doubt, however, but for that law the price of gold would have fluctuated as other things, according to the supply and demand; and it cannot but be deemed a great benefit to commercial interests to have, by means so simple, a ready and constant market for their bullion, at a price regular and certain.

Political economists disagree as to the cause of the high price of gold previously to the recoinage referred to. That eminent authority, ADAM SMITH, offers the following solution:—"By issuing too great a quantity of paper, of which the excess was continually returning, in order to be exchanged for gold and silver, the BANK OF ENGLAND was for many years together obliged to coin gold to the extent of between eight hundred thousand and a million a-year, or at an average about eight hundred and fifty thousand pounds. For this great coinage, the bank, in consequence of the worn and degraded state into which the gold coin had fallen a few years ago, was obliged frequently to purchase bullion at the high price of L.4 an ounce, which it soon after issued in coin at L.3, 17s. 10½d. an ounce, losing in this manner between 2½ and 3 per cent. upon the coinage of so very large a sum. Though the bank, therefore, paid no seignorage, though the government was properly at the expense of the coinage, this liberality of government did not prevent altogether the expense of the bank." Upon this passage RICARDO justly remarks, "On the principle above stated it appears most clear, that by not re-issuing the paper thus brought in, the value of the whole currency, of the degraded as well as the new gold coin, would have been raised, when all demands on the bank would have ceased," or in other words, the price of gold would have fallen to its mint price.

During the period of these important transactions the constitution of the mint remained unaltered. The various mints throughout the country appear to have fallen into disuse in the reign of ELIZABETH, but some of them were revived and reorganized by WILLIAM III. in order speedily to accomplish the great recoinage of silver during his reign. Subsequently to that period the provincial mints were abolished or consolidated with that in the Tower of London.

In the year of 1670, the CROWN, while it continued his salary to the master of the mint, restored to him further the contract for melting. On the other hand, an agreement was entered into between the master and company of moneyers, according to ancient custom, by which a rate per pound, graduated to each denomination of money coined, was allowed to the latter.

In 1702 the public appear to have assumed the expense of melting the bullion into bars in order to bring the metal to standard, provided it was near to the standard when imported into the mint ; whereas previously, it is thought, this preliminary expense was borne by the individual merchant or importer.

In 1799 the government withdrew altogether from the master of the mint the lucrative contract for melting, and wisely vested it in a subordinate and responsible officer, who, assuming all risk and waste, on consideration of certain *pro rata* allowances, relieved the CROWN, the master, and the public, from all responsibility whatsoever ; an arrangement obviously founded on the dictates of experience, as it is also consonant with the principles of common sense.

In the course of this century, the master, who had previously been a permanent officer supervising the coinage, and possessing therefore a practical knowledge of the business, gradually became a ministerial officer, and quitted office on any change of government. The duties of the office were in this manner circumscribed, and more nominal than real ; the *de facto* government of the mint devolving on a deputy whose office was permanent.

On the 7th February, 1798, his majesty GEO. III., by an order in council, appointed a committee of his privy-council " to take into consideration the state of the coins of this kingdom, and the present establishment and constitution of his Majesty's mint ; " and the result of their inquiries and deliberation was to advise the erection of a new mint, with improved machinery. This was carried into effect in or about the year 1810.

The old mint, which had existed in the Tower for centuries, was removed to a more spacious building on Tower Hill ; and the celebrated engineers, Messrs. BOULTON and WATT, of Soho, furnished it with engines and machinery of a character superior to any thing known at that time in connection with the fabrication of money. The steam-engine was substituted for horse-power, and most of the operations carried on slowly by manual labor were with greater speed and perfection effected by the agency of those ingenious contrivances, nice adaptations, and superior power, called forth by mechanical skill and invention.

Almost simultaneous with the erection of a new and more powerful mint, a new constitution and indenture were given to it in 1815, founded on a report drawn up and presented to the committee of the privy-council by Mr. W. WELLESLEY POLE (afterwards Lord MARYBOROUGH), who had been appointed master of the mint in the preceding year. These changes were rendered in some degree necessary by the circumstances of the case : by the enlarged establishment ; the increased duties of the officers ; and the necessity of a recoinage of the silver currency, as well as the introduction of new denominations of gold coin. The new organization of the mint consisted principally of an adaptation and enlargement of the old constitution, which, like that of the state, had grown up by degrees, and expanded with the wants of the public ; and like the constitution of the state, it exhibited, on minute examination, some anomalies and contradictions incidental to its origin. To the same cause may be attributed

3

its apparent want of simplicity, and clear definition of duties; but as it was found by experience adequate to encounter the greatest undertakings, and fully supply the public demands—in times, too, of great difficulty and danger—we may justly infer that if it were found wanting in latter times, the fault should rather be attributed to the management than to the constitution.

During the fourteenth and fifteenth centuries, we have it on record that a mint-board was constituted with legislative and executive functions, composed of the three heads of offices, the warden, the master, and comptroller. This governing body was enlarged by Lord MARYBOROUGH, and consisted of the master *ex officio*, his deputy virtually the president, the comptroller, the king's assay-master, the superintendent of machinery and clerk of the irons, and, finally, the king's clerk and clerk of the papers, who acted as secretary to the board.

In the operative departments, new agreements or contracts were entered into between the master on the one part, and the moneyers, and the melter and refiner, on the other; the latter office being judiciously separated from that of the deputy-master and his duties, with which it had been previously conjoined. These agreements, besides specifying the performance of duties and other obligations, secured certain fixed rates of payment to the moneyers and melter, for each denomination of coin delivered into the office of receipt, and in which rates were comprehended the repairs of machinery, the supply of labor and materials, as well as the waste or loss accruing in the various processes of coining and melting. And for the safety of the CROWN and master of the mint, large securities were required from the persons holding those responsible offices.

The fundamental principles had in view by Lord MARYBOROUGH, in thus remodeling the constitution and management of the mint in 1815, were a system of checks so perfect and complete, as to render fraud impossible; an arrangement with the moneyers and melter, which fully secured the public against all risk; responsibility in each distinct office; and greater efficiency and despatch as regards the coinage. These important changes having been satisfactorily accomplished, the great recoinage of silver commenced in 1816. An act was passed to call in the debased coin then in circulation; and it was enacted that the full nominal value in new money should be exchanged for the old silver brought to the mint, and the treasury was authorized to appoint receivers at various places throughout the kingdom.

The act of CHARLES II. as to coining silver brought to the mint without charge—the 7th and 8th of WILL. III. (1696–1697) relative to the weight and fineness of silver coin, under the mint indenture—and so much of the 14th of GEO. III. (1774), cap. 42, as requires 62 shillings to be made out of the pound troy of silver—were repealed; and it was enacted, that the pound troy of standard silver should henceforth be coined into 66 shillings, of which 62 shillings shall be delivered to the importer, and 4 shillings retained for assaying, loss, and charges of coinage; the surplus, if any, to be carried to the consolidated fund. The act, making silver a tender to L.25, and afterwards by weight, was also repealed, and the tender of this depreciated currency was limited to 40s.

The effect of these acts was, first, to withdraw any inducement to the public to coin silver; and secondly, to circumscribe the circulation of the currency in silver to the country, where it became a mere token exchangeable for a limited amount of gold. Formerly, gold and silver respectively were legal tenders to any amount; but by the 56th of GEO. III., cap. 68 (1816), gold coin is declared to be hereafter the only legal tender; and so it continues.

In the year 1817 the first sovereigns were struck at the new mint, and in process of time entirely superseded the old guinea coinage. The mint price of gold being L.3, 17s. 10½d. an ounce, sovereigns were coined at the rate of L.46, 14s. 6d. to the pound troy.

Concurrently with the erection of the new mint in LONDON (1807-1813), and the powerful machinery which enabled the government to prosecute with rapidity and success large coinages of both silver and gold, a refinery was established, as a necessary appendage to supply the mint with both metals in a fine state, to counterbalance the baseness of the gold and silver then brought to the mint, so as to bring them up to standard purity. This branch of business proved to be a great undertaking of itself, and for some years was extensively carried on at great cost to the public. Coarse silver was refined on the test by means of lead, and gold by the agency of nitric acid. But circumstances of a peculiar character were secretly operating to destroy the necessity for refining, for the special purpose referred to; because these tended to diminish the amount of coarse metal in the market, or rather to supply steadily large amounts of fine gold and silver.

In FRANCE a new and far cheaper process had been discovered and carried on clandestinely for many years, for refining both gold and silver by means of sulphuric acid, in large vessels of platinum; and a lucrative return for capital was found in simply extracting small portions of gold from silver, and silver from gold, which would not have yielded any profit under the old and expensive system. In consequence of this our sovereigns, alloyed partly with silver, were conveyed to PARIS and refined for the sake of the silver they contained, while all silver supposed to hold gold in combination was bought up in the ENGLISH market. To counteract in degree the exportation of gold coin, a refinery on the FRENCH system was established in the royal mint in 1829, as an experiment, in the first instance, at the sole expense of Mr. G. F. MATHISON, then melter and refiner; but subsequently he was indemnified for his outlay, and the refinery was adopted by the government under certain conditions. Mr. MATHISON was induced to undertake this meritorious work by the urgent persuasion of Mr. HERRIES, the then master of the mint, who properly conceived that no public establishment in this country should, on mere economical grounds, be so incomplete as to be unable to meet all requirements of a public nature, or lag behind in the general progress of science and art. By such undertakings, when liberally supported, enterprise is encouraged, skill called forth, and science promoted. But the government, influenced by an injudicious economy, which tends to destroy all public spirit, have judged differently; and the refinery, along with the engraving department in the mint, has been abolished as a public establishment.

In the year 1837, a committee of the HOUSE OF COMMONS was appointed, at the instance of Mr. JOSEPH HUME, to inquire into the management and expenses of the mint, with the view of reforming the alleged abuses and corruption of that establishment; but although very voluminous evidence was taken, no report was presented, in consequence of the abrupt termination of the sessions of parliament. The desire of reform was then most urgent; the abuses of the mint so great as to demand instant remedy; the expenses so extravagant as to require immediate attention ;—yet so fitful was this zeal for reform, that ten long years were allowed quietly to elapse before the inquiry was resumed.

Recoinage of light Gold Coin.

In 1842 commenced a large recoinage of light gold coin, which fully employed the machinery of the mint for a considerable period of time. This expensive undertaking was forced upon the government in consequence of the complaints and representations of the public, a great part of the gold currency having by wear fallen below its legal current weight. As the standard of value, and medium of exchange, the defective character of the gold coin influenced the foreign exchanges to the extent of its depreciation, and to the prejudice, therefore, of the foreign merchant. Moreover, the law making coin under the current weight no longer a legal tender, the embarrassment of the public would have been great if a speedy remedy had not been applied to meet the evil. The law of the case, therefore, was proclaimed and put in force; but the government on this occasion, instead of throwing the onus or loss on the individual holders of the light and defective coin, undertook to receive it from the BANK OF ENGLAND within a definite period, and recoin it at the public expense, returning new sovereigns weight for weight. The amount so withdrawn from circulation exceeded L.11,000,000; and the treasury not only bore the ordinary charges of coinage on this large amount, but the loss of weight, the waste in melting, the depreciation of standard, and the cost of assays. Notwithstanding this extensive purification of the currency, the evil was found to be only mitigated, not remedied; and the bank was authorized for the future to receive all light gold coin tendered at a fixed price per ounce (instead of sending it to the mint), which being thus withdrawn from circulation, is periodically melted down into bars, and treated simply as bullion. This process going on from time to time, if strictly adhered to, must eventually purify the currency, maintain the standard value of our coin, and therefore efface the reproach affixed to it here

and abroad. The renovation of the silver currency is also proceeding, though by slow degrees; but, as its circulation is limited to the
country, and the tender fixed by law to 40s., the evil arising from
its depreciation is of secondary importance.

New constitution of the British Mint.

We have now arrived at a period in the history of the mint and
of the coinage of considerable importance to the country, which comprehends a fundamental change in the constitution of the mint, and
a new organization of its management. The thirst for change, which
distinguishes this era, and marks all public measures, is not appeas-
ed by a simple reform; a revolution, radical and complete, can alone
satisfy this restless, if not dangerous, desire. It is easy to destroy
what is ancient, reared by the wisdom and sagacity of our forefath-
ers; but it needs wise men to construct and build up again. In the
zeal for change, conformable to what are called progressive ideas,
and the haste and imperfection incidental to modern legislation, we
lose sight of those precautions and prudential checks deemed by our
ancestors necessary to such an establishment as a mint. What fate
was to the ancients, economy is to the moderns; it overrules all by
an iron despotism, and subjects every principle to its sway. Before
it the appeal of reason is unheard, the dictates of judgment disregarded, and the teaching of experience despised. But it is not a
wise economy that is aimed at, or sought for, that implies security,
efficiency, and just principles; but cheapness, which is so little consistent with true economy, that eventually it proves to be its greatest enemy. The so-called principle of economy, now predominant in
public measures, before which every thing good, sound, and stable is
made to yield, will sometimes overreach itself; and experience may
teach us that if a saving be made in one direction, a loss tenfold
greater will accrue in another. It may be predicted safely, that with
regard to the new management of the mint, those principles will
hereafter be found peculiarly applicable.

On the 15th February, 1848, a commission was appointed by the
QUEEN to inquire into the constitution and management of the mint;
and, after collecting farther evidence of an unimportant character,
the royal commissioners presented their report to parliament in the
session of 1849.

Appended to the report, they published several papers or disqui-
sitions on mints and mint affairs of unequal merit: an admirable analysis of the constitution of the mint, by Sir EDWARD PINE COFFIN;
a treatise by Colonel FORBES, of the CALCUTTA mint, more commend-
able for its theory than its practical utility; and a very long, elab-
orate, and antiquarian paper by the secretary, the principal object
and purpose of which was to disprove the claim of the company of
moneyers to the title and distinction of a corporation. The report
itself, brief, clear, and explicit, proposes a thorough reform of the
mint in all its branches; recommends a revision of the constitution

of the mint and government, and at the same time a termination to the system of contracts, or more properly agreements, under which the operative departments of coining and melting had been carried on safely and efficiently for centuries. The only substantial charge brought against these departments was the great profits which had from time to time been derived from the coinage; but instead of diminishing the rates of charge, it was deemed expedient to place these departments on an entirely different footing.

The leading principles being laid down in the report of the commissioners, it was left to the treasury to devise the best means of giving them effect; and as a preliminary step the deputy-master, Sir JAMES MORRISON, who had served the public above half a century, was superseded by Captain HARNESS, of the engineers, on whose opinions and recommendations it is supposed the reform of the mint was finally accomplished. The responsibility, however, of the changes devolved on Sir JOHN HERSCHEL, who was subsequently appointed to fill the office of first permanent master of the mint, on the retirement of Mr. SHIEL, president of the commission.

An order in council, dated the 7th March, 1851, empowered the master of the mint, subject to the approval of the lords of the treasury, to alter the constitution and establishment of the mint.

One of the first acts consequent on this was the dissolution of the board, as constructed by Lord MARYBOROUGH in 1815; which seems to have exercised its functions without much influence or authority, and in a manner neither to inspire sentiments of dignity nor respect; and to the weakness and irresolution of its government may be attributed many of those abuses and anomalies which had by degrees grown up in the establishment.

Under the above order in council, power was taken to give legal notice, according to their agreements, for the termination of the contracts of the company of moneyers and the melter and refiner; and ultimately these officers vacated their offices, having compensation granted to them by the treasury for the loss of their privileges and emoluments; but it appears to us not in a manner to meet the justice of the case, as regards the company of moneyers, who had claims superior to all others.

Their claim to be considered a body corporate, if illusory or erroneous, did not necessarily invalidate the vested right which they had in their offices from time immemorial; and even assuming that an order in council had authority to dissolve the company in the summary way in which it was effected (which may be doubted), it appears somewhat unreasonable to regulate the retiring allowances of such functionaries by the law applicable to the superannuation of government clerks, &c.

As we have said, the main charge made against the moneyers and melter was the largeness of their emoluments; but no attempt was made to reduce them, and the fault therefore, if any, must rest with the government. No man or body of men are expected voluntarily to propose a reduction of emolument. And, moreover, as economy was supposed to be the ruling principle in the reform, it is a grave question whether the public interests would not have been better served by retaining the services of these officers for life, who had the advantage of long-tried experience, especially as by prematurely placing them on the pension list to the annual amount of L.8000, they have involuntarily become, as all pensioners must be, burdens to their country.

The office of the QUEEN's assay-master, one of the most ancient and most important in the mint, was also abolished, along with that of the master's assay-master. The QUEEN's clerk and clerk of the papers (formerly a board officer), and the weigher and teller, were converted into senior clerks.

Previously to Mr. SHIEL's retirement from office he was required by the treasury to report as to what measures he would recommend to carry out the reform of the mint; and in this document it appears he differed in opinion from the rest of the commissioners with regard to the abolition of all contracts in carrying on the practical operations of coining: and suggested that while the melter should be a salaried officer, the coining department might advantageously be farmed out, under certain conditions, to a respectable contractor, who would be required to give sureties to the amount of L.30,000. One of those conditions was that the government should supply the steam power, and the contractor labor, materials, &c., taking upon himself all risk and responsibility, and paying over to the government the waste of metal accruing in the various operations; and as an indemnity for this risk, loss and expenses of manufacture, it was stipulated that certain rates should be allowed on each denomination of money coined.

It was likewise suggested in the report, that a contract might advantageously be made with persons out of the mint for the supply of standard silver bars fit for coinage; and that the scissell, broken coin, and cuttings, arising from the manufacture, should be sold or exchanged.

With regard to the assay department, which in every other mint is deemed a necessary appendage, it is said, "It would be a better arrangement if several competent persons were appointed to act as assayers to the mint, on a fixed scale of fees, the master of the mint being empowered to call upon any of them to make, within separate laboratories, such independent assays as he may require, and the original reports of those assays being preserved as public records." These assayers, without any recognized official connection with the mint otherwise than their employment in that capacity, and, therefore, without any responsibility whatever beyond their characters as chemists, are in this manner intrusted with those important functions formerly discharged by the QUEEN's assay-master; and consequently the standard of the coin of the realm is in a great measure, if not altogether, made to depend on their fidelity.

The report referred to cannot but be deemed somewhat visionary

and inconsistent with all ideas of a well-managed and efficient establishment; nevertheless it received the acquiescence of Sir JOHN HER-
SCHEL, and the approval of the lords of the treasury. Its principal
feature is obviously one antagonistic to the very idea of perfection,
and the reverse of the practice prevalent in other well-regulated
mints,—namely, the dependence of the mint on operations performed external to it. Formerly, the principle advocated by Lord
MARYBOROUGH, and acted upon, was, that the mint should be capable of carrying on all the functions necessary to it : now, according
to this report, it is made to rely on the skill and ingenuity of persons employed elsewhere. Economy, or rather saving of money,
seems to have been the actuating motive in these preliminary
arrangements ; but time alone can prove whether the results of such
policy are consistent with true economical principles, as well as with
practical efficiency.

The project of a conditional contract for the coinage, as might
have been anticipated, proved a failure; not because enterprising
individuals were wanting to undertake such a business, but because
the rates were fixed at a price so inadequate to the duties and responsibilities, that ruin to the contractor was a contingency far from
improbable. In the report of Sir JOHN HERSCHEL, made to the treasury, it is said, "Before the contract with the moneyers had ceased,
a schedule for a contract for three years for the execution of the
principal part of the work performed by them, was prepared, and
advertisements issued to invite competition." But though offers
were made by respectable firms, the rates exceeded those fixed by
the government, except in one instance ; and the tenders were consequently rejected, the latter firm being unable to provide the necessary security.

The other proposed contract for the supply of silver bars was
abandoned, *ab initio*, probably because, on mature reflection, it was
found impracticable, if not extremely hazardous.

Viewing these measures in a practical light, we have no doubt
whatever that the operations of melting and coining should be carried on by contract, as safer, more efficient, and economical; and
the arguments employed by Mr. SMEE, in favor of such a system as
regards the coining are equally applicable to the operation of melting. The chief thing to be guarded against in the working of a
mint, is not so much the general expenses, such as labor, materials,
and salaries, as the loss of the precious metals ; for whatever saving
be made by cutting down salaries and wages, even to the point of
injustice, this will eventually be swallowed up by the waste of gold
and silver in the fabrication of the coin. Salaried officers, unlike
contractors, have no personal interest in the conduct of the business,
and when inadequately remunerated at the same time, it would be
folly and weakness to look for that vigilance and carefulness prompted
by the dictates of self-interest ; and without such checks patiently
and constantly applied, we may reasonably infer that the waste of
the precious metals will increase from year to year. If in such mat-

ters as coining and other collateral operations, we act agreeably to common sense, we should apply to them precisely the same principles as we apply to manufactories. The sense of duty in public officers is no doubt an element in the calculation; as also a conscientious regard for the public purse; but as these are not wholly or implicitly relied on in private matters, neither should they be in public. To the waste of gold and silver may also be added the increase of all other expenses; for it is contrary to all experience to suppose that government, by means of subordinate agents, can carry on a business like that of coining money with the economy of contractors, whose profits depend on studious attention to this principle.

These principles, however simple and obvious, have been disregarded in the reform of the mint; and we have reason to believe that already the consequences are apparent, however disguised from public inspection.

The system of contract best adapted to a mint appears to be that which combines the public officer and contractor, and which therefore differs in some respects from the system pursued in the FRENCH and UNITED STATES mints. In the former, one man contracts for the whole coinage, at a specified rate, and not only pays those under him, but supplies, out of his own capital, bullion for coinage. In the latter, the coiners and melters are remunerated by fixed salaries, and allowances are made for the waste of the precious metals, not exceeding a fixed rate.

As an improvement upon these plans, we propose that officers engaged in the operative departments should be paid moderate salaries; that the government should supply the steam-power, machinery, and every thing in the nature of *plant*, and keep the same in repair; and that a rate should be allowed, determined by experience and actual results, to the head of each department, out of which he should defray the cost of labor, materials, &c., and make good all waste arising from manufacture and other sources. By this simple process the CROWN, or master of the mint, would be relieved from all risk and responsibility. Officers acting under authority, and guarded by proper checks in the performance of their duties, are as likely to give general satisfaction, and may be as much confided in, as those employed on fixed salaries, while they would have every incitement to keep the waste and expenses within the limit allowed by government.

This practical suggestion is founded on the impression that waste of gold and silver is not only a very important element in the expenses of a mint, but that it is an indefinite expense, varying according to circumstances, yet coming on the average within certain limits. But the same circumstances which make it vary so as to baffle nice calculations, and render control over it helpless, may, and do actually, make it gradually increase; such, for example, as ignorance, carelessness, and want of vigilance. For the question is not about large amounts, obvious and tangible, arising from robbery and such like causes, which may be traced—but to minute portions, which, however apparently small and insignificant in ordinary manufacture, swell like arithmetical progression to great value on extensive coinages. For example, a loss of only 2 grains troy per pound of gold, or 1-2880th of the whole weight, over and above what is certified to be the usual waste, will, on the value of a million, amount to about L.400.

The constitution of the mint being abolished on the 26th July, 1851, orders were issued for the new constitution and establishment; amongst which it is said, "The peculiar distinction recognized by the indentures of the mint between the check and executive branches of the mint is abolished. All persons employed in the mint are equally the servants of the sovereign, and all will perform their duties under the immediate orders of the master of the mint." And it is further added, that every person so employed is to consider himself available for all its duties; an order quite inconsistent with the regulations prevailing in other public offices.

The moneyers having vacated their lucrative offices, and the tenders of independent contractors being rejected, measures were immediately taken to carry on the public service in the coining department by the appointment of officers on fixed salaries. Ultimately the office of clerk of the irons and superintendent of machinery was consolidated with that of the chief coiner, who has under him several assistants and clerks.

The melter and refiner having likewise retired on a pension, the same provision was made for the service in the melting department by the appointment of an officer called "senior clerk and melter," with assistants.

The offices of QUEEN's assay-master, and master's assay-master, having been abolished, a new office was created called the "resident assayer's office," the principal duty of which is the assay of the bullion imported for coinage. At the same time other parties carrying on the art of assaying out of the mint were appointed "assayers to the mint," paid by a fee on each assay, whose employment it is, in connection with the mint, to try the assays of the gold and silver bars melted for coinage, of the presumed standard, as well as the coin itself when fabricated.

The die department is an exception to the rule, for it remains unreformed—the only change made in it being the amalgamation of the head with the coinage department, the duties being supervised by a subordinate.

Circumstances of a peculiar kind for some time retarded the change contemplated in the engraving department; but the death of the chief engraver, suddenly and unexpectedly, precipitated the reform. Love of art and modern economical principles being at variance, the office of chief engraver was abolished, and a new one created, called the "resident engraver," whose duty is of a very circumscribed character. At the same time, the former assistant engraver and medalist, being dismissed from their offices, were appointed "non-resident engravers to the mint," with fixed salaries, and payments conditional on actual work executed.

We shall now proceed to give a practical outline of the various ingenious processes comprehended in the term coinage of money. For as it is said ten men are required to make a pin, so as many different operations are concerned in the manufacture of a single coin; such as, for example, weighing, assaying, melting, rolling, annealing, drawing, cutting-out, milling, blanching, and coining or stamping.

Although any person has by law the right or privilege to coin gold at the mint, the Bank of England is now the only importer of gold bullion; for, as by a recent act the bank is compelled to purchase all gold tendered to it at the fixed price of L.3, 17s. 9d. an ounce standard, the merchant or dealer has ceased to obtain any profit or advantage by taking his bullion to the mint. As before remarked, the difference between the mint and market price of gold, and any contingent profit obtained by the advanced value given to the importer's bullion by the assay, are neutralized by the loss of interest on his capital; while the bank, on the other hand, lessens the temptation to coin by making an immediate advance on the bullion tendered for sale. The bank may, therefore, be said to have the entire monopoly of the gold coinage of Great Britain; and, as coiners, they have virtually become the sole issuers of gold coin, being enabled thereby (as is asserted) to control and regulate more effectually the whole currency.

England, with regard to its coinage, differs from other countries in this,—that while they throw the burden of the coinage on the public, and charge a rate to defray the expense, she (by an act of Charles II., subsequently confirmed by one of George III.) pays the whole expense of the gold coinage out of the public treasury, charging nothing for the cost of manufacture. Consequently, gold bullion is coined by the mint at the rate of L.3, 17s. 10½d. an ounce, or 1½d. an ounce above the bank price; and the importer has returned to him in coin the exact equivalent of his bullion, standard weight for standard, having credit given to him, at the same time, for the enhanced value of his bullion computed by the mint assay,—arising from the difference paid to the merchant and the increased fineness allowed by the mint.

With regard to the silver and copper coinages, these are undertaken by the Crown as its peculiar prerogatives; because, as a considerable seignorage is charged on both, it is manifest the public cannot be permitted to participate in this profit or advantage. Silver is coined at the rate of 5s. 6d. an ounce, or 66s. per pound troy, which would be a seignorage of precisely 10 per cent. when the market price of bullion is 5s. an ounce. Copper is coined at the rate of L.224 a ton weight—more than 100 per cent. profit on the average price of copper. These coins, therefore, must be esteemed in the light of tokens rather than money; and by reason of their depreciation they are restricted in circulation necessarily to the country in which they are made, and are by law a legal tender only to a limited amount.

As the Crown, or the government as representative of the Crown, can alone coin silver and receive the seignorage, the bullion from which it is coined is purchased in the ordinary way in the market, and paid for out of the public treasury; and the Crown becomes liable for the expense of recoining the silver currency when worn out by wear and tear. Hence, when the bank "garbles" the silver coin, as it is technically called, and sends it to the mint to be melted and re-coined, the bank receives the value by tale, that is piece for piece, the cost of wear falling wholly on the public. Formerly the seignorage on the coinage was retained by the master of the mint to defray the expenses of the establishment; but by a recent act it is required to be paid in full to the consolidated fund, and the whole expenses of the mint are now voted annually by parliament.

Routine of business. Gold.

When the Bank of England require a coinage of gold, due notice is conveyed to the mint authorities, and the bullion is brought in by the bank in parcels of 100 ingots or bars, weighing about 200 ounces each, or in all about L.70,000 sterling. These deliveries of bullion are officially denominated importations; and their frequency depends entirely on the public exigencies. They ordinarily amount to four each week; but in 1852–53, when the bank treasures were drained by an unprecedented demand for gold coin consequent on the discovery of auriferous deposits in Australia, the amount received by the mint each week for several consecutive months was 900 ignots—value about L.650,000; and about the same amount was returned in coined sovereigns. This was by far the largest coinage ever undertaken by the mint as respects gold, and exhibits in one remarkable instance the enormous resources and wealth of Great Britain.

The bullion sent by the bank is weighed at the scale the same day, in presence of the bank clerk; and assay-pieces being cut from each bar of gold, they are sent to be tried by the mint assayer, along with the assay reports on which the bank purchased the bullion; and thus he is enabled to verify the reports, or note any important errors or deviations. In the meantime the bullion is taken charge of, and locked up under the keys of the master, deputy-master, and one of the senior clerks of the mint; the weight and number of each bar being first recorded in the official books. So soon as the assayer has completed the assays, he sends his reports written on a sheet of paper, side by side with the trade or bank reports, to the master of the mint, who, after inspection, refers them to the comptroller; and upon these the bullion is rated for coinage. It should, however, be remarked that the mint assayer, with the view of reducing the bullion to the standard of our currency—namely, 22 carats fine and 2 carats alloy—is required to report the whole contents of fine gold, as far as so delicate an operation will allow;

while, on the other hand, the trade assay takes no cognizance of fractional parts lower than one-eighth of a carat grain = 7$\frac{1}{2}$ grains troy. Thus, for example, a bar of gold reported by the trade assay B. 1·2$\frac{1}{4}$, will, by the mint assayer, be called B. 1·2$\frac{1}{4}$ + 6 grs.; that is to say, he finds six troy grains more per pound of fine gold than is indicated by the trade report; and it follows, if the bar were so much worse than it is better than standard, or Wo. 1·2$\frac{1}{4}$, the 6 grains, if discovered, would diminish the *worseness*, as it is called, to that extent.

Formerly, under the old system, these fractional differences were treated in a somewhat different manner, though the result was exactly the same. The masters' assay-master, whose province it was to examine the bullion at this stage, while he gave the benefit to the importer of the enhanced value of his bullion, carried off these fractions, in computing the standard, by combining the ingots or bars together and ordering them so to be melted; for example, two grains per pound *plus* would compensate for two grains *minus*.

The reports having been properly recorded in the journals against the number and weight of the ingots to which they belong, the computation is made of what is technically called the *betterness* or *worseness* of each ingot, as indicated by the assay; the former being placed in a column on the left, and the latter on the right of the journal, along with the excess grains or fractions beyond the ordinary report. This arithmetical process is called *rating*, and is more easily effected by constructing tables for the purpose, out of which the parts are taken and added together. The tables now in use are calculated decimally, though the complex notation of carats and carat grains is still retained in making the assay reports. If the importation of 100 ingots should consist of mixed gold, some of which are above, some under the standard, the columns are added separately, the excess grains added to the fineness, and then the worseness deducted from the betterness, or *vice versa*, and the difference either added to or deducted from the gross weight, which gives the standard weight, to be computed at the mint price of L.3, 17s. 10$\frac{1}{2}$d. an ounce.

A copy of this being sent to the bank and signed (called the mint-bill) shows the amount of standard bullion standing to the debit of the bank in the mint-books; and it will appear that in the total sum the value of the bullion is in excess of their own account by the surplus grains on each pound, and by an increase of weight gained at the mint-scale.

These preliminary processes completed in the manner described, the ingots are then classed in pots for melting, in a book called the pot-book, which affords an authenticated record of future proceedings. The importation of 100 ingots is generally divided into 16 pots, containing six or seven ingots each; and each pot is numbered accordingly. The pot-book, therefore, is an exact transcript of the journal broken up into 16 parts or sections; and the total of the one should agree with that of the other. Each pot shows the number and mark of the ingots, the gross weight of each; the better-ness and worseness and excess grains; and the quantity of alloy authorized to be added to bring the whole to standard.

The pot-book having been verified and signed by the appointed officers, and the weight debited to the melting department in the books of the mint-office, the gold bullion is then delivered over to the melter and arranged in trucks or boxes with square partitions, so that each pot is kept separate, and placed in order of its number—the marks and number of the ingots at the same time being com-pared with the pot-book.

The bullion thus consigned to the melting department, if not melted the same day, is locked up under the keys of the deputy-master or comptroller, the melter, and a junior clerk or assistant.

Gold-Melting.

Previously to the bullion being charged into the pots, the fur-naces are lighted by the workmen at an early hour, and the pots gradually annealed, as they are liable to crack by too sudden an application of heat. This is done in the following manner:—black-lead pots calculated to contain rather more than 100 lbs. weight of gold, are placed in a series of furnaces 14 inches square, and 20 inches deep from the grate. On the grate, formed of six movable iron bars, supported by cross-bars let into the brick-work, a stand is placed for the pot, usually cut from the bottom of an old pot, and the concavity being upwards it is filled with common coke-dust, to prevent the adhesion of the pot to the stand. To give depth to the pot in the furnace, and allow of as much fuel as the furnace will hold, a muffle formed of baked clay is placed on the pot in such a manner that the rim of each will exactly fit, and the mouth of the muffle is covered with a flat cover made generally of black-lead. The object of this contrivance is to give an additional depth of four inches of fuel above the pot, by which a more equal degree of heat is given to the melted gold (an object of great importance), other-wise there might not be a uniform mixture of the alloy and fine gold, which is easily effected at a proper degree of temperature.

The pot being thus placed upright in the furnace, coke to the depth of a few inches is sprinkled round the pot, and a layer of ignited charcoal, previously prepared in another furnace, is thrown upon the coke, and the furnace then filled up with fuel. To prevent too rapid combustion the door of the furnace is left open, and the damper communicating with the flue is nearly shut; but when the pot is supposed to be properly annealed the furnace door is then closed, and the damper drawn out about half its length. When the pot is heated to a bright red the gold may then be charged, which is done simply by removing the cover from the top of the muffle, and with a pair of tongs carefully placing the ingots on the bottom of the pot. The gold being charged, the copper alloy, weighed by the comptroller or his representative, and checked by the melter, is added to it before being melted; some pulverized charcoal is thrown in to neutralize oxidation; and the furnace having more fuel applied is then shut up, and the damper drawn out. When the metal is thoroughly melted and the temperature deemed adequate, it is well mixed or stirred with a rod of black-lead, fixed in tongs, heated to a bright-red before putting it into the metal. The pot is then withdrawn from the furnace by first drawing a bar from the grate on each side of the pot, and forcing all the fuel into the ash-pit; a pair of tongs is then made to encircle the pot, to which is attached a lever, by which the pot is lifted upon the top of the furnace. By another pair of tongs, encircling the pot nearly round the middle, it is carried by a man balancing the weight in his hand, and the metal cast into four moulds—a sling from the roof running over a pulley being attached to the side of the tongs, so as to relieve the man who pours, and add a greater degree of steadiness to the operation. The man who holds the sling in one hand, with the other removes the charcoal from the spout of the pot by means of a stick, so as to give a clear stream to the metal. The pot, emptied of its contents, is returned to the furnace, the bars that were withdrawn replaced, and the ignited fuel taken from the ash-pit, thrown into the furnace round the pot, which is again charged with more gold. Such a pot, if carefully treated, may be safely used eight or ten times in the course of the day.

The weight of each pot of gold is from 90 lbs. to 105 lbs. troy, and in this manner it is melted properly in one hour, making four long bars of about 25 lbs. each, measuring 27 inches in length, 1¼ inch in breadth, and nearly one inch in thickness. Formerly four furnaces were found adequate to supply a large coinage of gold, turning out 40 pots, or 4000 lbs. weight a-day, which was accomplished in 11 or 12 hours. More could have been done, by an addition of furnaces and men, but the material could not be supplied beyond the power of the assay office; it being a rule that all assays concerning the coinage should be made within the mint, and on the sole responsibility of one officer. But, under the new system, that restriction has been abolished, in degree at least; and during the late great pressure for coin, assays were sent to private parties out of the mint, which enabled that establishment greatly to extend the gold coinage beyond what was ever experienced; and, consequently, additional furnaces became necessary to keep pace with it, which augmented the amount of gold melted on each day to 5000 lbs., or nearly one quarter of a million sterling. During several months the amount of coined money delivered to the bank was L.630,000, or 13,500 lbs. weight; and assuming that the bars melted produced 50 per cent. of coin, it would be necessary, to meet this extraordinary demand, to melt at least 27,000 lbs. a-week, or 4500 lbs. a-day; but we believe it exceeded this considerably, as a change in the remedy of the coin greatly increased the number of spoiled pieces, while, on the other hand, the questionable alteration of the assay department caused an immense increase of damaged work in the melting department, from errors and irregularities in the assays.

From each gold pot melted in the way described, two samples are cut for the assay, one from the first and another from the fourth bar cast. These are taken in the presence of an authorized officer, weighed carefully, and put up in slips of paper marked with the number of the pot, and then delivered to the master of the mint. The bars of gold being trimmed and cleaned are marked with consecutive numbers and a distinguishing letter, so that if any error should appear the pot can be identified and its composition traced. They are then weighed, two at a time, and the weight is registered in the day-book; and at the end of the day the assays and clippings are added to the account, so as to show the apparent waste that has taken place. The bullion after this is locked up in the melting-house stronghold, under three keys, and remains there till such time as the assay trials have been made, and an order for delivery transmitted by the master of the mint. This being done, the bars are carried to the office of receipt, and weighed in presence of an officer or clerk, who gives a receipt to the melter on the part of the coining department. On the other hand, when the melter receives what is commonly called scissell, spoiled blanks, and other pieces of metal which cannot be made into money, from the coining department, he likewise gives in the same book a receipt for the amount, distinguishing what is scissell, ends, blanks, and brokages. This specification of these returns was at one time a record of great importance, and constituted a check on the proceedings of the moneyers, who were required by the mint indenture to coin of good money seven twelfths out of the bars delivered to them, minus the ends cut off, and hollow, brittle, or badly-melted bars. Consequently the amount of scissell returned to melt should not exceed five twelfths, and any amount beyond that was obviously to the prejudice of the melter. But now that the contract system no longer exists to cavil with carelessness and indifference, and no one's interest is affected by damaged work, the amount of scissell, by scrupulous nicety in the uniformity of the coin, has greatly increased, and consequently the expense of coinage, which is now defrayed out of the public treasury.

Silver.

When silver bullion is imported into the mint for coinage, it passes through the same preliminary stages as gold; but as the CROWN actually purchases the silver, it also claims the right of the importer of bullion to any benefit derived from the enhanced value given by the mint assay; and this, along with the seignorage, is carried to the public account. The average weight of silver ingots is about 1000 oz. troy; and they are marked, numbered, assayed, rated, and potted for melting, nearly in the same way as described of gold bullion. The weight of a silver pot is as near 420 lbs. as can practically be attained; and, generally, five such ingots constitute a pot, with the proper proportion of alloy. Silver ingots are reported in ounces and pennyweights, with excess grains over the half pennyweight, and the standard computed to that of 11 oz. 2 dwts. fine silver, and 18 dwts. alloy. And, when it is found the silver ingots so imported are mixed of fine and coarse, in whatever proportions, it is the practice to combine some of each together in the same pot, adding the necessary alloy, so as to facilitate the fusion of the metal, and diffuse the alloy more uniformly.

The silver hitherto has been melted in cast-iron pots of a strong fabric, weighing about 1¼ cwt. each; but these have recently been superseded by wrought-iron pots of about the same shape and dimensions, which possess some advantages over the others. The cast-iron pots referred to, and lifting and pouring machinery were introduced into the mint in 1811, and were deemed a prodigious improvement on the old, clumsy, and wasteful process of melting silver in small pots, while at the same time they enabled the mint with ease to cast 10,000 lbs. weight of silver daily into bars. At the same time iron moulds were brought into use, instead of those formerly used, which were made of sand.

The cast-iron pots, for many years after they were adopted, were found perfectly successful, and by means of them a great amount of bullion was melted safely, expeditiously, and economically, the waste of silver being much less than the usual allowance for loss by melting; but afterwards various circumstances, not originally foreseen, conspired to detract from the merit if not from the utility of this alteration. In the first place, the quality of iron seems everywhere to have deteriorated, consequent, as some would infer, on the introduction of the hot-blast in reducing the ore; but more probably from the haste and rapidity with which it is manufactured. Whether from the original quality of the iron, the ignorance or carelessness of the founder, or both combined, it is certain that in subsequent years the cast-iron pots lost by degrees all the great advantages ascribed to them. In the second place, concurrent with the falling off in the castings themselves, the silver ingot, originally of 60 lbs. weight, in process of time augmented to 80 lbs. and above; and this, coupled with an excess of fine silver in the market, caused by a cheap process of refinage, rendered the fusion far more difficult and hazardous in cast-iron pots, because the degree of temperature necessary to melt fine silver bars of 1000 ozs. each, is considerably higher than can safely be used with such a material; and in such cases the pot was found disabled before it had done a fourth part of the work required of it. Moreover, the iron melting and running from the bottom of the pot left large interior fissures partly filled with silver, difficult to extract, while, at the same time, the porous character of the iron caused a great absorption of the precious metal, which was recovered only in a small degree. The great care and attention, too, during the operation of melting under such circumstances, caused an excessive consumption of fuel, and a great loss of time.

4

In consequence of these defects and disadvantages, the subject was taken into consideration by Sir JOHN HERSCHEL, master of the mint; and, ultimately, forged iron pots, (manufactured by Messrs. HORTON of the works at Smithwick near Birmingham), were tried first experimentally, and then adopted; having, by the severest trial, proved eminently successful. The prime cost of such pots is of course four or five times greater than those of cast-iron; but it is conceived that is amply repaid in the end by a considerable saving of fuel, by greater safety, by economy of time and labor, and less waste of silver by accidents and absorption—to which may be added the greater amount of work of which they are capable. If we suppose the melting-power of a cast-iron pot to be $10 \times 400 = 4000$ lbs. weight, which on the average is not much underrated; by actual experiment, it has been found that the melting-power of a forged or wrought-iron pot is, on a large average, $40 \times 400 = 16,000$ lbs., or four times as great, which if maintained with regularity, would nearly compensate for the superior prime cost. It may, therefore, be assumed, that the latter pots will eventually supersede the former. The reason why they were not sooner introduced, or rather, why in former times they were tried and abandoned, is solely to be attributed to modern improvements, to skill, and perhaps science, applied to the manufacture of such articles.

In the silver melting-house there are eight melting furnaces, two cranes, and two pouring machines. Each crane stands in the centre of four furnaces, freely commanding the centre of each, and conveys the pots to the pouring-machine. The eight furnaces may be worked three or four times daily, with an adequate supply of moulds and workmen; but generally four are found ample to keep pace with an ordinary coinage. If the eight furnaces were put in work, and the pots charged only three times a-day, then about 10,000 lbs. weight of silver could easily be melted in eight or nine hours, and with greater economy of labor and fuel, and far less waste of silver, than by any other process. When the operation is performed skilfully, and the metal not retained too long in the fire, it has been found that the oxidation of the alloy is less than it would be if melted in a black-lead pot, or in a larger pot of iron, and the silver dipped out, as in the Paris mint, where copper is added from time to time to the fused metal in such proportions as shall compensate for the destruction of the alloy.

When the melting department was carried on under a contract, with fixed rates of payment, the melter bore all the waste arising from the various operations, and at the end of each year made up his account with the master of the mint, and made good all deficiency from that source. His situation was, therefore, one of considerable risk and responsibility; and as his profit or income depended on the proceeds of his office, deducting the various expenses, as well as losses, it was obviously his interest to conduct the business in the most economical manner. But the contract system having terminated, at the instance of modern ideas of improvement, the whole charges and expenses of this department are now borne by the government, and at the end of each quarter the account is made up and the loss of precious metal written off.

The assays of the gold and silver bars, referred to before, upon which the standard coin is manufactured, were formerly made or tried in the mint by the QUEEN's assay-master, who became responsible for the quality of the whole coinage; but under the new system the assays are sent by the master of the mint to persons out of the mint for examination, who are nominally attached to the establishment, but without any responsibility whatever. For this work they are paid a fee of 2s. 6d. for each assay; and when the coinage is considerable, very large emoluments are paid to these assayers, which has increased the expense of this branch beyond what it formerly was.

The master of the mint, on receiving the reports of the assays, orders the bullion which is represented by them to be delivered over for coinage, condemning such pots or bars as he finds may deviate from the standard beyond a certain amount; and these are either remelted with some addition of alloy or fine gold, or simply combined and mixed together. From some cause not ascertained, the amount of work so condemned exceeds that under the old system, and thereby enhances the cost of the coinage.

Operation of Rolling.

The first process to which the bars of gold and silver are subjected is that of flatting, rolling, or laminating, in the rolling-mill. Both descriptions are rolled cold; but as the operation hardens the metal, making it liable to crack at the edges, at a certain stage the bars are cut into shorter pieces, and are annealed in a reverberatory furnace, quenched suddenly in water, and cleaned with dilute acid. They are then passed repeatedly through the rollers, and gradually reduced to the thickness of the coin required.

Process of Pyxing.

By the process of pyxing, as it is technically called, the weight and fineness of the coined money is determined before it is delivered to the importer or to the public. It consists in taking from every journey-weight of gold and silver a pound in tale promiscuously, which is weighed in an accurate balance, the plus or minus over or under the standard weight being declared by the weigher, and recorded by the clerk. This determines within certain limits whether the money has been made within the remedy allowed by law. From the same pound weight of silver or gold, two pieces are taken, the one for the master of the mint, to be assayed, in order to test the fineness of the whole coin; the other for subsequent examination at the general trial of the pyx; and the coins so taken, one from each journey or bag, are sealed up in a packet, and put into a chest, called the pyx-box, locked up under the separate keys of the master and comptroller, there to remain until the general trial of the pyx referred to. When the assay-trial of the piece has been examined and proved to be of the legal standard, which, in this case, is taken as the average of the whole journey-weight, the master of the mint authorizes the money to be delivered to the importers of the bullion, who give a proper receipt for the same.

The general trial of the pyx in LONDON takes place at irregular periods before a jury selected by the lord chancellor, and comprehends an examination by weight and assay of all the money coined during a given time; and the verdict delivered by the foreman of the jury to the chancellor relieves the master of the mint from further responsibility as regards the past. While the company of moneyers were intrusted with the coinage of the money, the trial of the pyx was uniformly favorable to their skill and accuracy, as well as to the skill and vigilance of that important and responsible check officer, the QUEEN's assay-master; but as no trial has yet (1854) taken place under the new system, we are unable to draw any conclusion from it, either in point of skill or accuracy.

The company of moneyers, like the melter, carried on their business by a contract or agreement with the master of the mint for the time being, by which they were bound to make good all waste or loss accruing in their department, as well as to supply labor and materials. Now salaried officers conduct the various operations connected with coinage, the government taking upon itself the general expenses, the risk, and responsibility; and all waste in manufacture or loss from other causes is borne by the public, and defrayed out of the treasury. Formerly, the moneyers and melter gave heavy bonds of security to the master of the mint, as a guarantee against loss. Now no security whatever is exacted from any officer acting under the master, except from the person employed in superintending the melting department.

Under these circumstances, it is a question which time alone can solve, whether the government can manage an establishment like a mint (which, after all, is only a manufactory), as safely and economically as if carried on by contracts or agreements at moderate rates of payment.

Method of making the Dies.

An original die is engraven upon a piece of soft cast-steel of the size of the money to be coined. The device or design is, of course, cut into the steel, and its depth is proportionate to the relief ultimately wanted upon the coin. When the engraving is finished, the die, or matrix, as it is called, is hardened; a process requiring considerable care and attention. It frequently happens, that in this process, either from the steel being faulty or heated to excess, the die flies in pieces, and the whole labor of the artist is lost. When, however, the matrix proves to be perfect, it is placed in the multiplying die press, which works in every respect like a coining press, but is moved by men. An impression is taken from the matrix upon a blank die of cast steel, similar to the mode of impressing the money. The blank die is fixed as the lower die of the coining press, and by working the screw of the press, which has very long and heavily loaded arms, the matrix is made to strike the blank die with great force, and bring its impression in *relief* upon the surface. The hardness, by compression of the steel, is so great, that a perfect impression of the engraving cannot be obtained without annealing the die, perhaps twice or thrice in an iron pot with animal charcoal, allowing it to cool gradually. An impression taken in this way is called a puncheon die. When the engraver has given all the delicate outlines of the original to it, it is hardened in the same manner as its original, and used to give the impression to blank dies by a similar process; but in this case the impression is *sunk*, instead of being in *relief*. These are the dies employed to stamp the money.

The puncheon by which the die is stamped is therefore hard, and the blank die soft steel. The process of hardening is effected by immersing the puncheon in cold water after being heated; that of softening, by placing the dies in a pot covered with animal charcoal in a furnace, and then allowing them to cool slowly and gradually in the pot. The blank dies are formed of cylindrical pieces of steel nicely turned and polished, having one end square and the other of a conical shape. By the first blow given by the press the cone has disappeared, and the impression becomes visible on the surface. Several blows of the press are required to perfect a die; and between each the die is softened in the manner before described. After the first blow, the die is taken to a turning-lathe to shave off the rim of metal round the impression, so as to allow the second blow to deepen the impression without spreading the steel.

The amount of work done by the dies varies exceedingly; depending, first, on the quality of the steel, and, secondly, on the character of the metal to be stamped, which differs in hardness or softness according to the nature of the alloy contained in it.

By the officer presiding over the die department, an accurate register is kept of all dies manufactured, and he accounts also to the master of the mint for all matrixes, puncheons, and dies destroyed, as well as made, in the mint; so that none be surreptitiously used or carried away. A very large collection of the various dies used in the coinage of money, from an early period, is kept in the mint, affording to the connoisseur an interesting record of the progress of engraving in ENGLAND.

As a record of the coinage of the mint we append the following table, derived from authentic sources, which will be found useful:

By a return made by the company of moneyers to a committee of the HOUSE OF COMMONS in the year 1837, it appears that the amount of gold coined from 1558 to 1830, was L.154,762,335, 1s. 10d., and of silver, L.39,139,581, 0s. 8d.

SYNOPSIS

OF THE

ACTS OF CONGRESS

REGULATING THE MINT.

FROM BRIGHTLY'S "DIGEST OF THE LAWS OF THE UNITED STATES."
Published by KAY & BROTHER, Philadelphia.

THE MINT OF THE UNITED STATES.

I. OFFICERS OF THE MINT.—1, mint established; 2, located at Philadelphia; 3, appointment of officers; 4, duties of the director; 5, duties of the treasurer; 6, duties of the assayer; 7, duties of the melter and refiner; 8, duties of the chief coiner; 9, duties of the engraver; 10, appointment of assistants and clerks, their duties; 11, temporary appointments, workmen and servants; 12, oath of officers, etc.; 13, bonds of officers; 14, salaries; 15, pay of clerks may be increased; 16, director's annual report.

II. ASSAY AND COINAGE OF BULLION.—17, bullion, not intended for coinage, to be assayed; 18, bullion to be received for coinage; 19, to be weighed and receipted for; 20, to be assayed; 21, assayer to report; 22, charges for coinage; 23, certificate to be issued to depositor; 24, bullion to be formed into ingots; 25, ingots to be assayed; 26, deviation from standard in ingots; 27, treasurer's account with melter and refiner, allowance for waste; 28, ingots to be delivered to coiner; 29, deviation from standard weight in coining; 30, coin to be delivered to treasurer, his duties; 31, coins to be set apart for annual trial; 32, record of clippings, etc.; 33, treasurer's account with chief coiner, allowance for waste; 34, payment to depositors; 35, bullion fund, how applied; 36, annual trial of coinage, commissioners, their duties; 37, deviation allowed from standard weight of gold coin; 38, public moneys to be transferred to the mint for payment of depositors, no interest to be charged, bonds of treasurers, etc., may be renewed or increased; 39, silver bullion to be purchased for coinage, treasurer's account; 40, how silver coin to be paid out; 41, no deposits of silver bullion to be received for coinage; 42, bullion may be cast into ingots, charge therefor; 43, charge for casting into ingots; 44, amount of bullion received for refining to be gradually decreased; 45, profits to be paid into the treasury.

I. OFFICERS OF THE MINT

1. That a mint for the purpose of a national coinage be and the same is established ; to be situate and carried on at the seat of the government of the United States, for the time being.—*2d April,* 1792. § 1.

2. That the act, entitled " An act concerning the mint," approved March the 3d, 1801,* be and the same is hereby revived and con-

* This act directed that the mint should remain in the city of Philadelphia until 4 March, 1803.

tinued in force and operation, until otherwise provided by law.—
19*th May*, 1828. § 1.

Appointment of Officers.

3. The officers of the mint of the United States shall be a director, a treasurer, an assayer, a melter and refiner, a chief coiner, and
an engraver, to be appointed by the president of the United States,
by and with the advice and consent of the Senate.—18*th January*,
1837. § 1.

4. The respective duties of the officers of the mint shall be as
follows:

Duties of the Director.

First. The director shall have the control and management of the
mint, the superintendence of the officers and persons employed
therein, and the general regulation and supervision of the business
of the several branches. And in the month of January of every
year he shall make report to the president of the United States of
the operations of the mint and its branches for the year preceding;
and also to the secretary of the treasury, from time to time, as said
secretary shall require, setting forth all the operations of the mint
subsequent to the last report made upon the subject.

Duties of the Treasurer.

5. Second. The treasurer shall receive and safely keep all moneys which shall be for the use and support of the mint; shall keep
all the current accounts of the mint, and pay all moneys due by the
mint, on warrants from the director; he shall receive all bullion
brought to the mint for coinage; shall be the keeper of all bullion
and coin in the mint, except while the same is legally placed in the
hands of other officers; and shall, on warrants from the director,
deliver all coins struck at the mint to the persons to whom they
shall be legally payable. And he shall keep regular and faithful
accounts of all the transactions of the mint, in bullion and coins,
both with the officers of the mint and the depositors; and shall present, quarter-yearly, to the treasury department of the United States,
according to such forms as shall be prescribed by that department,
an account of the receipts and disbursements of the mint, for the
purpose of being adjusted and settled.

Duties of the Assayer, and the Melter and Refiner.

6. Third. The assayer shall carefully assay all metals used in
coinage, whenever such assays are required in the operations of the
mint; and he shall also make assays of coins whenever instructed
to do so by the director.—18 *Jan*, 1837.

7. Fourth. The melter and refiner shall execute all the operations
which are necessary in order to form ingots of standard silver or

gold, suitable for the chief coiner, from the metals legally delivered to him for that purpose.—*See Act 3 March*, 1795.

Duties of Chief Coiner and Engraver.

8. Fifth. The chief coiner shall execute all the operations which are necessary in order to form coins, conformable in all respects to the law, from the standard silver and gold ingots, [and the copper planchets,] legally delivered to him for this purpose.—*Ibid.*

9. Sixth. The engraver shall prepare and engrave, with the legal devices and inscriptions, all the dies used in the coinage of the mint and its branches.

Appointment of Assistants and Clerks.

10. The director shall appoint, with the approbation of the president, assistants to the assayer, melter and refiner, chief coiner, and engraver, and clerks for the director and treasurer, whenever, on representation made by the director to the president, it shall be the opinion of the president that such assistants or clerks are necessary. And it shall be the duty of the assistants to aid their principals in the execution of their respective offices, and of the clerks to perform such duties as shall be prescribed for them by the director.—1837.

11. Whenever any officer of the mint shall be temporarily absent, on account of sickness, or any other sufficient cause, it shall be lawful for the director, with the assent of said officer, to appoint some person attached to the mint, to act in the place of such officer during his absence; and the director shall employ such workmen and servants in the mint as he shall from time [to time] find necessary.—1837.

Oath of Officers.

12. Every officer, assistant and clerk of the mint, shall, before he enters upon the execution of his office, take an oath or affirmation before some judge of the United States, or judge of the superior court or any court of record of any state, faithfully and diligently to perform the duties thereof.—1837.

Bonds of Officers.

13. The following officers of the mint, before entering upon the execution of their respective offices,* shall become bound to the United States, with one or more sureties, to the satisfaction of the secretary of the treasury, in the sums hereinafter mentioned, with condition for the faithful and diligent performance of the duties of their offices, viz.: the treasurer in the sum of ten thousand dollars; the assayer in the sum of five thousand dollars; the melter and refiner in the sum of ten thousand dollars; the chief coiner in the

---

* They cannot legally execute their offices, unless they have given bonds for the faithful performance of their duties. 5 Opin. 687.

sum of ten thousand dollars. And similar bonds may also be required of the assistants and clerks, in such sums as the director shall determine, with the approbation of the secretary of the treasury.— *See Sect.* 38.

Salaries.

14. There shall be allowed to the officers of the mint the following salaries per annum : to the director for his services, including travelling expenses incurred in visiting the different branches, and all other charges whatever, three thousand five hundred dollars; to the treasurer, assayer, melter and refiner, chief coiner, and engraver, each two thousand dollars; to the assistants and clerks such annual salaries shall be allowed as the director may determine, with the approbation of the president : *Provided,* That an assistant shall not receive more than fifteen hundred dollars; and that a clerk shall not receive more than twelve hundred dollars. (See Sect. 15). To the workmen and servants shall be allowed such wages, to be determined by the director, as may be customary and reasonable according to their respective stations and occupations; and the salaries provided for in this section shall be payable in quarterly instalments.—18 *Jan.* 1837.

Pay of Clerks may be Increased.

15. That the seventh section of the act of January 18th, 1837, entitled "An act supplementary to the act entitled ' An act establishing a mint and regulating the coins of the United States,' " be so amended as to extend the limit for the annual salary of clerks in the mint of the United States to eighteen hundred dollars each, from and after the first of July, 1854, at the discretion of the officers authorized by law to appoint, with the approbation of the president of the United States, including also one clerk in the office of the assistant treasurer at Philadelphia ; and the salary of the chief clerk of the branch mint at New Orleans, shall be twenty-two hundred dollars from and after the first of July, 1854.—4 *August,* 1854.

Director's Annual Report.

16. The director of the mint shall make his annual report to the secretary of the treasury, up to the thirtieth of June in each year, so that the same may appear in his annual report to congress on the finances.—21 *Feb.* 1857.

II. ASSAY AND COINAGE OF BULLION.

17. It shall be lawful for the director of the mint to receive, and cause to be assayed, bullion not intended for coinage, and to cause certificates to be given of the fineness thereof by such officer as he shall designate for that purpose, at such rates of charge to be paid

by the owner of said bullion, and under such regulations as the said director may from time to time establish.—19 *May*, 1828. (*See No.* 44.)

Bullion to be Received for Coinage.

18. Gold and silver bullion brought to the mint for coinage, shall be received and coined by the proper officers, for the benefit of the depositor (*see* 41): *Provided*, That it shall be lawful to refuse at the mint, any deposit of less value than one hundred dollars, and any bullion so base as to be unsuitable for the operations of the mint: *And provided also*, That when gold and silver are combined, if either of these metals be in such small proportion that it cannot be separated advantageously, no allowance shall be made to the depositor for the value of such metal.—18 *Jan.* 1837

To be Weighed and Receipted for.

19. When bullion is brought to the mint for coinage, it shall be weighed by the treasurer in the presence of the depositor, when practicable, and a receipt given, which shall state the description and weight of the bullion: *Provided*, That when bullion is in such a state as to require melting before its value can be ascertained, the weight after melting shall be considered as the true weight of the bullion deposited.—*Ibid.*

To be Assayed.

20. From every parcel of bullion deposited for coinage, the treasurer shall deliver to the assayer a sufficient portion for the purpose of being assayed; but all such bullion remaining from the operations of the assay shall be returned to the treasurer by the assayer. —*Ibid.*

Assayer to Report.

21. The assayer shall report to the treasurer the quality or standard of the bullion assayed by him; and he shall also communicate to the treasurer such information as will enable him to estimate the amount of the charges hereinafter provided for, to be made to the depositor, for the expenses of converting the bullion into standard metal fit for coinage.—*Ibid.*

Charges for Coinage.

22. The only subjects of charge by the mint to the depositor shall be the following (*see* Nos. 42, 43): for refining when the bullion is below standard; for toughening when metals are contained in it which render it unfit for coinage; for copper used for alloy when the bullion is above standard; for silver introduced into the

alloy of gold; and for separating the gold and silver when these metals exist together in the bullion. And the rate of these charges shall be fixed from time to time by the director, with the concurrence of the secretary of the treasury, so as not to exceed, in their judgment, the actual expense to the mint of the materials and labor employed in each of the cases aforementioned; and the amount received from these charges shall be accounted for and appropriated for defraying the contingent expenses of the mint.—*Ibid.*

Certificate to be Issued to Depositor.

23. From the report of the assayer, and the weight of the bullion, the treasurer shall estimate the whole value of each deposit, and also the amount of the charges or deductions if any; of all which he shall give a detailed memorandum to the depositor; and he shall also give, at the same time, under his hand, a certificate of the net amount of the deposit, to be paid in coins of the same species of bullion as that deposited.—*Ibid.*

Bullion to be Formed into Ingots.

24. Parcels of bullion shall be from time to time transferred by the treasurer to the melter and refiner; a careful record of these transfers, noting the weight and character of the bullion, shall be kept; and the bullion thus placed in the hands of the melter and refiner shall be subjected to the several processes which may be necessary to form it into ingots of the legal standard, and of a quality suitable for coinage.—*Ibid.*

Ingots to be Assayed.

25. The ingots thus prepared shall be assayed by the assayer, and if they prove to be within the limits allowed for deviation from the standard, they shall be transferred by the melter and refiner to the treasurer, accompanied by the assayer's certificate of their fineness; and a careful record of the transfer shall be kept by the treasurer.—*Ibid.*

Deviation from Standard.

26. No ingots of gold shall be used for coinage of which the quality differs more than two-thousandths from the legal standard; and no ingots of silver shall be used for coinage of which the quality differs more than three-thousandths from the legal standard.—*Ibid.*

Treasurer's Account with Melter and Refiner.—Allowance for Waste.

27. In the treasurer's account with the melter and refiner, the melter and refiner shall be debited with the standard weight of all

the bullion placed in his hands, that is to say, with the weight of metal of legal standard fineness which it will make; and he shall be credited by the standard weight of all the ingots delivered by him to the treasurer. And once at least in every year, at such time as the director shall appoint, the melter and refiner shall deliver up to the treasurer all the bullion in his possession, in order that his accounts may be settled up to that time; and, in this settlement, he shall be entitled to a credit for the difference between the whole amount of bullion delivered to him, and received from him, since the last settlement, as an allowance for necessary waste: *Provided*, That this allowance shall not exceed two-thousandths of the whole amount of gold and silver bullion, respectively, that had been delivered to him by the treasurer.—*Ibid.*

Ingots to be delivered to Coiner.

28. The treasurer shall, from time to time, deliver over to the chief coiner, ingots for the purpose of coinage; he shall keep a careful record of these transfers, noting the weight and description of the ingots; and the ingots thus placed in the hands of the chief coiner shall be passed through the several processes necessary to make from them coins in all respects conformable to law.—*Ibid.*

Deviations from Standard Weight in Coining.

29. In adjusting the weights of the coins, the following deviations from the standard weight shall not be exceeded in any of the single pieces—in the dollar and half-dollar, one grain and a half; in the quarter dollar, one grain; in the dime and half-dime, half a grain; in the gold coins, one quarter of a grain; [in the copper coins, one grain in the pennyweight.] And in weighing a large number of pieces together, when delivered from the chief coiner to the treasurer, and from the treasurer to the depositors, the deviations from the standard weight shall not exceed the following limits —four pennyweights in one thousand dollars; three pennyweights in one thousand half-dollars; two pennyweights in one thousand quarter-dollars; one pennyweight in one thousand dimes; one pennyweight in one thousand half-dimes; two pennyweights in one thousand eagles; one and a half pennyweights in one thousand half-eagles; one pennyweight in one thousand quarter-eagles.—*Ibid.*

Coin to be delivered to Treasurer.—His duties.

30. The chief coiner shall, from time to time, as the coins are prepared, deliver them over to the treasurer, who shall keep a careful record of their kind, number and weight; and, in receiving the coins, it shall be the duty of the treasurer to see whether the coins of that delivery are within the legal limits of the standard weight; and if his trials for this purpose shall not prove satisfactory, he shall cause all the coins of this delivery to be weighed

separately, and such as are not of legal weight shall be delivered to the melter and refiner, as standard bullion, to be again formed into ingots and recoined.—*Ibid.*

Coins to be set apart for Annual Trial.

31. At every delivery of coins made by the chief coiner to the treasurer, it shall be the duty of the treasurer, in the presence of the assayer, to take indiscriminately, a certain number of pieces of each variety for the annual trial of coins, (the number being prescribed by the director) which shall be carefully labelled, and deposited in a chest appropriated for the purpose, kept under the joint care of the treasurer and assayer, and so secured that neither can have access to its contents without the presence of the other.—*Ibid.*

Record of Clippings, etc.

32. The chief coiner shall, from time to time, deliver to the treasurer the clippings and other portions of bullion remaining after the process of coining; and the treasurer shall keep a careful record of their amount.—*Ibid.*

Treasurer's account with Chief Coiner.—Allowance for Waste.

33. In the treasurer's account with the chief coiner, the chief coiner shall be debited with the amount in weight of standard metal of all the bullion placed in his hands, and credited with the amount, also by weight, of all the coins, clippings and other bullion delivered by him to the treasurer. And once at least in every year, at such time as the director shall appoint, the chief coiner shall deliver to the treasurer all the coins and bullion in his possession, so that his accounts may be settled up to that time; and, in this settlement, he shall be entitled to a credit for the difference between the whole amount of the ingots delivered to him, and of the coins and bullion received from him, since the last settlement, as an allowance for necessary waste: *Provided,* That this allowance shall not exceed two-thousandths of the whole amount of the silver, or one and one-half thousandths of the whole amount of the gold, that had been delivered to him by the treasurer.—*Ibid.*

Payment to Depositors.

34. When the coins which are the equivalent to any deposit of bullion are ready for delivery, they shall be paid over to the depositor, or his order, by the treasurer, on a warrant from the director; and the payment shall be made, if demanded, in the order in which the bullion shall have been brought to the mint, giving priority according to priority of deposit only. And in the denominations of coin delivered, the treasurer shall comply with the wishes of the

depositor, unless when impracticable or inconvenient to do so; in which case the denominations of coin shall be designated by the director.*—*Ibid.*

Bullion Fund.—How Applied.

35. For the purpose of enabling the mint to make returns to depositors with as little delay as possible (*see* No. 38), it shall be the duty of the secretary of the treasury to keep in the said mint, when the state of the treasury will admit thereof, a deposit of such amount of public money, or of bullion procured for the purpose, as he shall judge convenient and necessary, not exceeding one million of dollars; out of which those who bring bullion to the mint may be paid the value thereof, as soon as practicable, after this value has been ascertained. The bullion so deposited shall become the property of the United States; no discount or interest shall be charged on moneys so advanced; and the secretary of the treasury may at any time withdraw the said deposit, or any part thereof, or may, at his discretion, allow the coins formed at the mint to be given for their equivalent in other money.—*Ibid.*

Annual trial of Coinage.—Commissioners.—Their Duties.

36. To secure a due conformity in the gold and silver coins to their respective standards and weights, an annual trial shall be made of the pieces reserved for this purpose at the mint and its branches, before the judge of the district court of the United States for the eastern district of Pennsylvania, the attorney of the United States for the eastern district of Pennsylvania, and the collector of the port of Philadelphia, and such other persons as the president shall, from time to time, designate for that purpose; who shall meet as commissioners, for the performance of this duty, on the second Monday in February, annually, and may continue their meetings by adjournment, if necessary; and if a majority of the commissioners shall fail to attend at any time appointed for their meeting, then the director of the mint shall call a meeting of the commissioners at such other time as he may deem convenient. And before these commissioners, or a majority of them, and in the presence of the officers of the mint, such examination shall be made of the reserved pieces as shall be judged sufficient; and if it shall appear that these pieces do not differ from the standard fineness and weight by a greater quantity than is allowed by law, the trial shall be considered and reported as satisfactory; but if any greater deviation from the legal standard or weight shall appear, this fact shall be certified to the president of the United States; and if, on a view of the circumstances of the case, he shall so decide, the officer or officers implicated in the error shall

* The act 2 April 1792, § 15, which is hereby supplied, provided further that "if any preference shall be given contrary to the directions aforesaid, the officer by whom any undue preference shall be given shall, in each case, forfeit and pay $1000, to be recovered with costs of suit." 1 Stat. 249-50.

be thenceforward disqualified from holding their respective offices. -
Ibid.

Deviation allowed from Standard Weight of Gold Coin.

37. In adjusting the weights of gold coins henceforward, the following deviations from the standard weight shall not be exceeded
in any of the single pieces—namely, in the double-eagle, the eagle,
and the half-eagle, one-half of a grain, and in the quarter-eagle and
gold dollar, one-quarter of a grain. And in weighing a large number of pieces together, when delivered from the chief coiner to the
treasurer, and from the treasurer to the depositors, the deviation
from the standard weight shall not exceed three pennyweights in
one thousand double-eagles; two pennyweights in one thousand
eagles; one and one-half pennyweights in one thousand half-eagles;
one pennyweight in one thousand quarter-eagles; and one-half of a
pennyweight in one thousand gold dollars.—*2 March*, 1849.

Public Moneys to be transferred to the Mint for payment of Deposit-
ors.—No Interest to be Charged.—Bonds of Treasurers, etc., may be renewed or increased.

38. For the purpose of enabling the mint and branch mints of
the United States to make returns to depositors with as little delay
as possible, it shall be lawful for the president of the United States,
when the state of the treasury shall admit thereof, to direct transfers to be made from time to time to the mint and branch mints for
such sums of public money as he shall judge convenient and necessary; out of which those who bring bullion to the mint may be
paid the value thereof, as soon as practicable after this value has
been ascertained. The bullion so deposited shall become the
property of the United States; no discount or interest shall be
charged on money so advanced; and the secretary of the treasury
may at any time withdraw the said deposit, or any part thereof,
or may, at his discretion, allow the coins formed at the mint to be
given for their equivalent in other money: *Provided,* That the bonds
given by the United States' treasurers and superintendents of the
mint shall be renewed or increased at the discretion of the secretary
of the treasury, under the operation of this act.—*23 May*, 1850.

Silver Bullion to be purchased for Coinage.—Treasurer's Account.

39. In order to procure bullion for the requisite coinage of the
subdivisions of the dollar authorized by this act, the treasurer of
the mint shall, with the approval of the director, purchase such
bullion with the bullion fund of the mint. He shall charge himself
with the gain arising from the coinage of such bullion into coins of
a nominal value exceeding the intrinsic value thereof, and shall be
credited with the difference between such intrinsic value and the
price paid for said bullion, and with the expense of distributing said

coins as hereinafter provided. The balances to his credit, or the profits of said coinage, shall be, from time to time, on a warrant of the director of the mint, transferred to the account of the treasury of the United States.—21 *February*, 1853.

How Silver Coin to be paid out.

40. Such coins shall be paid out at the mint, in exchange for gold coins at par, in sums not less than one hundred dollars; and it shall be lawful, also, to transmit parcels of the same from time to time, to the assistant treasurers, depositaries and other officers of the United States, under general regulations, proposed by the director of the mint, and approved by the secretary of the treasury : *Provided, however,* That the amount coined into quarter-dollars, dimes and half-dimes, shall be regulated by the secretary of the treasury.—*Ibid.*

No deposits of Silver Bullion to be received.

41. No deposits for coinage into the half-dollar, quarter-dollar, dime and half-dime, shall hereafter be received, other than those made by the treasurer of the mint, as herein authorized, and upon account of the United States.—*Ibid.*

Bullion may be cast into Ingots.—Charge therefor.

42. At the option of the depositor, gold or silver may be cast into bars or ingots of either pure metal or of standard fineness, as the owner may prefer, with a stamp upon the same designating its weight and fineness; but no piece, of either gold or silver, shall be cast into bars or ingots of a less weight than ten ounces, except pieces of one ounce, of two ounces, of three ounces and of five ounces, all of which pieces of less weight than ten ounces shall be of the standard fineness, with their weight and fineness stamped upon them. But, in cases, whether the gold and silver deposited be coined or cast into bars or ingots, there shall be a charge to the depositor, in addition to the charge now made for refining or parting the metals, of one-half of one per centum (*see* 43) ; the money arising from this charge of one-half per centum shall be charged to the treasurer of the mint, and from time to time, on warrant of the director of the mint, shall be transferred into the treasury of the United States : *Provided, however,* That nothing contained in this section shall be considered as applying to the half-dollar, the quarter-dollar, the dime and half-dime.—*Ibid.*

Charge for casting Ingots, etc.

43. When gold or silver shall be cast into bars or ingots, or formed into disks at the mint of the United States, or any of the branches thereof, or at any assay office of the United States, the charge for refining, casting or forming said bars, ingots or disks shall be equal to,

5

but not exceed, the actual cost of the operation, including labor, wastage, use of machinery, materials, etc., to be regulated from time to time by the secretary of the treasury.—3 *March,* 1853

Amount of Bullion received for Refining to be gradually decreased.

44. When private establishments shall be made to refine gold bullion, the secretary of the treasury, if he shall deem them capable of executing such work, is hereby authorized and required to limit the amount thereof, which shall be refined in the mint at Philadelphia, from quarter to quarter, and to reduce the same progressively as such establishments shall be extended or multiplied; so as eventually, and as soon as may be, to exclude refining from the mint, and to require that every deposit of gold bullion made therein for coinage shall be adapted to said purpose, without need of refining: *Provided,* That no advances in coin shall be made upon bullion after this regulation shall be carried into effect, except upon bullion refined as herein prescribed.—*Ibid.*

Profits to be paid into the Treasury.

45. It shall be the duty of the superintendent of the mint to cause to be paid annually into the treasury of the United States the profits of the mint, and to present a quarterly account of the expenditures of the mint to the secretary of the treasury.— *Ibid.*

III. STANDARD WEIGHTS.
Troy pound.

46. For the purpose of securing a due conformity in weight of the coins of the United States, to the provisions of the ninth section of the act, passed the 2d of April, 1792, entitled "An act establishing a mint, and regulating the coins of the United States," the brass troy pound weight procured by the minister of the United States at London, in the year 1827, for the use of the mint, and now in the custody of the director thereof, shall be the standard troy pound of the mint of the United States, conformably to which the coinage thereof shall be regulated.—19 *May,* 1828.

Series of Standard Weights to be procured.— To be annually tested.

47. It shall be the duty of the director of the mint to procure, and safely to keep a series of standard weights, corresponding to the aforesaid troy pound, consisting of a one pound weight, and the requisite subdivisions and multiples thereof, from the hundredth part of a grain to twenty-five pounds. And the troy weights, ordinarily employed in the transactions of the mint, shall be regulated according to the above standards, at least once in every year, under his inspection; and their accuracy tested annually in the presence of the assay commissioners, on the day of the annual assay.—*Ibid.*

IV. BRANCHES OF THE MINT.

48. Branches of the mint of the United States shall be established as follows: one branch at the city of New Orleans for the coinage of gold and silver; one branch at the town of Charlotte in Mecklinburg county, in the state of North Carolina, for the coinage of gold only; and one branch at or near Dahlonega, in Lumpkin county, in the state of Georgia, also for the coinage of gold only.—3 *March,* 1835.

Officers to be appointed.—Clerks and workmen.—Salaries.

49. So soon as the necessary buildings are erected for the purpose of well conducting the business of each of the said branches, the following officers (*see* 53, 55) shall be appointed upon the nomination of the president, and with the advice and consent of the Senate: one superintendent, one treasurer, one assayer, one chief coiner, one melter and one refiner; and the superintendent of each mint shall engage and employ as many clerks (*see* 57) and as many subordinate workmen and servants as shall be provided for by law. And the salaries of the said officers and clerks shall be as follows: for the branch at New Orleans, to the superintendent, the sum of two thousand five hundred dollars; to the treasurer, the sum of two thousand dollars; to the chief coiner, the sum of two thousand dollars; to the assayer, melter and refiner, the sum of two thousand dollars each; to two clerks, the sum of twelve hundred dollars each; (*see* 15 and 65); to the subordinate workmen and servants, not exceeding twenty in number, such wages and allowances as are customary and reasonable, according to their respective stations and occupations. For the branches at Charlotte and Dahlonega, to the superintendents, each the sum of two thousand dollars, who shall respectively discharge the duty of treasurers; to the chief coiners, each the sum of one thousand five hundred dollars; to the assayers, melters and refiners, each the sum of one thousand five hundred dollars; to the clerks, not exceeding one at each branch, the sum of one thousand dollars; and to the subordinate workmen and servants, not exceeding the number of five at each of the said branches, such wages and allowances shall be paid as are customary and reasonable, according to their respective stations and occupations.—*Ibid.*

Oath of Office.—Bonds.

50. The officers and clerks to be appointed under this act, before entering upon the duties thereof, shall take an oath or affirmation before some judge of the United States (*see* 56), faithfully and diligently to perform the duties thereof; and shall each become bound to the United States of America, with one or more sureties, to the satisfaction of the director of the mint and the secretary of the treasury, with condition for the faithful and diligent performance of the duties of their offices.—*Ibid.*

Powers of the Director of the Mint.

51. The general direction of the business of the said branches of the mint of the United States shall be under the control and regulation of the director of the mint at Philadelphia, subject to the approbation of the secretary of the treasury ; and for that purpose, it shall be the duty of the said director to prescribe such regulations, and require such returns periodically, and occasionally, as shall appear to him to be necessary for the purpose of carrying into effect the intention of this act in establishing the said branches ; also for the purpose of discriminating the coin which shall be stamped at each branch, and at the mint itself ; also for the purpose of preserving uniformity of weight, form and fineness in the coins stamped at each place ; and for that purpose, to require the transmission and delivery to him at the mint, from time to time, such parcels of the coinage of each branch as he shall think proper to be subjected to such assays and tests as he shall direct.—*Ibid.*

Laws regulating the Mint, etc., to apply to the Branches.

52. All the laws and parts of laws made for the regulation of the mint of the United States, and for the government of the officers and persons employed therein, and for the punishment of all offences connected with the mint or coinage of the United States, shall be and the same are hereby declared to be in full force, in relation to each of the branches of the mint by this act established, so far as the same shall be applicable thereto.—*Ibid.*

Officers at New Orleans.—Salaries.

53. The officers of the branch mint at New Orleans shall be one superintendent, one treasurer, one assayer, one melter and refiner, and one coiner ; and the officers of the branch mints at Charlotte and Dahlonega severally, shall be one superintendent, who shall also perform the duties of treasurer ; one assayer, who shall also perform the duties of melter and refiner (see 55), and one coiner. And the annual salaries of the said officers shall be as follows : for the branch at New Orleans, to the superintendent, two thousand five hundred dollars ; to the treasurer, the assayer, the melter and refiner, and the coiner, each two thousand dollars ; for the branches at Charlotte and Dahlonega, to the superintendent, two thousand dollars ; and to the assayer and the coiner, each fifteen hundred dollars.—13 *March*, 1837.

Repeal

54. That so much of the act entitled " An act to establish branches of the mint of the United States," approved the 3d day of March, 1835, as is inconsistent with the provisions of this act, be and the same is hereby repealed.—*Ibid.*

Duties of Melter and Refiner transferred to Coiner at Dahlonega and Charlotte.

55. That an act passed the 13th day of February, 1837, to amend an act entitled "An act to establish branches of the mint of the United States," passed the 3d day of March, 1835, be and it is hereby altered and amended so as to transfer the duties of melter and refiner from the assayer to the coiner at the branches of Dahlonega in Georgia, and of Charlotte in North Carolina, respectively; and that all laws and parts of laws conflicting with this act be and they are hereby repealed.—27 *February*, 1843.

Before whom Oath of Office may be taken.

56. The oath or affirmation required by the third section of an act passed March 3d, 1835, entitled "An act to establish branches of the mint of the United States," may be taken before any judge of the superior court or of any court of record, in the state where the branch of which the person taking said oath is an officer or clerk, is situated.—2 *April*, 1844.

Treasurers to appoint their own Clerks. Subject to approval of Secretary.

57. That so much of the second section of the act approved March 3d, 1835, entitled "An act to establish branches of the mint of the United States," as vests the appointment of the clerks of the treasurer in the superintendent of each mint, be and the same is hereby repealed; and that the several treasurers of the United States mint be and they are hereby authorized to appoint their own clerks, subject, however, to the approval of the secretary of the treasury.—3 *March*, 1851.

58. That a branch of the mint of the United States be established in California, to be located by the secretary of the treasury, for the coinage of gold and silver.—*July*, 1852.

59. Suitable buildings shall be procured or erected, for carrying on the business of said branch mint; and the following officers shall be appointed, so soon as the public interests may require their services, upon the nomination of the president, [by] and with the advice and consent of the senate, to wit: one superintendent, one treasurer, one assayer, one melter and refiner, and one coiner; and the said superintendent shall engage and employ as many clerks, and as many subordinate workmen and servants, as shall be provided for by law. And until the 30th of June, 1855, the salaries of said officers and clerks shall be as follows: to the superintendent and to the treasurer, the sum of four thousand five hundred dollars each; to the assayer, to the melter and refiner, and to the coiner, the sum of three thousand dollars each; to the clerks, the sum of two thousand dollars each; to the subordinate workmen, such wages and allowances as are customary and reasonable, according to their respective stations and occupations.—3 *July*, 1852.

Oath.—Bonds.

60. The officers and clerks to be appointed under this act, before entering upon the duties thereof, shall take an oath or affirmation before some judge of the United States, or the supreme court of the State of California, faithfully and diligently to perform the duties thereof; and shall each become bound to the United States of America, with one or more sureties, to the satisfaction of the director of the mint and the secretary of the treasury, or the district attorney of the United States for the state of California, with condition for the faithful and diligent performance of their offices.—*Ibid.*

Powers of the Director of the Mint.

61. The general direction of the business of said branch of the mint of the United States shall be under the control and regulation of the director of the mint at Philadelphia, subject to the approbation of the secretary of the treasury; and, for that purpose, it shall be the duty of the said director to prescribe such regulations, and require such returns periodically and occasionally, as shall appear to him to be necessary for the purpose of carrying into effect the intention of this act in establishing the said branch; also, for the purpose of discriminating the coin which shall be stamped at said branch and at the mint itself; and also for the purpose of preserving uniformity of weight, form and fineness in the coins stamped at said branch; and for that purpose, to require the transmission and delivery to him at the mint, from time to time, of such parcels of the coinage of said branch as he shall think proper, to be subjected to such assays and tests as he shall direct.—*Ibid.*

Laws regulating the Mint, etc., to apply to this Branch.

62. That all the laws and parts of laws now in force for the regulation of the mint of the United States, and for the government of the officers and persons employed therein, and for the punishment of all offences connected with the mint or coinage of the United States, shall be and they are hereby declared to be in full force in relation to the branch of the mint by this act established, so far as the same may be applicable thereto.—*Ibid.*

To be the Depository of Public Moneys.—Duties and Liabilities of Treasurer.

63. The said branch mint shall be the place of deposit for the public moneys collected in the custom-houses in the state of California, and for such other public moneys as the secretary of the treasury may direct. And the treasurer of said branch mint shall have the custody of the same, and shall perform the duties of an assistant treasurer, and for that purpose shall be subject to all the provisions contained in an act entitled " An act to provide for the better organization of the treasury, and for the collection, safe-

keeping, transfer and disbursement of the public revenue," approved August the 6th, 1846, which relates to the treasurer of the branch mint at New Orleans.—*Ibid.*

Gold to be Refined and cast into Ingots.—Charges.

64. If required by the holder, gold in grain or lumps shall be refined, assayed, cast into bars or ingots, and stamped in said branch mint, or in the mint of the United States, or any of its branches, in such manner as may indicate the value and fineness of the bar or ingot; which shall be paid for by the owner or holder of said bullion, at such rates and charges, and under such regulations, as the director of the mint, under the control of the secretary of the treasury, may from time to time establish.—*Ibid.*

Pay of Clerks at New Orleans may be Increased.

65. That the seventh section of the act of 18th January, 1837, entitled " An act supplementary to an act establishing the mint, and regulating the coins of the United States," be so amended as to extend the allowance for the annual salary of the clerks in the branch mint of the United States at New Orleans, to eighteen hundred dollars each, from and after the first day of July, 1854, at the discretion of the officers authorized by law to appoint, with the approbation of the president of the United States.—3 *March,* 1855.

V.   ASSAY OFFICE, NEW YORK.

66. The secretary of the treasury is hereby authorized and required to establish in the city of New York an office for the receipt and for the melting, refining, parting, and assaying of gold and silver bullion and foreign coin, and for casting the same into bars, ingots, or disks. The assistant treasurer of the United States in New York shall be treasurer of the said assay office; and the secretary of the treasury shall, with the approbation and consent of the president of the United States, appoint such other officers and clerks, authorize the employment of such assistants, workmen, and servants as shall be necessary for the proper conduct and management of the said office, and of the business pertaining thereto, at such compensation as shall be approved by the president: *Provided,* That the same shall not exceed that allowed for corresponding services under existing laws relating to the mint of the United States and its branches.—3 *March,* 1853.

Bullion.—Certificates.—Ingots, etc.

67. The owner or owners of any gold or silver bullion, in dust or otherwise, or of any foreign coin, shall be entitled to deposit the same in the said office, and the treasurer thereof shall give a receipt, stating the weight and description thereof, in the manner and under the regulations that are or may be provided in like cases of deposits at the mint of the United States with the treasurer thereof. And

such bullion shall, without delay, be melted, parted, refined, and assayed, and the net value thereof, and of all foreign coins deposited in said office, shall be ascertained; and the treasurer shall thereupon forthwith issue his certificate of the net value thereof, payable in coins of the same metal as that deposited, either at the office of the assistant treasurer of the United States, in New York, or at the mint of the United States, at the option of the depositor, to be expressed in the certificate; which certificates shall be receivable at any time, within sixty days from the date thereof, in payment of all debts due to the United States at the port of New York, for the full sum therein certified. All gold or silver bullion and foreign coin deposited, melted, parted, refined, or assayed as aforesaid, shall, at the option of the depositor, be cast in the said office into bars, ingots, or disks, either of pure metal or of standard fineness (as the owner may prefer), with a stamp thereon of such form and device as shall be prescribed by the secretary of the treasury, accurately designating its weight and fineness: *Provided,* That no ingot, bar, or disk shall be cast of less weight than five ounces, unless the same be of standard fineness, and of either one, two, or three ounces in weight. And all gold or silver bullion and foreign coin intended by the depositor to be converted into the coins of the United States, shall, as soon as assayed and its net value certified as above provided, be transferred to the mint of the United States, under such directions as shall be made by the secretary of the treasury, and at the expense of the contingent fund of the mint, and shall there be coined. And the secretary of the treasury is hereby authorized, with the approval of the president of the United States, to make the necessary regulations for the adjustment of the accounts between the respective officers, upon the transfer of any bullion or coin between the assay office, the mint, and assistant treasurer in New York.—*Ibid.*

Powers of Director of the Mint.

68. The operations of melting, parting, refining, and assaying in the said office shall be under the general directions of the director of the mint, in subordination to the secretary of the treasury; and it shall be the duty of the said director to prescribe such regulations, and to order such tests, as shall be requisite to insure faithfulness, accuracy, and uniformity in the operations of the said office.—*Ibid.*

Laws regulating the Mint, &c., to apply to this Office.

69. The laws of the United States for the government of the mint and its officers in relation to the receipt, payment, custody of deposits and settlement of accounts, the duties and responsibilities of officers and others employed therein, the oath to be taken and the bond and sureties to be given by them (as far as the same may be applicable), shall extend to the assay office hereby established, and to its officers, assistants, clerks, workmen, and others employed therein.—*Ibid.*

Charges for Refining, etc.

70. The same charges shall be made and demanded at the said assay office for refining, parting, casting into bars, ingots, or disks, and for alloy, as are or shall be made and demanded at the mint (see Sec. 43) ; and no other charges shall be made to depositors than by law are authorized to be made at the mint. And the amount received from the charges hereby authorized shall be accounted for and appropriated for defraying the contingent expenses of the said office.—*Ibid.*

Buildings and Machinery.

71. The secretary of the treasury is authorized to procure, by rent, lease, or otherwise, a building or apartments in the city of New York, suitable for the operations of said office, unless he shall be of opinion that suitable apartments in the custom-house in that city may be assigned for this purpose. And he is also hereby authorized and directed to procure the necessary machinery and implements for carrying on the operations and business of the said office.—*Ibid.*

CHAPTER SECOND.

VI. ASSAY AND COINAGE OF BULLION.

1. The provisions of the 5th section of chapter 97 of the act of Congress approved March 3d, 1853 (*see* 44), requiring the secretary of the treasury to limit the amount of refining at the mint, whenever private establishments shall be capable of refining bullion, shall be extended to the several branches of the mint, and to the United States assay office at New York, in all cases where deposits of bullion are made for coins or fine bars.—20 *February,* 1861.

2. The mint of the United States and branches shall continue to refine gold and silver bullion, and no contract to exchange crude or unparted bullion for refined bars shall be made until authorized by law.—20 *July,* 1868.

VII. BRANCHES OF THE MINT.

3. That a branch of the mint of the United States be located and established at Denver, in the territory of Colorado, for the coinage of gold.—21 *April,* 1862.

Officers of branch Mint at Denver.

4. For carrying on the business of said branch, the following officers shall be appointed, as soon as the public interest shall require their service, upon the nomination of the president, by and with the advice and consent of the senate, namely: one superintendent, one assayer, one melter and refiner, and one coiner; and the said superintendent shall employ as many clerks, subordinate workmen and laborers, under the direction of the secretary of the

treasury, as may be required. The salaries of the said officers shall be as follows: to the superintendent, the sum of two thousand dollars; to the assayer, the sum of eighteen hundred dollars; to the melter and refiner, eighteen hundred dollars; to the coiner, eighteen hundred dollars; to the clerks, subordinate workmen and laborers, such wages and allowances as are customary, according to their respective stations and occupations.—*Ibid.*

To give Bond.

5. The officers and clerks to be appointed under this act, before entering upon the execution of their offices, shall take an oath or affirmation, before some judge of the United States, or of the supreme court of said territory, faithfully and diligently to perform the duties of their offices; and shall each become bound to the United States of America, with one or more sureties, to the satisfaction of the director of the mint, or the secretary of the territory of Colorado, and of the secretary of the treasury, with the condition of the faithful performance of the duties of their offices.—*Ibid.*

Powers of Director of the Mint.

6. The general direction of the business of said branch of the mint of the United States shall be under the control and regulation of the director of the mint at Philadelphia, subject to the approbation of the secretary of the treasury; and for that purpose, it shall be the duty of the said director to prescribe such regulations, and require such returns periodically and occasionally, and to establish such charges for parting, assaying, refining and coining, as shall appear to him to be necessary for the purpose of carrying into effect the intention of this act in establishing said branch; also for the purpose of preserving uniformity of weight, form and finish in the coin stamped at said branch.—*Ibid.*

To be a Depository for Public Moneys.

7. Said branch mint shall be a place of deposit for such public moneys as the secretary of the treasury may direct; and the superintendent of said branch mint, who shall perform the duties of treasurer thereof, shall have the custody of the same, and also perform the duties of assistant treasurer; and for that purpose shall be subject to all the provisions contained in an act entitled "An act to provide for the better organization of the treasury, and for the collection, safe-keeping, transfer and disbursement of the public revenue," approved August 6th, 1846 (*see* Sec. 43, 62), which relates to the treasury of the branch mint at New Orleans.—*Ibid.*

Certificates of Deposit.

8. That the superintendent of said branch mint be authorized, under the direction of the secretary of the treasury, and on terms to be prescribed by him, to issue in payment of the gold dust and

bullion deposited for assay and coinage or bars, drafts or certificates of deposit, payable at the treasury or any sub-treasury of the United States, to any depositor electing to receive payment in that form.— *Ibid.*

General Laws extended to this Branch.

9. All the laws and parts of laws now in force for the regulation of the mint of the United States, and for the government of the officers and persons employed therein, and for the punishment of all offences connected with the mint or coinage of the United States, shall be and they are hereby declared to be in full force in relation to the branch of the mint by this act established, as far as the same may be applicable thereto.—*Ibid.*

Branch Mint at Carson City.

10. That a branch of the mint of the United States be located and established at Carson City, in the territory of Nevada, for the coinage of gold and silver.—*3 March*, 1863.

Appointment of Officers.—Salaries.

11. For carrying on the business of said branch, the following officers shall be appointed, as soon as the public interest shall require their service, upon the nomination of the president, by and with the advice and consent of the senate, namely : one superintendent, one assayer, one melter and refiner, and one coiner ; and the said superintendent shall employ as many clerks, subordinate workmen and laborers, under the direction of the secretary of the treasury, as may be required. The salaries of the said officers shall be as follows : to the superintendent, the sum of two thousand dollars ; to the assayer, the sum of eighteen hundred dollars ; to the melter and refiner, eighteen hundred dollars ; to the clerks, subordinate workmen, and laborers, such wages and allowances as are customary, according to their respective stations and occupations.—*Ibid.*

Oath of Office.—Bonds.

12. The officers and clerks to be appointed under this act, before entering upon the execution of their offices, shall take an oath or affirmation, before some judge of the United States, or of the supreme court of said territory, faithfully and diligently to perform the duties of their offices ; and shall each become bound to the United States of America, with one or more sureties, to the satisfaction of the director of the mint, or the secretary of the territory of Nevada, and of the secretary of the treasury, with the condition of the faithful performance of the duties of the offices.—*Ibid.*

Powers of Director of the Mint.

13. The general direction of the business of said branch of the mint of the United States shall be under the control and regulation

of the director of the mint at Philadelphia, subject to the approbation of the secretary of the treasury; and for that purpose, it shall be the duty of the said director to prescribe such regulations and require such returns periodically and occasionally, and to establish such charges for parting, assaying, refining and coining as shall appear to him to be necessary for the purpose of carrying into effect the intention of this act in establishing said branch; also for the purpose of preserving uniformity of weight, form and finish in the coin stamped at said branch.—*Ibid.*

To be a Public Depository.

14. Said branch mint shall be a place of deposit for such public moneys as the secretary of the treasury may direct; and the superintendent of said branch mint, who shall perform the duties of treasurer thereof, shall have the custody of the same, and also perform the duties of assistant treasurer; and for that purpose shall be subject to all the provisions contained in an act entitled " An act to provide for the better organization of the treasury, and for the collection, safe-keeping, transfer and disbursement of the public revenue," approved August 6th, 1846, which relates to the treasury of the branch mint at New Orleans.—*Ibid.*

Drafts to be issued for Gold Dust.

15. That the superintendent of said branch mint be authorized, under the direction of the secretary of the treasury, and on terms to be prescribed by him, to issue in payment of the gold dust and bullion deposited for assay and coinage or bars, drafts or certificates of deposit, payable at the treasury or any sub-treasury of the United States, to any depositor electing to receive payment in that form.—*Ibid.*

Laws Regulating the Mint extended to this Branch.

16. All the laws and parts of laws now in force for the regulation of the mint of the United States, and for the government of the officers and persons employed therein, and for the punishment of all offences connected with the mint or coinage of the United States, shall be and they are hereby declared to be in full force in relation to the branch of the mint by this act established, as far as the same may be applicable thereto.—*Ibid.*

Branch Mint at Dalles City.

17. That a branch of the mint of the United States be located and established at Dalles City, in the state of Oregon, for the coinage of gold and silver.—*4th July*, 1864.

Salaries.

18. For carrying on the business of the said branch the following officers shall be appointed, as soon as the public interest shall require their service, upon the nomination of the president, by and with the

advice and consent of the senate, namely: one superintendent, one assayer and one melter and refiner and one coiner; and the superintendent shall employ as many clerks, subordinate workmen and laborers, under the direction of the secretary of the treasury, as may be required. The salaries of the said officers and clerks shall be as follows: to the superintendent, the sum of two thousand dollars; to the assayer, the sum of eighteen hundred dollars; to the melter and refiner, eighteen hundred dollars; to the clerks, subordinate workmen and laborers, such wages and allowances as are customary, according to their respective stations and occupations.—*Ibid.*

Oath of Office.—Bonds.

19. The officers and clerks to be appointed under this act, before entering upon the execution of their offices, shall take an oath or affirmation before some judge of the United States, or of the supreme court of said state, faithfully and diligently to perform the duties of their offices; and shall each become bound to the United States of America, with one or more sureties, to the satisfaction of the director of the mint, or the district judge of the United States for the district of Oregon, and of the secretary of the treasury, with the condition of the faithful performance of the duties of their offices.—*Ibid.*

Powers of Director of the Mint.

20. The general direction of the business of said branch mint of the United States shall be under the control and regulation of the director of the mint, at Philadelphia, subject to the approbation of the secretary of the treasury; and for that purpose, it shall be the duty of the said director to prescribe such regulations, and to require such returns, periodically and occasionally, and to establish such charges for parting, assaying, refining, and coining, as shall appear to him to be necessary for the purpose of carrying into effect the intention of this act in establishing said branch; also for the purpose of preserving uniformity of weight, form, and finish in the coin stamped at said branch.—*Ibid.*

To be a Public Depository.

21. Said branch mint shall be a place of deposit for such public moneys as the secretary of the treasury may direct; and the superintendent of said branch mint, who shall perform the duties of treasurer thereof, shall have the custody of the same, and also perform the duties of assistant treasurer; and for that purpose shall be subject to all the provisions contained in an act entitled " An act to provide for the better organization of the treasury, and for the collection, safe-keeping, transfer, and disbursement of the public revenue," approved August 6, 1846, which relates to the treasury of the branch mint at New Orleans.—*Ibid.*

Drafts to be issued for Gold dust and Bullion.

22. That the superintendent of said branch mint be authorized, under the direction of the secretary of the treasury, and on terms to be prescribed by him, to issue in the payment of the gold dust and bullion deposited for assay and coinage, or bars, drafts, or certificates of deposit, payable at the treasury or any sub-treasury of the United States, to any depositor electing to receive payment in that form.—*Ibid.*

Laws regulating the Mint extended to this Branch.

23. All the laws and parts of laws now in force for the regulation of the mint of the United States, and for the government of the officers and persons employed therein, and for the punishment of all offences connected with the mint or coinage of the United States, shall be and they are hereby declared to be in full force in relation to the branch of the mint by this act established, as far as the same may be applicable thereto.—*Ibid.*

VIII. ASSAY OFFICE, BOISE CITY.

24. That a United States assay office be located and established at Boise City, in the territory of Idaho, for the assaying of gold and silver. For the carrying on of the business of said office the following officers shall be appointed, as soon as the public interest shall require their service, upon the nomination of the president, by and with the advice and consent of the senate, namely : one superintendent, one assayer, and one melter and refiner, and two clerks ; and the superintendent may employ as many subordinate workmen and laborers, under the direction of the secretary of the treasury, as may be required. The salaries of the said officers and clerks shall be as follows : to the superintendent, the sum of two thousand dollars ; to the assayer, the sum of eighteen hundred dollars ; to the melter and refiner, eighteen hundred dollars ; to the clerks, one eighteen hundred dollars and one sixteen hundred dollars ; to the subordinate workmen and laborers such wages and allowances as are customary, according to their respective stations and occupations.—*19th Feb.* 1869.

Oath of Office.—Bond.

25. The officers and clerks to be appointed under this act, before entering upon the execution of their offices, shall take an oath or affirmation before some judge of the United States, or of the supreme court of said territory, as prescribed by the act of July 2, 1862, and each become bound to the United States of America, with one or more sureties, to the satisfaction of the director of the mint, or of one of the judges of the supreme court of Idaho territory, and of the secretary of the treasury, with the condition of the faithful performance of the duties of their offices.—*Ibid.*

To be Subject to the Control of the Director of the Mint.

26. The general direction of the business of said assay office of the United States shall be under the control and regulation of the director of the mint at Philadelphia, subject to the approbation of the secretary; and for that purpose, it shall be the duty of the said director to prescribe such regulations, and to require such returns, periodically and occasionally, and to establish such charges for parting, assaying, melting and refining, as shall appear to him to be necessary for the purpose of carrying into effect the intention of this act in establishing said assay office.—*Ibid.*

To be a Public Depository.

27. Said assay office shall be a place of deposit for such public moneys as the secretary of the treasury may direct; and the superintendent of said assay office, who shall perform the duties of treasurer thereof, shall have the custody of the same, and also perform the duties of assistant treasurer; and for that purpose shall be subject to all the provisions contained in an act [entitled] "An act to provide for the better organization of the treasury, and for the collection, safe-keeping, transfer and disbursement of the public revenue," approved August 6, 1846, which relates to the treasury of the branch mint of New Orleans. (See Sec. 44).—*Ibid.*

Certificates of Deposit to be Issued for Bullion.

28. That the superintendent of said assay office be authorized, under the direction of the secretary of the treasury, and on terms to be prescribed by him, to issue in payment of the gold dust and bullion deposited for assay and coinage or bars, drafts or certificates of deposit, in sums of not less than one hundred dollars, payable at the treasury, or any sub-treasury of the United States, to any depositor electing to receive payment in that form.—*Ibid.*

Certain Laws extended to this Office.

29. All the laws and parts of laws now in force for the regulation of the United States assay office at New York, and for the government of the officers and persons employed therein, and for the punishment of all offences connected with said assay office, or with the mint of the United States, shall be and they are hereby declared to be in full force in relation to the assay office by this act located and established, so far as the same may be applicable thereto.—*Ibid.*

THE

NUMISMATIC DICTIONARY,

OR,

COLLECTION OF THE NAMES OF ALL THE COINS KNOWN,

FROM THE EARLIEST PERIOD UP TO THE PRESENT

DAY, WITH THEIR COUNTRIES, VALUES,

MULTIPLES, DIVISIONS, ETC.

ABACUS, the Roman calculation Table.

ABASSI, Persian, Silver, value 6d.   Qu. Shahee.

ABBEY PIECES, various countries, Brass, possibly current for small sums, but chiefly used in computation as Jetons.

ABDI, Silver, half rupee of Mysore.

ABRA, Polish, Silver, value 1s.

ABUQUELP, Egyptian, Silver, value 30 medini, 1s. 6d.   See Griscio.

ACHESON, Scots Billon, value 8d., named from Atkinson, mint master.

ACHTZEHNER, Swedish, Silver.

ACKEY, colonial, Silver, coined in 1818.

ACKIE, Ashantee, Gold, value 5s. 4d. from Ackee, seed of Guinea, Af.

ADHÀ, Silver of Nepaul, equal to a quarter *Rupee*.

ADLEA, Tripoli. A billon coin, issued in 1827, plated with Gold, forced upon the people as the equivalent of a Dollar.

AES, Roman, term for money in general, Brass.

AEFORTIATI, Roman, Senatorian coins of the 12th and 13th centuries.

AFTABY, scallop shaped gold coin of the Mogul dynasty, said to have been coined in the reign of Akbar, A.D. 1014.

AHMEDI, Gold coin of Mysore (Hindustan) about 31 to 32s. sterling.

AHMULAHS, Abyssinian salt money, various sizes, new, 20 to a Dollar.

AIGNEL, Anglo-Gallic, Gold.   Bearing the Agnus Dei.

AKHTER, Copper, quarter of the *Pice* of Mysore.

AKCHEH, Turkish silver, very small, value about $\frac{1}{4}$ of the Para.

ALBERT, Flemish, Gold.   Also Dollars and Groschen.

Albus, German, Copper, value 12 Hellers, at Cassel, Cologne, etc.

Alfazzat, Persian, Silver.

Allevure, Swedish, Copper, the smallest value.

Almond, Hindostan. The nut is current, 40 to a Piece. See Baddam.

Altin, Russian, Silver.

Altmichlic, Turkish, Silver, value 3s., 60 Paras.

Angel, English, Gold, value 6s. 8d., bearing St. Michael and Dragon.

Angelet, English, Gold, the half Angel, value 3s. 4d.

Angster, Swiss, Copper, also Rapp, value half a Rapen. Zurich.

Ankosee, Chinsoree, a Rupee of Silver, current in the Deccan.

Anna, or Ana, Hindostan, Silver, 16 to a Rupee.

Aperhias, Maltese.

Archer, Persian, Gold, the Daric.

Ardite, Spanish, Copper, ancient and of small value. Catalonia.

Argenteus Antoninianus, large Silver of Caracalla (Roman), about 60 to the then Roman pound.

Armoodi, Turkish, Gold.

As, Roman, Brass, value varied, literally 1lb. of 12 oz., but reduced, 216 B.C., to one ounce.

Ashereh, Modern Egypt, Silver, =10 Paras, 01¼.

Ashrafi, Persian, Gold, value 9s. sterling currency. There is also the treble Ashrafi, called "*Muhr-Ashrafi.*"

Ashruffy, Hindostan, Gold, value 12s. 6d. Nepaul.

Ashreneah, Modern Egypt, Silver, =20 Paras, 02½.

As Libralis, As Grave. Other names for the weighty As.

Aspar, Aspre, or Mina, Turkish, Silver. 120 to a Piastre.

Assarius, Small Roman Copper, appearing in the reign of Diocletian.

Assignats, French notes, first issued April 19th, 1790.

Assarion, Greek, Brass, rendered farthing.

Attine, Polish, Silver, value 5d.

August D'or, Saxony, Gold, value 16s. 3d.

Aureus, Roman, Gold, value 16s. 8d. The Bezant also.

Autonomous, Coins of Cities in Greece, enjoying their own laws.

Baat, Siamese, Sliver, value 2s. 6d., nut shaped.

Baboyères, Silver, coin current in Lorraine about A.D. 1511.

Bache, Zurich, Billon, value 1¾d.

Baddam, Hindostan, the almond of Persia, current on the Malabar coast.

Bagattino, Venetian, Copper, value half Soldi, ¼d.

Bagoglee, Persian, Gold, a ducat. Bajoglee.

Baiocco, Papal, Copper, value ½d.

Baiochello, Papal, Billon, single value 1d., double value 2d.

Bahadry, Hindostan, Gold, the Star Pagoda, in the Mysore, so called.

Bajoire, Genevese, Silver, value 4s. 6d.

Bákri, Silver, quarter Rupee of Mysore.

Banco, Genoese, Bank money. The word Bank is derived from the Lombards, the Bench for transacting business.

Banco-daler, Swedish, paper money issued by the National Bank, equivalent to about 35 cents.

Band, African, weight for gold dust, 2 oz.

Bank Dollar, Hamburg, Silver,
   In England, the Spanish Dollar, re-stamped and issued, as a Token, by the Bank, in 1804.

Barbone, Luccese, Silver, value 6d.   Qu. Bearded head.

Bars, Siamese, Siver, current.

Bars, W. African, Iron, current.

Basarmo, Hindostan, Tin.

Basaruco, Hindostan, Tin, Malabar coast, value 10 to 1d., see Budgerook.

Batz, Swiss, Copper silvered, value 1¼d., 10 Rappen.

Bawbee, Scots, Copper, value ½d.   Qu. Bas Piece.

Beard Coins, Russian, Copper.   Receipt for being shaved.

Bedidlik, Modern Egypt, Gold, = 100 piastres, $4 97.

Beka, Jewish, Silver.   The half Shekel.   Baka, divided.

Bell Dollar, Brunswick, Silver, D. Augustus 1643, with and without clapper.

Benda, Ashantee, Gold, value £10 13s. 4d.

Bendiky, Morocco, Gold, value 9s.

Bener-Penny, Anglo-Saxon, Silver, given in charity.   See Mærra.

Bes or *Bessis*, Roman, piece of 8 *unciae.*

Beshlik, Turkish, Silver, value 5 paras.

Bestic or Beslic, Turkish, Silver, value 5 aspers, 3d.

Bezant.   The Byzantine ducat, Gold.   Also silver Bezantines, Imperial coins from the 5th century after Christ, each value 2s.

Bezzo, Venetian, Copper, value ¼d.   Bezzi money.

Bia, Siamese, Copper, round and thick, value 200 cowries.

Bigati, Roman, Silver, the denarius bearing a two-horsed car.

Bigota, Chili, Gold.   Qu. Mustachio.

Billon, coins of mixed metal, silver and copper.   Bas Billon the worst.

Bisti, Persian, Silver, value, 2d.

Bit, the Spanish Real, Silver, in Jamaica: also the Portuguese Testone; there are also Half Bits, silver cut from Dollars.

Black Dog, St. Christopher's, Billon.   The Cut Dollar, also so called.

Black Mail, Scots protection money.
   Blanque Maille, French, bad Silver.

Black Money, English, the Bas Billon, denounced, temp. Edward I.

Black Peake, Indian.   Rare shells strung, value 2s. 6d. a cubit.

Blaffert, Cologne, a small coin.

Blamuser, Westphalia, money of account.

Blanc, French, a silver coin, value 4d.
   The Ecu Blanc, the French crown piece.

Blanca, Spanish, money of account in Malaga.

BLANK, English Billon. The Gros Blanc, Anglo-Gallic, temp. Henry VI.

BLANQUILLE, Barbary, Silver, value 2½d.

BODLE, Scots, Copper, the half Plack. From Bothwell, mint master.

BOHMEN, or Bohemian, Prague, Silver, value 3 Kreutzers.

BOLIVIANO, the new peso or dollar of Bolivia, equal to five francs.

BOLOGNINO, Luccese, Billon, value 1d. Also at Bologna.

BON-GROS, Hesse-Cassel, Silver, value 2d.

BONNET-PIECE, Scots, Gold, temp. K. James I. from the Cap then worn.

BORAGE GROAT, Scots, Silver, 1467, value 12d. Qu. From Borax used in it.

BORBI, Egyptian, Copper, value 3 aspers. Qu. Burbi, see Bourbe.

BORDHALFPENNY, paid for a stall in a market.

BORJOOKES, Abyssinian, glass beads, current for small money.

Bos, the Greek Didrachm, Silver, bearing an ox.

BOUTTETEEN, Tripoli, Silver = to 30 paras.

BOVELLA, Persian, Silver, value 16s.

BUNTAGUI, Morocco, gold, equal to about $2 00.

BOUGES, African, cowries are so called.

BOUHAMSTASH, Tripoli, =15 paras.

BOURBE, Barbary, money of account at Tunis, value half asper.

BOUSEBBATASH, Tripoli, =7½ paras.

BRABANT, English, Base coin, temp. K. Edward I.

BRABANT KRONE, Austrian, Silver, value 4s. 6d., 2g. 15k.

BRACTIATE, Roman, and other coins, impressed on one side only, from Bractia, a spangle.

BROAD PIECE, English, Gold, value 20s. The Unit, temp. K. James I.

BUDGEROOK, Hindostan, money of account on the Malabar coast, 6 to a Pice.

BUGNE, Silver Coin, current in Loraine about A. D. 1511. Struck in Metz.

BUISPERNAL, Silver Coin, current in Loraine about A. D. 1511.

BUSHE, Aix-la-Chapelle, Copper, value 4 Hellers.

BUSSORA, Crux, Turkish, Silver, value 16d.

CABESQUIS, Persian, Silver, value 1d. Casbesquis, Kasbequis.

CACAO, Mexico, Grains current, 100 to a Medio, 3½d.

CAGLIARESCO, Sardinian, Copper, value 6 to Soldi.

CAHAUN, Bengal, Silver, value 7½d. Cahuse, a quarter Rupee.

CALDERILLA, Spanish, Copper, the Cuarto, value 4 Maravedis.

CANDARINE, Chinese, money of account. 100 to a Tael, value ⅞d.

CANTEROY, Hindostan, the Sultany Fanam, so called in the Mysore.

CAPELLONE, Modena, Silver, value 3d.

CARAT, Arabian, a small coin of very base silver at Mocha.

The carat weight for gold, named from the red bean of Abyssinia, the fruit of the Kuara. 4 grains.

CARAGRONCH, Mod. Greece, Silver, value 5s.

CARDECU, French, Silver, the quart D'Ecu, so called in England.

CARIVAL, Bombay, valued 12 Pice.

CARL D'OR, Brunswick, Gold, value 16s. 4d.

CARLINO, Sardinian, Gold, value £1 18s. 10d.

CARLINO, Italian, Silver, value 5d. Coined first in 1490, by King Charles VIII. of France.

CARLO, Lombardy, Silver, value 5s.

CAROBA, Barbary. A coin of Tunis.

CAROLIN, new Gold coin of Sweden, equal to ten francs.

CAROLIN D'OR, Bavarian, Gold, value £1 0s. 8d.

CAROLINE, Swedish, Silver, value 1s. 6d.

CAROLUS, English, Gold, value 23s. The Laureat, temp. King Charles II. Carube money of account in Algiers.

CASH, Chinese, Brass, coins for stringing, cast, 1000 Cash, 100 Candarines, 10 Mace = 1 Tael. See Tseen.

CASTILLON, Spanish, Gold, probably from bearing the arms of Castile.

CASTELLANO, Spanish, Gold, the ancient coin.

CATAA HAMSEE, Modern Egypt, gold = 5 piastres. 25.

CATI, Chinese, value, 16 Taels, or £5 6s. 8d. Also Catty.

CAVALIER, Swedish, Silver.

CAVALLO, Sardinian, Billeon. Cavalli and Cavalluci, Naples.

CAVALLOTTO, Genoese, Billon, value 2d.

CAVEER, Arabian, money of account at Mocha. 40 to a Dollar. Cabeer or Carear, value 1½d.

CENT, Dutch, Copper, 100 to a Guilder.

CENT, American, Copper, 100 to a Dollar.

CENTIME, French, Copper, 100 to a Franc; also in Belgium and Ionian Islands.

CENTENTIONALIS, Roman, a silver coin issued by Constantine the Great, weight about 50 grains.

CENTESIMO, Italian, Copper. Lombardy, value one-twelfth of a penny, 100 to a Lira.

CENTESSIMO, Copper, Uruguay.

CENTUSSIS, Roman, 100 As, value in account 40 Sesterces 10 Deniers, or 6s. 3d.

CHAISE, Anglo-Gallic, Gold, temp. K. Edward III. The French Coin of Philip le Bel, the Royal Dur, hard coin.

CHALCUS, Greek, Brass. The earliest of that metal. 431 B. C.

CHALLIES, Ceylon, Copper, value 4 to a farthing. From Chally, Copper.

CHAPPEE, East Indies, Silver. The Rupee, when marked or chopped.

CHAYE, Persian, Silver. The Shaki, value 6d.

CHEDA, Tartary, Tin.

CHEGO, Portuguese, a weight for gold, 4 carats.

CHELON, Polish, Billon.

CHEQUIN, Turkish, Gold, value 9s. 6d.

CHERASIS, Persian, Gold, various value. The Tela, a medal.

CHIDA, Hindu, Tin, when round, value ½d., but if octagonal, value 2d.

CHIH TSIH, Chinese, a peculiar coin, struck by Woo Te of the Han dynasty.

CHOUSTACK, Polish, Billon, value 2d.

CHRISTIAN, Danish, Gold, value 16s. 5d.

CHRISTINE, Swedish, Silver, value 1s. 2d.

CHRYSUS, Greek, Gold, equivalent to the Stater.

CINQ FRANCS, French, Silver, value nearly 4s.

CINQUINO, Neapolitan.

CISTOPHORUS, Greek, Silver, bearing the Cista, or Chest, of Bacchus. Ancient Cistophori, of cities in Asia. Tri-drachms.

CLACO, Mexican. Elaco.

CLOTH, Abyssinia. Blue Surat cloth, a cubit in length, folded in a three-cornered packet, value half a dollar. See Wadmal.

COAL MONEY, British, found at Kimmeridge, coast of Dorsetshire; it is not quite proven that this was money.

COB, rough Silver pieces made in Mexico and South America, before the introduction of machinery.

COCKIEN, Japanese, value £10.

COINS, probably originally tokens given at Temples. The earliest are of religious character in their devices.

COLONATO, Spanish, Silver; the Pillar Dollar is so called.

COLONIAL COINS, Greek money struck for the Roman Colonies; also English, struck for Canada, the Indies, etc.

COLOGNE, the Mark of, Weight, the Standard of Germany, 8 oz. Troy.

COMMASSEE, Arabian, Copper, but contains a little silver. 60 to a dollar at Mocha.

CONDOR, Chili, Gold, 10 Pesos, value £1 17s. 3d.

CONDORIN, Japanese, Copper, value ¾d.

CONSTITUTION COINS, Germany, about 1738.

CONSULAR COINS, Roman, Silver, Denarii struck under the Government of Consuls. Family Medals.

CONTO, Portuguese, computation. 1000 Millreis.

CONTORNIATI, Roman, Tickets, not current.

CONVENTION COINS, German, about 1763, also 1848.

COPFSTUCK, Austrian, Silver, value 9d., 20 Kreutzers. Copstick.

COPANG, Japanese, Gold, value £2 4s. 2d. Also Silver, 4s. 6d. Qu. Oubans.

CORNADO, Spanish, Copper, value small. "No vale un Cornado," is, "not worth a farthing."

CORONILLA, Spanish, Gold. Vientin D'Oro, value 20 Reals.

COURONNES DU SOLEIL, French, Gold, 1546, current in England, as Crowns of the Sun, temp. K. Edward VI.

COWRIES, Bengal and Africa, small shells from the Maldives.

COZ, Persian, Copper, value 10 to a Shaki. Coz Bagues.

CRAZIA, Tuscan, value ¾d. An old coin.

CREUTZER, or CRUITZER. See Kreutzer.

CRIMBAL, W. Indies, Silver, value 7½d. The Isle du Vent. Bit.

CROAT, Spanish, Silver. The Gros D'Argent of Arragon, origin of English Groat.

CROCARD, English, Base coin, temp. K. Edward I.

CROCIATO, Genoese, Silver, named from the arms. The Croisat, value 4s. 4d.

CROON, Flemish, Silver.

CRORE, Bengal computation, 160 Lacs, or 10 million Rupees.

CROSS, all money bearing a cross. The Cross Dollar, of Spain, bears the Burgundy cross.

CROWN, English, Gold, temp. K. Henry VIII. Crowns of the double rose, Thistle Crowns.

CROWN, English, Silver, temp. K. Edward VI., value 5s.

CRUCHE, Swiss, Billon, value ½d.

CRUSADO, Portuguese, Gold and Silver, various value, the Crusado Novo, Silver, value 2s. 2d.

CU, thin Brass, bearing a shield ; the Ecu, half-farthing.

CUARTA, Spanish, Copper, value 4 Maravedis, the Calderilla.

CUFIC COINS, Arabian, named from Kufa, on the Euphrates.

CUNETTI COINS, Anglo-Saxon, Silver. Pennies struck at Cunetium, Marlborough.

CUT MONEY, Brazilian, Silver. Plata Macuquina.

CZARSONITCH, Russian, Gold, value 9s. 3d.

DAELDER, Dutch, Silver, value 2s. 6d.

DAEZAJIE, Persian, Silver, value 5s.

DAHAB, Abyssinian, Silver. See Harf.

DALER, Swedish, the Silver, in Silfermynt; the Copper, Kopparmynt.

DALER RIX, value 3s. 8d. See Dollar.

DAMA, Hindu, Copper. Nepaul.

DANAJO, Lombardy, Copper; or Danajuolo, the smallest money. Danaro.

DANDY PRAT, English, Silver, temp. K. Henry VII. dwarf coin.

DANE MONEY, Roman Coins found in Northamptonshire, so called.

DANIM, Arabian, current at Bussora, value ½d.

DARIC, Persian, Gold, named from Darius. Greek Darics.

DÉCADRACHM, Attic, Silver, equivalent to the Demi-stater of Gold.

DECIME, French, Copper, value 1d., the tenth of a Franc.

DECIMO, La Plata, Copper, value ½d., the tenth of a Medio.

DECUPLO, Sicilian, Gold.

DECUSSIS, Roman, Silver, marked X. 10 Asses, same as Denarius.

DENAING, Russian, Copper. Copees or Pence.

DENAR, Silesia, Copper, the Pfening of Breslau.

DENARIUS, Roman, Silver, marked X. Denos Æres, value 8d. ; it was lowered both in weight and value.

DENARIUS, Anglo-Saxon, as Denarii S. Petri, the Peter Pence, a golden Denarius, temp. K. Henry III.

DENARO, Italian, money of account, value, one 24th of a penny.

DENGA, Russian, Copper, the half Copee. Also Dengop and Denushka.

DEMY, Scots, Gold, like the English half noble. There are Demi-Pistoles, Louis, and Sequins in Gold.

DENIER, French, Copper, the twelfth part of a Sou. Also Swiss, the Deniers d'Argent, ancient coins; also the Deniers D'Or; the Double Denier, Anglo-Gallic, both of Silver, and Billon.

DENIER DE GROS, Flemish, the Groote, or Penny.

DENUSHKA, Russian, Copper, the half Copec.

DERHEM SEGAR, Barbary, Copper.

DERLINGUE, Venetian, Silver, half the Scudo.

DEVIL'S HEAD MONEY, Chinese, Silver. Spanish Dollars, so called.

DICHALCOS, Greek, Silver, the smallest coin.

DICKENS, Swiss, Silver.

DIDRACHM, Attic Silver, the Stater Aureus, or Philippus.

DIKOLLYBON, Greek, Copper.

DIME, American, Silver, value, the tenth of a Dollar, 5d.

DINAR, Arabian, Gold, value, 8s. Denar.

DINERO, Spanish, money of account. "Tener dinero," to be rich. DINERAL and DINERADA, a large sum of money.

DINERUELO, Spanish, Copper, current in Aragon.

DIOBOLUS, Attic Silver, division of the Pentobolus.

DIRHEM, Arabian, Silver.

DITTO BOLO, Ionian Islands, Copper.

DIWANI, Abyssinian money.

DOBRAO, Portuguese, Gold, value, £6 14s., the Dobra.

DOBLON, or Doubloon, Spanish, Gold, value, 5 Dollars; the Doblons de Acuatra, and De Ocho, are value, 8 and 16 Dollars.

DOBLON, Mexican, the gold onza, value, £3 4s.

DODEE, Bengal, Copper, the half Pice. Doudon. Dudu.

DODKIN, English, Copper, the small Duyt, once current.

DODRANS, Roman, piece of nine unciae, copper.

DOG, W. Indies, Copper, value, 3d. The half Dog, value, 1½d.

DOIT, Hindostan, Copper, 120 to a Rupee.

DOLLAR, Spanish, Silver, the Peso Duro, the Piastre, or Piece of Eight, an ounce, value, 4s. 3d.

DOLLAR, American, Silver, value, 4s. 1¼d., 10 Dimes, 100 Cents, 1000 Mills.

SPECIE DOLLAR, Norwegian, value, 4s. 6d.

DOLLAR, Swedish, Copper. In 1679, square, the legend and date in a circle, a crown in the corners. The Double Dollar is 9 inches square.

DOOGANEY, Bombay, Copper, a Pice.

DOPPIA, Papal, Gold, value, 13s.

DOPPIETTA, Sardinian, Gold.

DOPPIO, MODEA, Portuguese, Gold, value, £2 14s. The Double Pistole.

DOREA, Bombay, Copper, value, a farthing.

DORM PENNIES, Roman coins, found in Dorsetshire, so called.

DOS REALES, Mexican, Silver, value, 1s. 2 Reals.

DOUBLA, Barbary, value 4s. 6d. 80 aspers.

DOUBLE, French, Copper, value, 2 Deniers, the Double Denier.

DOUBLE, Guernsey, Copper, value, half farthing.
DOUBLE CROWN, English, Gold, 1604, value, 10s.
DOUBLE DUCAT, various, Gold, value, 18s. 8d.
DOUZAIN, French, Copper, value, 12 Deniers, the Sous.
DRACHM, Greek, Silver, value, 8d., literally a handful, 6 oboles.
DRACHM, Jewish, Silver, the half Shekel, so called by the Greeks.
DRACHMA, Modern Greek, value, 100 Lepta.
DREYER, Silesian, Copper, the half Kreutzer of Breslau.
DREYLING, Danish, Copper, the quarter Skilling.
DRITTEL, Mecklenburgh, Silver, value, 1s., one third of Rix Dollar.
DUBBEL, Batavia, money of account.
DUBBELTJE, Dutch, Copper, value, 2 Stivers.
DUBS, Hindu, Copper.   See Dudee, or Dodee.
DUCAT, various, the coin of a Dukedom, first coined at Venice, Gold,
    value, 9s. 4d., Silver, 3s. 5d.
DUCATELLO, Venetian, Silver.
DUCATO DI BANCO, Neapolitan, Silver, value, 5 Tarins, 3s. 6d.
DUCATONE, Flemish, Silver, the crown; value, 5s. 3d. also, in Parma,
    the Scudo, value, 4s. 3d.
DUETTO, Italian, Billon, 2 quattrini.
DUMAREE, Hindu, Copper, 12 to a Pice, on the Malabar coast.
DUPONDIUS, Roman, Brass, the double As.
DUTGEN, Dantzic, Silver, value, 3 Groschen.
DURO, Spanish, Silver, the hard Dollar, the Cob.
DUYT, Dutch, Copper, the eighth of a stiver.   Doit.
DYNG, Burmah, Silver as above.   Worth about 5 per cent. more than
    Huetnee.   *Exceedingly pure.*

EAGLE, English, Silver, base coin, temp. K. Edward I.
EAGLE, American, Gold, value, 10 Dollars, £2 1s.
ECU, Anglo-Gallic, Gold, temp. K. Edward III.   The chaise.
ECU, French, Silver, the Crown, the Ecu Blanc, and Gros Ecu.
EBBOEER, Danish, Silver, value, 14 Skillings.   The Justus Judex.
EFFECTIVE, money in Spain and Portugal, so called.
EGISTALER, Hungarian, Silver, the Dollar.
ELECTRUM, coins in metal, partly Silver and partly Gold.
ESCA, a Gold coin, current in Lorraine about A. D. 1511.
ESCALIN, Netherlands, base silver; and name for the Bit, in West
    Indies.
ESCALIN, Liege, Silver, value, 10d. and money of account in Basle.
ESCUDO, Spain, Gold, value, 8s.
ESTERLING, English, Silver, the Anglo-Norman penny, whence Ster-
    ling.

FALOO, Madras, Copper, value, 5 Cash.
FAMILY COINS, Roman, Silver.   Denarii struck under Consuls.

FANAM, Hindu, Silver, value, 1¼d.   Fanon and Fano.   There is

FANAM, Indian, Gold, with alloy, on the Malabar coast, value, 6d.

FARDO, Indian, Silver, value, 2s. 9d.   Qu. Pardo.

FARTHING, English, Copper, 1672; some previously of pewter, tokens, value, 960 to the £1.

FARUKI, Hindu, Gold, the quarter Mohur.

FEDERAL MONEY, American and Federation money, German, 1838.

FELDKLIPPE, Netherlands, Silver, a siege piece of William, Duke of Julich, 1543.

FELOUK, Barbary, Copper, value, a farthing.

FELS, a small Copper coin.   Persian *pul.*   Arabic *fils*, said to be the same as the Turkish *Mangur.*

FENIM, Swiss, money of account.

FETTMANGEN, Flemish, money of account at Cleves.

FEORTHLING, Anglo-Saxon, Silver, literally a fraction, the fourth part of a penny, hence derived farthing.

FERDING, Russian, Silver.   Money of account at Libau.

FILLIPO, Italian, Silver.   Milan, value, 4s. 11d.

FIORINO, Tuscan, Gold, named from the Fleur-de-Lis, arms of Florence, value, 1s. 1½d.

FISCA, Canary Isles, Silver.

FIVE POUND PIECE, English, Gold, various reigns.

FLINDERKE, Hanoverian, money of account at Emden.

FLINRICH, Bremen, money of account.

FLITTER, Brunswick, Copper, small, literally, a spangle.

FLOOSE, Arabian, value, one twentieth of a penny, money of account at Bussorah, and in Barbary.

      Fluce, Flouche.

FLOREN, Flemish, Silver, value, 1s. 8d., the Guilder.

FLORIN, English, Gold, temp. K. Edward III.   The gold florin, struck by German States.

FLORIN, English, Silver, 1849, a tenth of the Pound.

FLORIN, Polish, Silver, value, 6d.   The Zlot.

FOANG, Siamese, Silver.   Fuang, Fouang.

FOLLIS, Roman, Brass, weight, ½oz.

FONDUCLI, Turkish, Gold, value, 7s. 6d.

FORLI, Egyptian, Copper.

FORTY PENCE.   Ten groats was a fee for a Lawyer, or Priest.

FOUR ANGEL PIECE, Scots, Gold, temp. K. James IV.

FRANC, French, Silver, value, 9½d.   The unit also of Belgium, Switzerland, and Sardinia.

FRANCISCONE, Tuscan, Silver, value, 4s. 4d.

FRANKEN, Swiss, old money of account, value, 1s. 2¼d.

FREDERICK D'OR, Prussian, Gold, value, 16s. 6d.

FUDDAH, Egyptian, Silver.   The Para.

FUDDEA, Bombay, Copper.   The double Pice, 1d.

FUNDUK, Turkish, Gold, weight about 52 grs.

FYRKE, Danish, Copper.

GALL, Cochin China, Silver, value, 4d.

GASSA, Persian. 20 to a Mamoodi.

GARI, Hindu. About 4000 Rupees.

GAZ, Turkish, Silver. The Para.

GAZZETTA, Venetian, Copper, value, ¾d.

GENOVINO, Genoese, Silver, value, 4s. 4d. The Scudo.

GENOVINO, Genoese, Gold, value, £3 2s. 8d., 96 Lire, Genovino.

GENEVOISE, Geneva, Silver.

GEORGE D'OR, Hanoverian, value, 16s. 3d.

GEORGINO, Modena, Silver, value, 2¼d.

GERAH, Jewish, Silver, the smallest money, 20th of a shekel.

GHERISH, Turkish, Billon, also called Piastre.

GIGLIATO, Tuscan, Gold. The Zequin.

GIULIO, Papal, Silver, value, 6d., as the Paulo, and Leono.

GIUSTINA, Venetian.

GIUSTINIANO, Venetian, Silver.

GOESGEN, Hanoverian, money of account.

GOLCHUTS, Chinese, Gold, in canoe-shaped ingots. The Dutch name.

GOLD DUST, Africa, current in Tibbar, in the central part.

GOLD LUMPS, Ashantee, current.

GOLD PENNY, English, temp. K. Henry III.

GOURDS, Spanish and American Dollars, are so called in the West Indies.

GOZ, Arabian.

GRAIN, Troy weight, the smallest, 24 to a pennyweight; the fourth of a Siliqua, or Carat.

GRANO, Maltese, Copper. Also Neapolitan. Value, one third of a penny.

GRISCIO, Egyptian, Silver, value, 1s. 6d., 30 medini.

GRIWNA, Russian, Silver, value, 10 copees, 3½d. Grieve, Grieven.

GROAT, English, Silver, from temp. K. Edward III. Grossum, Greater. Croat, Gros.

    Broadfaced groats, Rex groats, Dominus groats, and Cross Key groats, as well as White groats, so base that a shilling is worth nine of them.

GROOT, Dutch, Copper, value, ½d.

GROS, Flemish, Silver.

GROS, Anglo-Gallic, Billon. Also Gros Blanc.

GROS ECU, Geneva, Silver, value, 4s. 8d.

GROSCHEN, Prussian, Billon, value, 30 to a Thaler, 1½d. Also Russian and Polish.

GROSSETTO, Venetian, money of account.

GROSSO, Luccese, Billon, value, 3d. Mezzo-Grosso, 1½d.

GROTE, Bremen, value, ½d., 96 Grotes to a Specie Rix Dollar, also Flemish, 12 to a shilling.

GROUCH, Turkish, Silver, the Piastre. Guerche, Goorooch.

GROUPE, Turkish, computation. A bag of money.

GRUESO, Spanish, money of account at Navarre.

GUBBER, Bengal, Gold, the Dutch Ducat, so called. The Sequin

GUIENNOIS, Anglo-Gallic, Gold, temp. K. Edward III.

GUINEA, English, Gold, 1662, value, 20s., afterward 21s. First struck in gold from the Guinea coast.

GUILDER, Flemish, Silver, value, 1s. 8d. The Gulden.

GUILLOT, Brabant, Copper, one sixth of a Sou.

GULDEN, Germany, Silver, value, 1s. 8d. 60 Kreutzers, Austrian, Silver Gulden, 2s., Florin.

GUNDA, Bengal, value, 4 cowries.

GUN MONEY, Irish, Brass, temp. K. James II. Made from cannon.

GUT GROSCHE, Prussian, Hanoverian, 24 to a Thaler.

HALF-PENNY, English, Silver, from temp. K. Edward I. Also Copper, from temp. King Charles II.

HARD HEAD, Scots, Billon, value, 1½, the Hardie.

HARDI, French, Copper, 1270, the Liard of Philip le Hardi.

HARDIE, English, Billon, temp. K. Edward III.

HARDIT, Anglo-Gallic, Gold, temp. K. Richard II. Double and Half Hardits.

HARF, African. Qu. Haraff. The Dahal.

HARPER, Irish, Silver, value, 9d. A familiar term.

HASER DENARIE, Persian, Silver. Huza Deenar.

HASSHAHSHAH, African, Iron, anchor-shaped. Hashia.

HECTAE, or HEKTALE, Greek, Gold, ⅓ of the Stater and divisions, small as the $\frac{1}{16}$ of the Hectae.

HEIDERI, Silver, Double Rupee of Mysore.

HELFLING, Anglo-Saxon, Silver. The Halfpenny.

HELLER, German, Copper. 4 Hellers—1 Kreutzer, 60 Kreutzers—1 Gulden.

HEMICHRYSUS, Greek, Gold, equivalent to half Stater.

HEMI-DRACHM, Greek, Gold, value, 6 silver Drachmæ, 3s. 9d.

HEMI-OBOLUS, Attic, Silver, one-half of the Obolus.

HEMI-OBOLUS, Greek, Silver, the half Obolus, one twelfth of a Drachm. Hemi Drachm, or Triobolum.

HEMI-STATER, Greek, Gold, one-half of the Stater.

HOG, Irish, Silver, the English Shilling, so called.

HOGS PENCE, Roman coins, found in Leicestershire, so called as turned up by swine.

HOON, Madras, Silver. The Pagoda.

HORSE, Danish, Silver, value, 1s. 2d.

HUET-NEE, Burmah—or translated "flower silver"—paid out by weight and quality, for trade purposes, and worth about 15 per cent more than the rupee silver of Hindustan.

HUITIEME, Genoese, Gold, value, 8s. 4d.

HUNA, Hindu, money of account on the Malabar coast. Qu. Anna.

HUZAR DEENAR, Persian, Gold. Haser Denarie.

IKILIK, Turkish, Silver, equal to two piastres.

IMANI, small Silver coin of Mysore.

IMPERIAL, Russian, Gold, 10 Rubles, value, £1 12s. 7d., also Flemish, Gold, value, 11s. 3d.

INDEPENDENT DOLLAR, Chili, 1817, Silver.

INDERMILLE, Hindu, Silver, value, 10d. Nepaul.

INFORTIATI, Roman, Senatorian coins of the 12th and 13th centuries.

INGOT, Japan and Burman Empire, current, unwrought, both of Gold and Silver.

INGOT, a few were issued by the Bank of England on resuming cash payments, in 1816.

INGOT, a thin bar of Gold or Silver, to be rolled and made into coin ; sometimes applied to small commercial bars.

IRON, Angola, now current, in bars. Also Lacedamonian money.

ITAGANNES, Japan, Silver, in lumps.

ITZIK, Japan, Gold, value, 8s. 9d. Bean shaped. Itjib, Itchebo.

IZELOTTE, German, Silver, value, 2s. 9d.

JACOBUS, English, Gold, value, 25s. temp. K. James I.

JÀFARI, small Silver coin of Mysore.

JAGHIRE, Hindu.

JAKU, Jewish, Gold.

JANE, English, Billon. Coins brought from Genoa.

JETON, Flemish, Brass, counter, from Jeter, to cast.

JETTAL, Hindu, Copper, on Malabar coast. Settle. Jetul.

JILÀLEH, Silver coin, square form. Mogul dynasty, equal to the Rupee in value.

JOANESE, Portuguese, Gold, value, £3 11s. 2d. Commonly termed the Joe.

JULIO, the Papal, and Justiniano, the Venetian, Silver coins. See G.

JUSTINIANO, Venetian, Silver, value, 4s. 11d.

JUX, Turkish, 100,000 Aspers. Juck.

KABEAN, Tavoy Hindostan, Copper, value, a farthing. 40 Kabeans =1 Rupee.

KAIRIE BASHIREH, Modern Egypt, Gold=10 piastres. 48.

KAIRIE HASHREEN, Modern Egypt, Gold=20 piastres. 1.01.

KAISER GROSCHE, Bohemian, Silver, value, 1½d.

KALTIS, Lydian, Gold.

KAPANG, Sumatra, Copper, small.

KATIB, Copper, one-eighth of the *Pice* of Mysore.

KASBEKI, or KASBEGI, Persian, Copper coin.

KÀZMI, small Silver coin of Mysore.

KAZNEH, Egyptian, a Treasury of 1000 Purses, value £5,000.

KEES, Egyptian, a Purse of 500 Piastres, £5.

KEFEB, Turkish.

KEEPING, Sumatra.

KESITAH, Canaanite, Silver, bearing a lamb.

KHEYREEYEH, Egyptian, Gold, value, 1s. 9d.
KHODÁBANDI, Persian, Silver, value about 7d. stlg.
KIBEAR, Abyssinian.
KIN-TAO-TSIEN, Chinese, knife-money.
KITZE, Turkish, Gold. A Bag, value, 30,000 Piastres.
KIZRI, very small Silver coin of Mysore.
KLIPPINGE, Danish, Silver.
KOBANG, Japanese, Gold, value, 27s. 4d.; it varies.
KODAMA, Japanese, Silver, a globular lump bearing characters.
KOLA, nut, Africa. Current on the Western Coast.
KOMPOW, Chinese, Linen, current in the Philippine Isles.
KOLLYBON, Greek, Copper.
KOPEK, Russian, Copper, also Copeck and Kopaika, value, three
    eighths of a penny.
KOPY, Bohemian, money of account.
KOPFSTUCK, Austrian, Silver. 20 Kreutzers.
KOPFSTÜCK, Bavarian, Silver, value about 16 cents.
KOROOMS, Persian, Silver. Keran. Kran.
KORSHVIDE, Danish, Silver.
KRAN, Arabian, also Karaun, 500 equal to 10,000 Piastres.
KREUTZER, Austrian, Copper, value, one third of a penny, from
    Kreutz, Cross. See Heller.
KRONEN THALER, German, Silver. The Brabant Crown or Dollar,
    value, 4s. 5d.
KRUMSTERK, Hanoverian. At Emden.

LAC, Bengal computation, 100,000 Rupees, etc. Lakh.
LAND MUNTZ, German, Billon, money circulating only in the State
    where coined.
LARGE BRASS, Roman. The Sestertius, value, about 2d.
LARIN, Arabian, Silver, value, 1s. Laree. Persian.
LAUB THALER, Prussian, Silver. The Dollar with a wreath.
LAUREAT, English, Gold. Temp. K. Jas. I. Laurel, value, 20s.
LAXSAN, Batavian, money of account.
LEADEN COINS, Roman. Nummi plumbei, and current in the
    Birman Empire, also Tokens English.
LEAM, Chinese, Silver, in Ingots, each value, 6s. 8d.
LEATHER COINS, Roman. Ases Scorteos, and English Tokens.
LEONINE, English, base foreign coin, temp. King Edward I., value, ¼d.
LEOPARD, Anglo-Gallic. Gold, temp. K. Edward III.
LEOPOLD, Belgium, Gold, value, 19s. 4½d., when issued 25 Francs,
    now 24¼ Francs.
LEOPOLDINO, Tuscan, Silver, value, 4s. 5d.
LEPTON, Greek, Copper, ancient; modern Lepta, 100 to a Drachma.
LIARD, French, Copper, value, 3 Deniers.
LIBELLA, Roman, Brass. The As of diminished weight.
LIBRA JAQUESA, Spanish, value, 3s. 1d., money of account in Arra-
    gon, and Balearic Isles.

LION, Scots, Gold.   Le Lion, an early French coin, and Anglo-Gallic in Billon.   LION DOLLAR is Dutch.

LIRA, Italian, Silver.   Lira Nouva, value, 9½d., Lira Austriaca, value, 8d.

LIRAZZA, Venetian, Silver, base, value, 1s. 3d., 30 Soldi.

LISBONINE, Portuguese, Gold, value, 25s.

LIVONINA, Russian, old coin.

LIVORNINO, Tuscan, Silver, value, 4s. 4d., also Lantern, or Tower Dollar.

LIVRE, Old French computation, value, 10d., 20 sous.   Livre Tournois, a coin of Tours.

LOUIS D'OR, French, Gold, value, 18s. 8d.

LOUIS D'ARGENT, French, Silver, value, 60 sous.

LUBS, the money of Lubeck.

LUCULLEA, Roman.   Money struck in Greece by Lucullus, by order of Sylla.

LUNGA, the currency of Leghorn, as distinguished from that of Florence.

LUSBURGER, Luxemburg, Silver penny, temp. K. Edward I.; forbidden in England, temp. Edward III.

LYANG, Chinese, money of account.

MAAMBE, Egyptian, Silver, value, 2 Piastres, 8d.

MACE, Sumatra, Batavia, and China, value, 8d.

MACUQUINA, Brazilian, Silver, the cut money, quina of arms 5 shields Portugal.

MACUTA, Portuguese, Africa, Silver, value, 2¾d., 2000 zimbis or cowries.

MADONINA, Genoese, Silver, value, 1s. 6¾d.   The double Lira.

MÆRRA, Anglo-Saxon, Silver.   The Bener penny.

MAHBUB, Tripoli, Gold, value, 1s. ¼d., also Mahboob.

MAHHBOUL, African, value, 4s. 2d.

MAILE, English, Silver, the Half Sterling, temp. Henry IV.

MAILLE, French, Billon, base coin of smallest value.

MAJORINA PECUNIA, Roman, Brass.   Lower Empire.

MALLA, Spanish, Copper, 2 Mallas—1 Denier.   The smallest coin at Barcelona.

MALTIER, German, Billon, value, half a Marien Groschen.

MAMOUDA, Arabian, Silver, value, 5½d., 10 Floose—1 Danim, 10 Danims—1 Mamouda.   Also Mamoodi.

MANCANZA, Neapolitan, Gold, value, 15s., 4 Ducati.

MAMCOUSCH, Arabian, Gold.

MANCUS, Anglo-Saxon, Gold, value, 30 pence.   From the Arabian Mancush.

MANEH, Jewish, equal to 50 or 60 Shekels.

MANGÛR, Greek, 4 to an Asper.

MANILLA, African, Copper, current on Western Coast, also of Iron and of Tin.

MARABOTIN, Spanish, Silver. Arabic Dirhem.

MARADOE, Chinese, Silver, value, 600 Cash.

MARAVEDI, Spanish, Copper, 34 Maravedis—1 Real, 20 Reals—1 Dollar.

MARC, Danish, Silver, Marc of Currency, value, 4½d., specie Marc, value, 1s. 6d., Marc of Hambro and Lubeck, 1s. 6d. Also Mare.

MARC, Norwegian, Silver, specie Marc, value, 10½d., 24 Skillings.

MARCHETTO, Venetian, Billon, value, ⅓d. Marcucci, the St. Mark.

MARENGO, Lombardy, Gold, value, 14s. 7d. Eridania 1801.

MARIEN GROSCHEN, German, Billon, value, ⅔d., 36 to a Thaler, Marien Gulden, at Brunswick.

MARK, English Computation, 13s. 4d. Mearc, Anglo-Saxon, also Danish and Swedish.

MARK, Scots, Silver, 1581.

MARK OF COLOGNE, German weight, 8 oz. Troy.

MARQUE, Mauritius, Copper.

MAS. Qn. Mace, Chinese and Indian Silver, value, 100 Cash. The Masse, 14 Rupees.

MASSE, French, Gold, 1314. The Chaise. From the Mace or Scepter.

MATH, Hindoo. Money of account at Rangoon.

MATTAPAN, Venetian, Silver, value, 3d. Coined at Cape Mattapan, 1203.

MATTIER, Hanoverian, Silver. Matthier, Copper.

MAUNDY MONEY, English, Silver. The Silver 1d., 2d., 3d., and 4d., coined for Royal Charity on Maundy Thursday.

MAX D'OR, Bavarian, Gold, value, 13s. 7d., MAXIMILIAN, 1½ Ducats.

MAYON, Siamese, Silver, the 4th of the *tical.*

MEDAL, a term for a coin, not struck for currency.

MEDIA ONZO, Mexican, Gold, value, £1 12s. Also Media quarta de Onza.

MEDIAN, Barbary, Gold.

MEDINO, Egyptian, Silver, the Para. The Turkish Medin or Meidein.

MEDIO PESA, Mexican, Silver, value, 2s. 1½d. The half Dollar.

MEDJEDEER, Turkish, Silver, value, 3s. 5d., 20 Piastres.

MEHRÁBI, an oblong gold coin or medal of the Mogul Dynasty of Hindustan, about 6dwt. 22grs. weight.

MEISSNER GULDEN, Saxony. Money of account at Leipsic.

MENIAN, Barbary, Silver, value, 2s. 7d., 50 Aspers.

MERAU, French, Lead. A Token at Religious festivals.

MERIGAL, Barbary, Gold, value, 18s.

MERK, Scots, Silver, value, 1s. 1d.

MESS VALUTA, Tyrol, money of account at Bolsano.

METICAL, Barbary, Gold, value various.

METALLINE, Roman, Copper washed with Silver, so called.

MEZZO SCUDO, Lucca, Silver, half Scudo.

MIDDLE BRASS, Roman. Size of Semis.

MIL, proposed name for the thousandth part of the Pound.

MILL, United States, money of account. 1000 to a Dollar.
MILLIARENSIS, Silver of Constantine the Great, equal to 24 *follis.*
MILREA, Portuguese, Gold, value, 4s. 5d.
MILREI, Portuguese, Silver, value, 4s. 5d.   1000 Reis.
MILREI, Brazil, Silver, value, formerly 4s. 5d., now 2s. 1d.
MIMOEDA, Portuguese, Gold, value, 13s. 6d.   The half-moidore.
MINA, Greek, Greek money of account, or 100 drachmæ.
MINUTA, Anglo-Saxon, Copper.   The Styca.
MIOBOLO, Ionian Islands, Copper.
MIRLITOF, French, Gold.
MISCAL, Arabian, Gold.
MISSILIA, Roman.   Coins scattered at the Games.
MITE, English, Copper, value, one third of a farthing.
MITKUL, Barbary, Gold, value, 9s., 24 Fluces—1 Blankeel, 4 Blan-
     keels—1 Ounce, 10 Ounces—1 Mitkul.   Bendiky, Miscal, or Du-
     cat.
MITRE, English, base silver, temp. K. Edward I.
MOBOGS, Hindu, seeds used for weighing gold.
MOCO, West Indies, Silver, value, 1s. 1½d.   A piece cut from a
     Dollar.
MOHUR, Hindu, Gold, value, £1 9s. 1d., the Mohur Sicca, 32s.   Mohr,
     Mohar, and Moore.
MOIDORE, Portuguese, Gold, value, 27s.   The Moeda D'Oro.
MONACO, Italian, Silver, value, 4s. 4d.   The Monk.
MONZONNAH, Barbary, Silver, value, 1d.
MORELOS DOLLARS, Mexican, Silver Dollar, coined in 1812 or '13 by
     the Rep. Gen. Morelos.
MOSTOSKA, Russian, Copper, 4 to a Kopek.
MOUTON, Anglo-Gallic, Gold.   Bearing Agnus Dei.
MUSKET BALLS, American, value, a farthing, current in Massachu-
     setts, 1656.
MURAGLIOLI, Modena, Copper, value, 1d.
MYNET, Anglo-Saxon, whence mint.
MURAJOLA, Bologna.
MUNTZE, German.   The small coins.

NANDIOGINS, Japanese, Silver.   A lump.
NAPOLEON, French, Gold, 1803, value, 15s. 10d., 20 Francs.
NASARA, Tunis, Silver, value, 2½d.
NAULUM, Greek, money put into mouths of deceased persons.   The
     freight.
NEWEMEEN, Ashantee, Gold, value, £4 5s. 4d. an ounce.
NISFIAH, Turkish, Gold, weight about 20 grains.
NOBLE, English, Gold, 1344, value, 6s. 8d ; there are George, Rose
     Nobles, etc.
NOUMIA, Roman, small Copper, only 10 grains weight, later days of
     the Empire.
NUMMUS, Roman, the Sestertius, also the Generic name for money

Nusf, Modern Egypt, Silver=10 Piastres, 48 cts.
Nusflik, Modern Egypt, Gold=50 Piastres, $2.49.
Noir, French West Indies, Billon, 1½d., the black dog, so called.

Oban, Japan, Gold. Ouban.
Obolus, Greek, Brass, also Anglo-Saxon, and English, temp. K.
    Henry III., base.
Obolus, Rhenish, Gold. Also Silver, value, 1s. 2d.
Obolo, Ionian Islands, Copper.
Obsidional, money struck during a siege.
Ochava, Mexican, Copper, value, ⅜d., 8 Ochavas—1 Rial, 8 Rials—1
    Dollar.
Ochavo, Spanish, Copper, value, ½d. The Chavo and Chovy.
Ochello, Venetian, Gold, value, £1 17s. 8d., 4 Zecchine.
Ochosen, Spanish. The smallest old coin.
Octagon, California. See Slug.
Oertogs, Swedish, Silver.
On-beshlik, Turkish, Silver=15 Paras.
Oncetta, Neapolitan, Gold, value, 10s. 3d.. Onza.
Oncia, Italian, Gold, value, 10s. 3d. in Sicily.
Onikilik, Turkish, Gold, value, about 90 cents.
Onlik, Turkish, Silver=10 Paras.
Onza de Oro, Mexican, Gold, value, £3 4s. The Doblon.
Onzaro, Papal, Gold, value, 9s. 4d., the Ducat. Ongaro.
Or, Persian, Silver, value, 6s. 8d.
Ora, Anglo-Saxon, computation, an ounce, 20 pennies. Also
    Danish.
Or, or Ore, Swedish, Copper, and Silver, value, 1d. Koppar Ore,
    the Rundstyck. Silver, the Styfer.
Ort, Danish, the fourth; as Ort Groschen, fourth of a Groat.
Ortje, Flemish, Copper.
Osella, Venetian, Gold. Oselle, Venetian, Silver, value, 3s. 2d.
    Osell.
Ostic, Greek, value, 6d.
Oustava, Portuguese. A division of the Mark.
Owl, Greek, Silver. The Tetradrachm.

Padens, Hindoo, nuts from Persia, current at Surat. The Bad-
    dams.
Pagoda, Hindoo, Gold, and also Silver. Star Pagoda, value, 7s. 4d.
    Arcot Pagoda, value, 4s. 11d.
Paï, a Chinese Medal.
Paisah, Hindoo, Copper. Nepaul.
Paolo, Papal, Silver, value, 5d., 10 Pauli—1 Scudo.
Paparina, Roman, coins of 12th and 13th centuries, also called
    Provisini.

7

Papetto, Papal, Silver, value, 10½d.
Papirolo, Sardinian, Billon.
Para, Turkish, Billon, 40 Paras to a Piastre. Parat.
Pardo, Barbary, Silver, value, 1s. 3d. Pardao. Also Indian.
Pargo, Portuguese India, Silver, value, 2s. 5d., 4 Tangas.
Parisis D'Or, French, 1350. And Parisis d'Argent, 1350.
Parpajolo, Lombardy, Billon, value, 1d., 8 to a Lira.
Pasteboard, Dutch. Siege money at Leyden, 1574.
Pataque, another name for the Turkish Silver, *Yuzlik.*
Pataca, Portuguese and Brazilian, Silver, value, 1s. 5d., Patacao or Selo.
Patack, Batavian.
Patacon, Spanish, Silver, value, 4s. 3d.
Patagon, Dutch, Silver, value, 4s. 1d., 50 Stuyver Piece, or Leg Dollar. Swiss, value, 3s. 10d.
Patard, Flemish, Copper, value, 1d. Patar, the Stiver.
Patty, Hindoo, inferior coin of Trangania.
Paunchea, Bombay, money of account, value, 5 Rupees.
Pavillon, Anglo-Gallic, Gold, temp. K. Edward III.
Pecco, Java. Money of account.
Pecha, Tartary, Copper. Pessa, Pice.
Pecunia, Roman money, from Pecus, cattle.
Penebad, Silver of Persia, present weight about 41 grains.
Penge, Danish, Pence, money.
Penguin, Ashantee, Gold, value, £11 16s. 4d.
Pening, Dutch, Copper, the half-farthing, coin in general in many countries.
Penny, Anglo-Saxon, Silver; English, Gold, temp. K. Henry III., also Copper, from temp. K. George III., 240 to a Pound.
Penny of St. Paul, Westphalia, Silver, 1260. Munster.
Pennyyard, Penny, Silver, English coins in heraldry so called. Spence, arms.
Pentadrachm, Greek, Silver, value, 3s. 6d. Drachmæ.
Pentachalkon, Attic, Silver, ⅝ of the Obolus.
Pentobolus, Attic, Silver, piece of 5 Oboles.
Perpero, Ragusa, Silver. Perpera, Greek, Gold, value, 10s.
Peseta, Spanish, Silver, value, 1s. 0½d., 5 Reals; the Mexican quarter dollar.
Peso Duro, Spanish, Silver, value, 4s. 3d. The Hard Dollar.
Pessa, Hindoo, Copper, value, ½d. Pecha, Pice.
Petermengen, Germany Triers, Billon, value, ¾d.
Petit Florin, Tuscan, Gold, 1340:
Petit Ryal, French, Gold, 1314.
Pezza, Tuscan, Silver, value, 3s. 8d. Pezza, Leghorn, Gold, value, 4s., Pezzi Solidi, Piasters.
Pfennig, German, Copper, 12 Pfennings—1 Groschen, 30 Groschen —1 Thaler.
Phai'nung, Siamese, weight for gold.
Philip, Flemish, Gold. The Ryder. Phillipo, Lombardy, Silver.
Phœnix, Mod. Greek, Silver, value, 8d.

PIASTER, Spanish, Silver, the Dollar, value, 4s. 3d.

PIASTRA, a la Rose, Tuscan, Silver. The Neapolitan Dollar.

PIASTRE, Turkish, Silver, value, 3d.

PIATAK, Russian, Copper, value, 5 Kopeks.

PIC, Chinese, value, 100 Catties.

PICE, Hindoo, Copper, 12 Pice—1 Anna, 16 Annas—1 Rupee.

PICCHALEON, Sardinian, Copper. The Centisimo.

PICCOLA, Maltese, Copper, 6 to a Grano, the smallest coin.

PIECE OF EIGHT, Spanish Silver, value, 4s. 3d., the Dollar, or Piaster, formerly 8 Reals, now 20 Reals.

PIED-FORT, French, a standard coin, or Pattern.

PIGNATELLO, Papal, Billon, temp. P. Innocent XII.

PILLAR DOLLAR, Spanish, Silver. The Dollar with the Pillars, value, 4s. 3d.

PINA, Peruvian, Silver Bullion.

PISTAREEN, Spanish, Silver, value, 10d., the fifth of the Dollar, 4 Reals.

PISTOLE, Spanish, Gold, value, 16s., formerly 32 Reals, now 80.

PISTOLE, German, various States, Gold, value, 16s. 3d.

PISTOLE, Scots, Gold, 1701.

PITE, or BOURGEOISE, French, Billon, temp. St. Louis of France, ½ of the Denier.

PITIES, Batavian, leaden coins.

PLACK, Scots, Billon, one third of a penny.

PLATINUM, Russian, 3 Rouble piece, current value, 8s. 10d., intrinsic value, 6s.

PLAPPART, Swiss, Copper, a Bernese coin, 1458.

PLAPPERT, German, Billon, value, 2d., 4 Albus.

PLAQUETTE, Flemish, Billon.

PLATA, Mexican, Silver money. Plata Macuquina, Brazilian strips.

PLATES, Swedish, Copper. The large coins.

PLOTT, Swedish, Silver, value, 1s. 6d. Plat.

PLUMBEI NUMMI, Roman, leaden coins. Temp. Saturnalia.

POLLARD, English. A Poll head, clipped coin.

POLONAISE, Polish, Gold.

POLTIN, Russian, Silver, value, 1s. 6d., the half Ruble. Polpoltin, the quarter Rouble.

POLTURAT, Hungarian, Copper.

POLUSKA, Russian, Copper. The quarter Kopek.

PONDO, Roman, Brass. The As.

PONE, Tartary, Copper, value, ½d.

PONTE, Sicilian. Money of account.

POOT, Junk, Ceylon, Tin money.

PORCELAIN, a shell, current in W. Indies.

PORTCULLIS, English, Silver, at Bombay; Crown, Half-crown, Shilling, and Sixpence, temp. Q. Elizabeth.

PORTUGALESE, Lubec, Gold.

POTIN, Egyptian, coins of a mixture of lead, copper, and tin.

POU, or PAO, ancient Chinese coins. The word signifying to distribute.

Poul, Tartary, Copper.   Poul e Siaho, Persian, Copper.
Pound, Anglo-Saxon and English, computation, value, 20s.
Provisini. Roman, Senatorian coins of the 12th and 13th centuries.
Publico, Neapolitan, Copper.
Pul, Persian, Copper.   The general name for coins of that metal.
Pulzlaty, Hungarian, Silver, the half Florin.
Punn, Bengal, value, 20 cowries.
Puon-Leang, ancient Chinese coins of the Tsin dynasty.
Purse, Turkish, 500 Piastres.
Pysa, Asiatic, Copper, value, 50th of Mamoud.   Qu. Pice.

Quadrans, Brass, Roman 4th of the As.   Small brass.
Quadrigati, Roman, Silver, denarii with four-horse car.
Quadruple, Spanish, Gold, 4 Pistoles, value, £3 4s.
Quadruple, Sardinian, Gold, 80 Lire, value, £3 3s. 4d.
Quadrussis, Roman, Brass, value, 4 Asses.   The As Grave.
Quan, Cochin China, Silver, value, 4s. 6d.
Quart Crown, Bavarian, Silver, value, 1s. 1d.
Quarta Onza, Mexican, Gold, value, 16s.   Quarto de Peso, Peru-
    vian, Copper.
Quarentino, Modena, Silver, value, 1s. 8d.
Quarter Guinea, English, Gold, value, 5s. 3d.   K. George I. and
    III.
Quartillo, Mexican, Silver.   Quarter Real.
Quartinho, Portuguese, Gold.
Quarto, Gibraltar, Copper, value, farthing, 16 Quartos—1 Rial, 12
    Rials—1 Dollar, from the Spanish Cuarta.
Quattrini, Venetian, Silver, very small.
Quattrino, Italian, Copper, value, farthing.   Quattrinello.
Quilate, Spanish.   The Carat.
Quinarius, Roman, Silver.   The half Denarius, marked V.   Also
    of Gold.
Quincunx, Roman, Brass, piece of five Unciae.
Quincussis, piece of 5 Asses.
Quinto di Scudo, Lucca, Silver, value, 10½d.
Quintuple, Neapolitan, Gold, 5 Ducati, value, 17s. 1d., 5 Scudi,
    value, 19s. 2d.

Rader Florin, German.   Money of account at Cologne.
Ragusina, Ragusa, Silver.
Rapp, Swiss, Copper, 10 Rappen—1 Batz.   Angster.
Rathspraesentger, German, Silver, value, 8d.   Aix la Chapelle.
Ratisbonina, Ratisbon.   Money of account.
Ratiti, Roman, Silver.   The Denarius bearing a Ratis.   Raft.
Real, Spanish, Silver, the Rial, value, 2½d.   20 Reals—1 Dollar.
Real, Persian, Silver.   The Rupee.

REALE, Sardinian, Silver, value, 4½d. The Florentine.

REBIA, Turkish, Gold, weight about 13¼ grains.

RED WOOD, Angola, now current.

REGENSBURGER, Ratisbon. Money of account.

REI, Portuguese, Copper, value, one-fifth of a farthing. Rez, Reis, computation, 1000 Reis—1 Milbrei.

REICHS GULDEN, Saxony, Silver, value, 1s. 8d. Two-thirds of Rix Dollar.

REICHS THALER, Prussian, Silver, value, 2s. 11d.

BESELLADO, Spanish. Money re-coined.

RIAL, English, Gold. The Rose Noble, temp. K. Edward IV.

RIAL, Mexico, Silver, value, 6½d., 8 Rials—1 Dollar.

RIDDY, Ceylon. Silver, bent wire, value, 7d. Rheedy.

RIDER, Scots, Gold. Temp. K. James IV. Ryder.

RIKS DALER, Danish, Silver, specie value, 4s. 7d. The Rigsbank Dollar, value, 2s. 3d.

RIKSGALD-DALER, Swedish, paper money, equal to about 25 cents.

RING MONEY, Gold, Silver, Iron, and Tin, Celtic. Now in Africa.

RIX DOLLAR, Hanse Towns, Silver, specie value, 3s. 10¼d., and current value, 2s. 11d.

RIX DOLLAR, Sweden, Silver, specie value, 4s. 6d., Rix Dollar Banco, value, 1s. 8d.

ROANOKE, Indian shells strung, value, 6d. a cubit, or 18 inches.

ROOKIE, Turkish, Silver, value, 1s. 8d. Qu. Gold.

ROSARIE. A base coin, perhaps Abbey piece.

ROSE NOBLE, English, Gold, value, 6s. 8d., and in temp. K. James I., Rose Royal, value, 30s.

ROSINA, Tuscan, Gold, value, 18s. 3d. Mezza Rosina.

ROUT, Polish, Silver, value, 5d.

RUBA, Modern Egypt, Silver, = 5 piastres, 24.

RUME, Turkish, Gold, value, 1s. 9d. 35 Aspers. Rubieh.

RUBLE, Russian, Silver, value, 3s., 100 Copecks. Rouble.

RUNSTYCK, Swedish, Copper, value, one sixth of a farthing. Koppar Ore.

RUPEE, Hindostan, value, 1s. 11d., 16 Annas. Inscription in Oriental characters; the oldest are square.

RUSPONE, Tuscan, Gold, value, £1 8s. 6d., from Ruspo, newly coined.

RYAL, French, Gold. See Rial.

RYDER, Flemish, Gold, value, £1 4s. 9d. Also Silver, value, 5s. 4d. The Ducatoon. See Rider.

RYKSORT, Danish, Silver.

SAADEEYEH, Egyptian, Gold, value, 1s.

SADIKI, Gold of Mysore, weight about 4 dwt. 10 grs.

SAHIB-KORAN, or Real of Silver, Persia, weight about 143 to 159 grains, value, 1s. 2d.

SAIME, Barbary. Money of account at Algiers.

SAINT ANDREW, Scots, Gold.

SAINT JOHN THE BAPTIST, Genoese, Silver.

SAINT MARK, Venetian, Silver. The Crociato, or Scudo.

SAINT THOMAS, Portuguese, Gold, value, 9s. At Goa, in India.

SAINT STEPHEN, Portuguese, Gold, value, 30s. The Milrea.

SALDING, English. Base coin, temp. K. Edward I. Scalding.

SALUNG, Siamese, value, 2 Foangs.

SALUT, Anglo-Gallic, Gold, value, 13s. 4d.

SANNAR, Persian.

SANTA, Chinese computation, 9d. 200 Cash.

SATTALIE, Bencoolen, also Sattellee, money of account, 3 Sattalies— 1 Succos, 4 Succos—1 Dollar.

SCARABEI, Egyptian, clay-baked, beetle-shaped, probably current money; also Greek, Gold, and Silver.

SCEATTA, or SKEATTA, Anglo-Saxon, Billon or Silver.

SCHAFF, Hanoverian. Money of account at Emden.

SCHALIN, Dutch, Silver, value, 7d.

SCHELLING, Flemish, Billon.

SCHERFFE, Brunswick, Money of account.

SCHILLING, Hanse Towns, Billon, value 1d.

SCHLANTE, Swedish, Copper, value, ½d. Slantar or Lös penningar, Copper.

SCHLECH THALER, German. Money of account at Aix-la-Chapelle.

SCHOCK, Saxony, money of account.

SCHOT, early Prussian Silver.

SCHUITE, Japanese, Silver, boat-shaped, value, 25s. 3d.

SCHWARE, Bremen, Copper, 5 to the Grote.

SCHWARTZ, Hanse Towns, 5 Schwartzen—1 Grote.

SCORTEOS ASES, Roman, Leather coins.

SCUDINO, Modena, Gold.

SCUDO, Italian, Silver, value, 4s. 2d., 10 Paoli.

SCUDO D'ORO, Genoese, value, 4s.

SCUTE, English, temp. Q. Elizabeth.

SCYLLINGA, Anglo-Saxon. Computation.

SEAOU, Pwang Leang. Ancient Chinese coin. *"Little half Leangs."*

SECHSER, German, Copper, value, 2d., literally a sixer, or Kreutzer piece.

SECHSLING, Hamburg, Copper.

SECHSTELS, Saxony, Silver, value, 5d., 4 good Groschen.

SEGROS, Polish, Billon, value, 4d.

SELAH, Jewish, Silver. 2 Shekels.

SELLO, Brazil, Silver, value, 2s. 9d. See Pataca.

SEMBRELLA, Roman, Brass. Selibra, Semi Libella.

SEMIS, Roman, Brass. The Semi As or Semiuncia, and Semi Aureus, Gold.

SEMISIS, Gold. Half of the Byzantine *Solidus.*

SENI, Japanese, Copper. The Cas. 600 to a Tael.

SEPECK, Anam Emp. Brass.

SEQUIN, Turkish, Gold, value, 9s. 3d., Chequin or Sultany. Also Italian, Zequin, or Zechino.

SERRATA, Roman. Coins with the edges notched.

SESSINO, Parma, Copper. Sesino.

SESTERTIUM, 1000 Sestertii (HS), Roman money of account.

SESTERTIUS, Roman, Silver, 4th of Denarius, also Large Brass.

SESTHALF, Dutch, Silver, value, 5d.

SEVEN SHILLINGS, English, Gold, temp. K. George III.

SEXTANS, Roman, Brass. 6th of the As.

SEXTULA, Roman, Brass.

SHAHEE, Persian, Silver, value, ½d., 4 Shahis—1 Piastre, 5 Piastres—1 Karaun, 10 Karauns—1 Tamaun. Shahi.

SHAHEE, Copper, of Persia, 10 of them equal to one Penebad.

SHAKEE, Turkish, Silver, value, 3½d.

SHATREE, Persian, Silver.

SHARI, Kabul, Silver, value, 5d.

SHEKEL, Jewish, Silver, value, 3s. Also in Gold. Also called Kesitah in Book of Job.

SHILLING, English, Silver. 20 to a Pound.

SHOE, Chinese, Gold and Silver Ingots, value various, from one half to 100 Taels. Dutch name, Schuit.

SHOSTACK, German, money of account in Prussia, Poland, etc. Shustack.

SIANI, Syria. Money of account at Aleppo, 24 Siani—1 Asper.

SICCA, Persian, Gold, at Delhi: means a Die, a coin.

SICCA RUPEE, Bengal, Silver, value, 2s. 1d.; Sicca, a weight.

SICLE, Jewish, Silver. The Shekel.

SIGILLE, Roman, Brass; also leaden counters at the Saturnalia.

SILBER GROSCHEN, Prussian, base metal, value, 1¼., 30 to a Thaler.

SILIQUA, the Carob Bean. The Carat weight.

SILVER SOVEREIGN, Spanish. The Dollar, so called.

SINGPNAI, Siamese, value, 2 Phainungs.

SLET DOLLAR, Danish. Schlecht, a 4 Mark Piece.

SLIPS, English, Base money, temp. K. Edward VI., value 1½d.

SLUG, California, Gold, value, £10 5s. 2d.; 50 Dollars, Octagon.

SMALL BRASS, Roman. The size of the Sextans.

SNAPHANE, Brabant, Silver, 1489.

SOL., old French Copper. The Sou.

SOLDO, Italian, Copper.

SOLIDUS, Roman, Gold, value 12s. Solidus, the Anglo-Saxon shilling.

SOLOTA, Greek, value 1s.

SOMPAYE, Siamese, Silver.

SONG-PAYE, Siamese, Silver, weighs about 15 grains.

SOVEREIGN, English, Gold, 1485, value, £1 5s.; 1816, value, £1.

SOVEREIGN, Austrian, Gold, value, £1 7s. 10d., 3 Ducats.

SPINTRLE, Roman, Brass, obscene tickets, not current.

SPUR ROYAL, English, Gold, value, 15s. The Spurred Groat, Scots. Silver, value 16d.

STAMBUL, name given to the Turkish Gold, *Zer-mahbüb*, coined in Constantinople, as the name *Misr* is given to those coined at Cairo.

STATER, Greek, Gold, value, about £1 3s., Greek for standard. Early name, Chrysus; also Hemistater (or Half Stater), the Distater (or Double Stater.)

STEPING, English, Base coin, temp. K. Edward I.

STERLING, Anglo-Norman, Silver. Steore, Standard.

STIVER, Flemish, Copper. Stuyver, Dutch, Billon, value 1d.

STUBER, German, Copper. The Stiver. Styfer, Swedish, Billon.

STYCA, small Copper coin of the Northumbrian (Anglo-Saxon) kings.

STYKKER, Danish.

SUCCO, Bencoolen, money of account, quarter Dollar.

SUADO, Austrian, Silver, value, 4s. 8d.

SUELDO, Catalonia and Majorca, money of account, 12 Dineros—1
   Sueldo, 12 Sueldos—1 Libra, value 2d.

SUKA, Silver of Nepaul, weighing 22 grains.

SUSKIN, English. The diminutive of the French Son.

SWINE PENNIES, Roman coins found in Lincolnshire, so called.

SYCEE, Chinese, Silver Ingots, canoe-shaped, Chinese standard silver.

SYFERT, Hanoverian, Copper, current at Embden.

TAEL, Chinese, Silver, value, 6s. 8d., 1000 Cash. Thail, Japan, Tell.

TALLA, Spanish, Copper, value, the 4th of a Real.

TALARO, Tuscan, Silver, the Dollar; the Thalaro of the Levant, 16
   Piastres. Turkey.

TALENT, Hebrew, computation, 60 Shekels.

TALENT, Greek, weight 60 Minæ, the value of the Attic Mina was
   £4 1s. 3d.

TANGA, Indian, Gold, value, 7½d., 4 Tangas—1 Pargo.

TAOU, Chinese, Knife coins, early brass, cast.

TA-POU, ancient, Chinese coin, great *pou.*

TAR, Silver, Hindoo, value ½, current on the coast of Malabar   Tare.

TARTEMORION, Attic Silver, ⅛ of the Obolus.

TARIN, Sicilian, Maltese, Silver, value, 20 Grani, 5th of a Ducat.

TARO, Sicilian, Silver, value, 8½d., 5 Tari—1 Ducat; and Malta
   value, 1½d.

TCHAO, Chinese paper money.

TELA, Persian, Various value. The Tilla.

TEMASHA, small uneven Silver coin of Sinagur, in the northern
   range of the Hindustan mountains.

TERUNCIUS, Roman, Brass, 3 oz. 4th of Libella.

TESSERÉS, tokens or tickets used for admission to the ancient games
   and theatres.

TESTER, English, Silver. Coin with a head upon it.

TESTON, Italian, Silver, value, 1s. 6d.

TESTONE, Portuguese, Silver, value, 5¾d., 100 Reis.

TETRA DRACHM, Greek, Silver, value, 4 Drachmæ; the Stater
   Argenteus, value, 3s. 3d.

TETROBOLUS, Greek, Silver, value, 4 Oboli, 6d.

THALER, German, Silver, value, 2s. 11d. First coined in Joachim's
   Thal, a valley in Bohemia.

THIRD OF A GUINEA, English, Gold, value 7s.

THRIMSA, Anglo-Saxon. Three-fifths of a shilling.

TICAL, Siamese, Silver, nut-shaped. The Baat.

TILLA, Persian, Gold, value, 13s. 4d. The Tela and Tila.

TINFE, Polish, Silver, value, 1s. 3d. Timpfe.

TI-POU, ancient Chinese coin.

TOGHRALI, name given such Turkish pieces as are distinguished by the *toghra*, or royal cypher.

TOKENS, English, Copper, issued by tradesmen in the 16th and 18th centuries; also Silver, English, temp. K. George III.

TOKOO, Ashantee, Silver, value 8d.

TOMAN, Persian, Gold, value, 10s. 3d., 50 Abassis or Piastres. Touman and Tomaun.

TOMPONG, Malacca.

TONGA, Persian, Silver, value, 7s. 6d.

TORNESE, Neapolitan, Copper. 2 to the Grano.

TOUGH PIECES, English, Silver. Given to persons touched for King's evil. Also Gold.

TOURNAY GROAT, Anglo-Gallic, Silver, temp. K. Henry VIII.

TOWN PIECES, English, Copper, tokens issued by towns.

TRARO, Venetian, Billon, value 2d., 4 to the Lira Austriaca.

TREMISSIS, Roman, Gold, value, one-third of the Solidus, 4s.

TRIDRACHM, Greek, Silver, value, 3 Drachmæ.

TRIENS, Roman. Value, one-third of the As.

TRIENTES, Gold coins of the Gothic kings of Spain.

TRIHEMITARTEMORION, Attic Silver, ⅓ of the Obolus.

TRIKOLLYBON, Greek Copper.

TRIGROSS, Polish. Value, 2d.

TRIOBOLUS, Greek, Silver. The Hemidrachm, value, 4¼d.

TRIQUETRA, a type of coins, bearing three joined legs, originating in Sicily.

TRIPONDIUS, Roman, Brass, value, 3 Ases.

TRITEMORION, *or* TRITARTEMORION, Attic Silver, ¾ of the Obolus.

TSEEN, Chinese, Brass. The Cash.

TURNER, Scots, Copper. A base coin. Qu. Tournois, coined at Tours.

TSE-POU, ancient Chinese coin, later *pou*.

TURNOSE, German Silver.

TWENTY SHILLING PIECE, English, Silver, temp. K. Charles I.

TWO GUINEA PIECE, English, Gold, from temp. K. Charles II.

TWO PENNY PIECE, English, Copper, temp. K. George III.

TUNKA, Hindoo, Silver, value 2s.

TYMFE, Prussia, Silver, value, 8¼d., 18 Old Gross.

UCHU, Peruvian, species of Capsicum. The Pod, used as a coin.

UDLI, Hindoo, Silver.

UNCIA, Roman, Brass. Ounce, 12th of As.

UNICORN, Scots, Gold, temp. K. James III.

UNIT, English, Gold, value 20s., temp. K. James I. Laureled pieces.

URDEE, Bombay, Copper.

UTA, Batavian. At Java.

VARAHA, Gold, coin of Mysore, value, about 8s.

VARGAS, Dollars.   Mexican Silver Dollars, coined in 1811 and 1812 by the Republican General, Vargos.

VEINTEN, or Coronilla, a Spanish gold Dollar.

VELLON, Spanish, Copper. Or Billon.

VICTORIATUS, Roman, Silver, value 4d.   The Quinarius, with a fiure of Victory.

VINTEM, Portuguese, Copper, value, 1d., 50 to the Milreis, 20 Reis. Vintin. at Goa ; Vintem, Spanish, Gold coin.

VIZ, Bengal, Copper.

WAMPAM, Peage, American, shells strung, current in Pennsylvania, 10s. a fathom

WADMAL, African, woolen cloth made in Iceland, and current.

WHITE PEAKE, Indian, shells strung, 4s. a cubit, 18 inches.

WILLIAM, Dutch, Gold, value, 16s. 5d., formerly 10 Guilders.

WITTEN, Hanoverian, Silver, 10 Wittens—1 Stiver, current at Embden.   Witten Penning, Danish, Silver.

WISSE MUNTZEN, Bavarian, Billon, inferior to current coin.

WOOD, Angola, a red kind from Malemba, current.

WOO TSZE TSEEN, Chinese money, without inscription ; of the CHOW dynasty.

XERAPHIN, Hindoo, Silver, value, 2s. 1d.

XERIPH, Greece, value, 10s.

YERMEEBESHLEK, Turkish, Gold, value, 12s. 6d.

YUZLIK, Turkish, Silver, value, 2½ Piastres, or 100 Paras, value, about 63 cents.

ZAHL PFENNIG, German, Brass, the Jeton, or reckoning penny.

ZARIMLIK, Turkish, Silver, =20 Paras.

ZARMAHBUB, Greece, Gold, value, 6s.   Zermahub, Turkish, Gold, the Sequin.

ZEHNER, Austrian, Silver, = 10 Kreutzers, value, 8 cents.

ZECCHINO, Venetian, Gold, value, 9s. 5d., from Zecca, the mint, the Sequin of Turkey.

ZENZERLI, Turkish.   Current in Egypt.

ZIAM, Barbary, Gold, value, 5s. 2d.

ZIMBI, Angola, Shell.   The Cowrie.

ZLATY, Hungarian, Silver.   The Florin.

ZLOT, Polish, Silver, value 6d., 30 Groschen, 15 Kopecs.

ZODIAC RUPEES, Hindoo, value, 4s. 11½d., bear the different signs of the Zodiac ; there are also Zodiac Mohurs.

ZOLOTAH, Turkish, Silver, equal to 30 Paras.

ZUZA, Jewish, Silver.   4th of a Shekel.

ZWANZIGER, Austrian, Silver, value 8d., 20 Kreutzers.

ZWEYDRITTEL, Mecklenburg, Silver, value, 2s.   Two-thirds of Rix Dollar.   Danish, value, 2s. 10d.

GOLD AND SILVER DEPOSITS FOR COINAGE.

Statement of Domestic Gold and Silver Deposited at the United States Mint and Branches, for Coinage, to June 30, 1870.

FROM.	Gold.	Silver.	Gold and silver.
California....................	$ 630,575,666 05	$ 33,053 93	$ 630,608,719 98
Montana....................	24,075,557 98	70,714 51	24,146,272 49
Colorado...................	17,666,867 21	482,211 94	18,149,079 15
Idaho.....................	15,424,434 90	284,986 40	15,709,421 30
North Carolina..............	9,654,622 33	43,763 86	9,698,386 19
Oregon....................	10,738,133 87	1,764 19	10,739,898 06
Georgia....................	7,151,235 56	403 83	7,151,639 39
Virginia...................	1,615,736 38	....	1,615,736 38
South Carolina.............	1,371,383 76	....	1,371,383 76
Nevada....................	366,724 58	4,969,761 35	5,336,485 93
Alabama	206,040 57	....	206,040 57
Arizona...................	566,107 12	38,107 93	604,215 05
New Mexico................	523,133 29	....	523,133 29
Utah	98,987 86	....	98,987 86
Tennessee.................	81,529 69	....	81,529 69
Washington Territory........	61,711 71	....	61,711 71
Dakota	5,760 00	....	5,760 00
Nebraska..................	14,748 31	....	14,748 31
Vermont..................	5,459 88	....	5,459 88
Other Sources.............	43,676,058 14	....	43,676,058 14
Parted from Silver..........	4,045,251 39	....	4,045,251 39
Lake Superior..............	....	251,471 70	251,471 70
New Mexico and Sonora......	....	6,193 93	6,193 93
Sitka.....................	397 64	....	397 64
Wyoming Territory..........	88,543 21	74 25	88,617 46
Maryland..................	89 15	....	89 15
Kansas....................	846 36	468 00	1,314 36
Fine Bars	....	767,447 66	767,447 66
Parted from Gold...........	....	5,607,820 70	5,607,820 70
Total to June 30, 1870......	$ 768,015,026 91	$ 12,558,244 18	$ 780,573,271 12

COINAGE OF THE MINT AND BRANCHES TO THE CLOSE OF THE YEAR, ENDING JUNE 30, 1870.

MINTS.		Gold.	Silver.	Copper.	Pieces.	Value.
Philadelphia..	1793	$ 448,047,892 41	$ 101,382,781 86	$ 11,019,008 55	1,089,841,949	$ 560,449,182 82
San Francisco.	1854	288,440,706 81	7,684,457 17	....	30,726,649	296,125,163 98
New Orleans..	1838	40,381,615 00	29,890,037 13	....	94,890,695	70,271,652 13
Charlotte.....	1838	5,048,641 50	....	....	1,206,954	5,048,641 50
Dahlonega....	1838	6,121,919 00	....	....	1,851,750	6,121,919 00
New York....	1854	179,780,145 58	4,580,015 17	....	... .	184,360,160 75
Denver.......	1863	3,592,305 53	....	....	....	8,592,305 53
Carson City...	1870	110,576 05	19,793 00	....	88,566	82,369 05
Charlotte.....	1869	19,269 00	322 61	....	....	19,591 61
Total.......		$ 971,482,571 88	$ 143,557,406 94	$ 11,019,008 55	1,218,087,593	$ 1,126,058,987 37

COINAGE OF THE UNITED STATES.

Coinage of the Mint of the United States, from the year 1792, in-cluding the Coinage of the Branch Mints from the commence-ment of their operations, and of the Assay Office.

Years.	Gold, Value.	Silver, Value.	Copper, Value.	WHOLE COINAGE.	
				No. of Pieces.	Value.
1793–5	$ 71,485 00	$ 370,683 80	$ 11,373 00	1,834,420	$ 453,541 80
1796	102,727 50	79,077 50	10,324 40	1,219,370	192,129 40
1797	103,422 50	12,591 45	9,510 34	1,095,165	125,524 29
1798	205,610 00	330,291 00	9,797 00	1,368,241	545,698 00
1799	213,285 00	423,515 00	9,106 68	1,365,681	645,906 68
1800	317,760 00	224,296 00	29,279 40	3,337,972	571,335 40
1801	422,570 00	74,758 00	13,628 37	1,571,390	510,956 37
1802	423,310 00	58,343 00	34,422 83	3,615,869	516,075 83
1803	258,377 50	87,118 00	25,203 03	2,780,830	370,698 53
1804	258,642 50	100,340 50	12,844 94	2,046,839	371,827 94
1805	170,367 50	149,388 50	13,483 48	2,260,361	333,239 48
1806	324,505 00	471,319 00	5,260 00	1,815,409	801,084 00
1807	437,495 00	597,448 75	9,652 21	2,731,345	1,044,595 96
1808	284,665 00	684,300 00	13,090 00	2,935,888	982,055 00
1809	169,375 00	707,376 00	8,001 53	2,861,834	884,752 53
1810	501,435 00	638,773 50	15,660 00	3,056,418	1,155,868 50
1811	497,905 00	608,340 00	2,495 95	1,649,570	1,108,740 95
1812	290,435 00	814,029 50	10,755 00	2,761,646	1,115,219 50
1813	477,140 00	620,951 50	4,180 00	1,755,331	1,102,275 50
1814	77,270 00	561,687 50	3,578 30	1,833,859	642,535 80
1815	3,175 00	17,308 00	. . . . . .	69,867	20,483 00
1816	. . . .	28,575 75	28,209 82	2,888,135	56,785 57
1817	. . . . . .	607,783 50	39,484 00	5,163,967	647,267 50
1818	242,940 00	1,070,454 50	31,670 00	5,537,084	1,345,064 50
1819	258,615 00	1,140,000 00	26,710 00	5,074,723	1,425,325 00
1820	1,319,030 00	501,680 70	44,075 50	6,492,509	1,864,786 20
1821	189,325 00	825,762 45	3,890 00	3,139,249	1,018,977 45
1822	88,980 00	805,806 50	20,723 39	3,813,788	915,509 89
1823	72,425 00	895,550 00	. . . . . .	2,166,485	967,975 00
1824	93,200 00	1,752,477 00	12,620 00	4,786,894	1,858,297 00
1825	156,385 00	1,564,583 00	14,926 00	5,178,760	1,735,894 00
1826	92,245 00	2,002,090 00	16,344 25	5,774,434	2,110,679 25
1827	131,565 00	2,869,200 00	23,557 32	9,097,845	3,024,342 32
1828	140,145 00	1,575,600 00	25,636 24	6,196,853	1,741,381 24
1829	295,717 50	1,994,578 00	16,580 00	7,674,501	2,306,875 50
1830	643,105 00	2,495,400 00	17,115 00	8,357,191	3,155,620 00
1831	714,270 00	3,175,600 00	33,603 60	11,792,284	3,923,473 60
1832	798,435 00	2,579,000 00	23,620 00	9,128,387	3,401,055 00

COINAGE OF THE UNITED STATES.—*Continued.*

Years.	Gold, Value.	Silver, Value.	Copper, Value.	Whole Coinage.	
				No. of Pieces.	Value.
1833	$ 978,550 00	$ 2,759,000 00	$ 28,160 00	10,307,790	$ 3,765,710 00
1834	3,954,270 00	3,415,002 00	19,151 00	11,637,643	7,388,423 00
1835	2,186,175 00	3,443,003 00	39,489 00	15,996,342	5,668,667 00
1836	4,135,700 00	3,606,100 00	23,100 00	13,719,333	7,764,900 00
1837	.1,148,305 00	2,096,010 00	55,583 00	13,010,721	3,299,898 00
1838	1,809,593 00	2,315,250 00	53,702 00	15,780,311	4,178,547 00
1839	1,375,760 00	2,098,636 00	31,286 61	11,811,594	3,505,682 61
1840	1,690,802 00	1,712,178 00	24,627 00	10,558,240	3,427,607 50
1841	1,102,197 50	1,115,875 00	15,973 67	8,811,968	2,233,946 17
1842	1,833,170 50	2,325,750 00	23,833 90	11,743,153	4,182,754 40
1843	8,302,787 50	3,722,250 00	24,287 20	4,640,582	11,967,830 70
1844	5,428,230 00	2,235,550 00	23,587 52	9,051,834	7,687,767 52
1845	3,756,447 50	1,873,200 00	38,948 04	1,806,196	5,668,595 54
1846	4,034,177 50	2,558,580 00	41,208 00	10,133,515	6,633,965 50
1847	20,221,385 00	2,374,450 00	61,836 69	15,392,344	22,657,671 69
1848	3,775,512 50	2,040,050 00	64,157 99	12,649,790	5,879,720 49
1849	9,007,761 50	2,114,950 00	41,984 32	12,666,659	11,164,695 82
1850	31,981,738 50	1,866,100 00	44,467 50	14,588,220	33,892,306 00
1851	62,614,492 50	774,397 00	99,635 43	28,791,958	63,488,524 93
1852	56,846,187 50	999,410 00	50,630 94	32,964,019	57,896,228 44
1853	55,213,906 94	9,077,571 00	67,059 78	76,484,062	64,358,537 78
1854	52,094,595 47	8,619,270 00	42,638 35	44,645,011	60,756,503 82
1855	52,795,457 20	3,501,245 00	16,030 79	16,997,807	56,312,732 99
1856	59,343,365 35	5,196,670 17	27,106 78	33,870,966	64,567,142 30
1857**	25,183,138 68	1,601,644 46	63,510 46	19,440,547	26,848,293 60
1858*	52,889,800 29	8,233,287 77	234,006 00	56,491,655	61,357,088 06
1859*	30,409,953 70	6,833,631 47	307,000 00	53,550,522	37,550,585 17
1860*	23,447,283 35	3,250,635 26	342,000 00	27,101,598	27,039,918 61
1861*	80,708,400 64	2,883,706 94	101,660 00	23,724,713	83,693,767 58
1793 to 1861	$ 669,116,406 62	$ 128,159,481 97	$ 2,617,473 55	800,602,475	$ 799,923,362 14
1862*	61,676,576 55	3,231,081 51	116,000 00	28,296,899	65,023,658 06
1863*	22,645,729 90	1,564,297 22	478,450 00	51,980,575	24,688,477 12
1864*	23,982,748 31	850,086 99	463,800 00	46,981,396	25,296,635 30
1865*	30,685,699 95	950,218 69	1,183,330 00	87,323,851	32,819,248 64
1866*	37,429,430 46	1,596,646 58	646,570 00	38,427,923	39,672,647 04
1867*	39,838,878 82	1,562,694 18	1,879,540 00	54,110,384	43,281,113 00
1868*	24,141,235 06	1,592,986 48	1,713,385 00	49,735,840	27,447,606 54
1869*	32,027,966 03	1,574,937 17	1,279,055 00	36,666,668	34,881,958 20
1870*	30,103,364 75	2,670,054 16	611,445 00	23,961,29.	33,384,863 91
1862 to 1870	$ 302,531,629 83	$ 15,593,002 98	$ 8,371,575 00	417,486,828	$ 326,406,207 81
1793 to 1870	$ 971,648,036 45	$ 143,752,484 95	$ 11,019,048 55	1,218,149,303	$ 1,126,419,569 95

** Six months to June 30, 1857.   * For the fiscal year ending June 30.

THE DAILY PREMIUM ON **GOLD** AT NEW YORK IN THE YEAR **1862.**

Those quotations in full-face type indicate the lowest and highest rates of each month.

	Jan. 1862.	Feb. 1862.	Mar. 1862.	April, 1862.	May, 1862.	June, 1862.	July, 1862.	Aug. 1862.	Sept. 1862.	Oct. 1862.	Nov. 1862.	Dec. 1862.
1	Holiday.	3½ a 3¾	2⅝ a **2¾**	1⅞ a 2	**2¼** a 2½	Sunday.	**8¾** a 9¼	15⅛ a 15¾	16½ a 17⅛	**22** a 22¾	29⅝ a 31¼	**28½** a 31½
2	**1½** a 2	Sunday.	Sunday.	2 2¼	2⅜ 2⅜	**3½** a 3⅝	9¼ 9½	15 15⅛	16½ 17	22⅜ 23	Sunday.	31 31½
3	2 2	3⅜ 3⅝	2 2⅜	1⅞ 1⅞	2½ 2¾	3½ ..	10⅛ 10½	Sunday.	17¾ 19	22⅜ 22⅝	30½ 31½	31 32
4	.. ..	3½ 3⅞	1¾ 2	1⅞ 1⅞	Sunday.	3½ 3⅝	Holiday.	14⅝ 15	17⅞ 18½	22½ 23	29¼ 31½	33 **34**
5	Sunday.	3⅜ 3½	2 2	1⅞ 2	3⅛ 3½	3¾ 4	9¾ 10	14½ 14¾	18¼ 19⅛	Sunday.	31½ 32¾	31½ 32½
6	.. ..	3⅜ 3⅝	2 2¼	Sunday.	2⅞ 3⅜	4 4⅛	Sunday.	14⅜ 14½	18⅜ 19	23 23⅛	31½ 32	30½ 32
7	.. ..	3⅛ 3⅜	2 2⅛	2⅛ **2¼**	2⅞ 2⅞	4 4⅛	10 10¼	14½ 14½	Sunday.	23½ 24	31½ 32	Sunday.
8	3½ 4½	3¼ 3¾	1⅞ 2	2 2¼	2⅞ 3	Sunday.	10¾ 11¼	12¾ 13¼	19 19½	24½ 25	32 32¼	31⅜ 31½
9	4½ **5**	Sunday.	Sunday.	1¾ 1⅞	3¼ 3½	4¼ 4⅜	13¼ 16½	**12½** 12¾	18¾ 19¼	26 26⅝	Sunday.	32⅝ 33¼
10	4 4½	3⅞ 4	2 2	1¾ 1⅞	3⅜ 3⅜	4⅛ 4⅜	15⅝ 17½	Sunday.	18⅝ 18¾	27 29	32¼ **33¼**	32½ 32½
11	.. ..	3⅞ 4½	1⅞ 1⅞	1⅞ 1⅞	Sunday.	4⅜ 4⅝	14¾ 16	13⅝ 14	18¾ 19	28 28⅞	31 32¾	32⅛ 32½
12	Sunday.	4 4⅜	1⅞ 1⅞	1¾ 2	3⅜ 3⅜	4⅞ 5⅛	13⅞ 14½	13½ 14	19 19⅜	Sunday.	31½ 32	31½ 31¾
13	2½ 4	4 4⅛	1¼ 1⅞	Sunday.	3⅛ 3⅜	5⅛ 5⅛	Sunday.	14 14½	18⅝ 19	29 30⅝	31½ 32	31⅛ 32
14	2¾ 3¼	4⅛ 4¾	1¼ 1⅝	1¾ 1⅞	3⅛ 3⅜	5⅜ 5¾	15½ 16½	15 16	Sunday.	32 33½	32 33	Sunday.
15	2 2½	4⅜ **4⅞**	1⅜ 1½	1¾ 1⅞	3⅛ 3⅜	Sunday.	17 ..	14¾ 15½	17½ 17⅞	34 37⅝	31¾ 32	31⅞ 32¼
16	2½ 2½	Sunday.	Sunday.	1⅝ 1⅞	3 3⅛	6½ 6¾	16¾ 17½	14⅞ 15¼	16½ 17¾	32½ 35	Sunday.	32 32⅛
17	1⅞ 2	3¾ 4½	1¼ 1⅜	1⅝ 1⅞	3 3⅛	6 6⅛	18 19	Sunday.	16⅞ 17¾	32 33	32 32¼	32¾ 33
18	1⅞ 2	3⅜ 3¾	1⅜ 1⅝	1⅝ 1¾	Sunday.	5¾ 6⅛	19 19¾	15 15½	16¾ 17½	29 30	31⅜ 32	32½ 32¾
19	Sunday.	3 3½	1¼ 1⅜	1⅜ 1½	[illegible]	6⅛ 6⅜	18¼ 19	14⅞ 15½	**16⅛** 17¾	Sunday.	30 31	32½ 32¾
20	2¼ 2½	3 3¼	1⅛ 1⅜	Sunday.	[illegible]	6⅜ 6⅝	Sunday.	15 15½	16¾ 17½	27 29	30½ 30½	32 32⅛
21	2 2½	3⅜ 3¾	1⅛ 1¼	1½ 1⅝	[illegible]	6⅜ 6¼	20 20¼	15½ 16	Sunday.	28¾ 32	30½ 30⅝	Sunday.
22	2½ 3	No Board.	**1⅛** 1⅜	1⅛ 1⅜	[illegible]	Sunday.	19¾ **20¾**	15 **16¼**	16¾ 17⅛	33 **34**	30½ 30¾	32½ 32⅝
23	3 3¾	Sunday.	Sunday.	1⅛ 1¼	[illegible]	6¾ ..	19 19½	15½ 15¾	17⅜ 18	32½ 33	Sunday.	32⅛ 32½
24	3⅛ 3⅝	3¼ 3½	1¼ 1⅜	1¼ 1⅜	[illegible]	7⅜ 8¾	17 17½	Sunday.	18⅜ 19	30¼ 32½	30⅛ 30¾	32 32⅛
25	3 3⅞	3 3¾	1¼ 1⅜	**1⅛** 1¼	4 **4**	8⅛ 8¾	14 17¼	15¼ 15¾	20 20¾	30 31⅛	29⅞ 30	Holiday.
26	Sunday.	2⅞ 3⅛	1⅛ 1¼	1⅜ 1⅜	Sunday.	8⅞ 9⅛	17½ 18	15½ 15¾	20½ 20½	Sunday.	29¼ 29½	31⅞ 32
27	3 3½	2⅞ 3	1⅛ 1¼	Sunday.	4 4½	9⅜ **9½**	Sunday.	15½ 15¾	21⅜ 21½	30 31¼	T'giving	31⅞ 32⅝
28	3¾ 3⅞	**2⅛** 2½	1⅛ 1¼	1⅜ 1¾	3⅞ 4	9 9⅛	16⅝ 17⅜	15½ 15⅝	Sunday.	31⅝ 32½	29¼ 29½	Sunday.
29	3½ 3¾	.. ..	1⅛ 1¼	1¾ 1⅞	3⅞ 3⅞	Sunday.	15¾ 16½	16 16½	21¾ 23½	31½ 31¾	**28¾** 29¼	31½ 32¾
30	3⅛ 3⅛	.. ..	Sunday.	2 2	.. ..	8⅞ 9⅛	14¼ 14½	15⅝ 16	21½ **24**	30½ 30¾	Sunday.	32⅝ 33
31	3⅛ 3⅜	.. ..	1⅜ 1¾	.. ..	3½ 3⅝	.. ..	15 16	Sunday.	... ...	29½ 30	... ...	33½ 33⅝

THE DAILY PREMIUM ON **GOLD** AT NEW YORK IN THE YEAR **1863.**

These quotations in full-face type indicate the lowest and highest rates of each month.

	Jan. 1863.	Feb. 1863.	Mar. 1863.	April, 1863.	May, 1863.	June, 1863.	July, 1863.	Aug. 1863.	Sept. 1863.	Oct. 1863.	Nov. 1863.	Dec. 1863.
1	Holiday.	Sunday.	Sunday.	56⅜ a **57**½	50¾ 51½	46 a **47**½	44¾ a **45**	29½ a **29**¾	**26**½ a 27⅞	**40**⅛ 40⅜	Sunday.	**47**¾ a 48⅜
2	**33**⅝ a 35	56¾ a 57½	71 a 71½	53¼ 57	49⅛ 50⅛	46¾ 47¼	43⅞ 44½	Sunday.	27½ 28	43 43¼	45⅞ a 46½	48½ 48⅜
3	33⅝ 34¾	54½ 55	71⅜ **71**¾	53 53½	Sunday.	46¾ 46½	44 44¼	27½ 27¾	29½ 31¼	43 43⅛	46⅛ 46¼	51½ 52¼
4	Sunday.	57 57½	65 68	54¾ 55¼	48½ 50	46 46½	Holiday.	28¼ 28⅝	33½ 34½	Sunday.	46 46½	52¼ 52¾
5	34⅝ 35	56¾ 57½	57 58	Sunday.	48½ 51½	46 46¾	Sunday.	27¾ 27⅞	31½ 31¾	44 44¾	46¼ 47¼	51¼ 52
6	34 34½	57⅞ 57½	50 54	51 52⅞	52¼ 54	45⅛ 45⅞	38 39¼	Fast Day.	Sunday.	46 47¼	48 48¾	Sunday.
7	34¼ 35	56⅞ 57¼	54¾ 55½	50 52½	54¼ **55**⅜	Sunday.	32½ 38½	27 27¾	33 33¼	46¼ 46½	46⅛ 47⅛	51 52⅛
8	35⅝ 36⅝	Sunday.	Sunday.	**45**½ 47	52⅜ 54½	43 43½	30⅞ 31¾	26¼	32 32½	46 46⅞	Sunday.	48¾ 49⅛
9	37¾ 38¼	55¼ 55¾	55¾ 57¼	46½ 48	49 50¼	42⅝ 42¾	31¼ 31⅝	Sunday.	32¾ 32⅞	46¾ 47	46¼ 46⅝	48½ 48⅝
10	38⅛ 39	**52**¼ 53¾	60 63	46½ 49	Sunday.	**40**½ 40¾	32¼ 33	26⅛ 26¾	31⅛ 31⅜	48⅛ 48½	45 45⅜	48¾ 49⅜
11	Sunday.	52½ 56	57⅞ 58½	50⅛ 52⅛	48½ 49	41¾ 42	32¼ 32½	26⅝ 26¼	29⅞ 29¾	Sunday.	45⅜ 45¾	51 51⅛
12	40¾ 42	54⅛ 54½	58½ 60½	Sunday.	48⅝ 49¼	41¼ 41¾	Sunday.	26¼ 26⅝	28⅞ 29	49½ 50¼	46⅝ 47	50 50⅜
13	42 44	55½ 55⅞	59½ 62	57 57⅝	49¾ 49¼	42¼ 42½	31¼ 31⅝	26⅝ 27	Sunday.	53¾ 54¾	47 47⅜	Sunday.
14	46½ 47¼	55½ 55¾	57¾ 58¾	55 55¼	49¾ 50⅛	Sunday.	31 31½	25½ 26¼	30⅞ 31⅝	52½ 53¾	46⅝ 47	49¾ 50⅜
15	48 48¼	Sunday.	Sunday.	52 54	49¾ 50	44½ 46½	28⅛ 29¼	25⅜ 25½	31 32⅛	56 **56**⅛	Sunday.	50¾ ...
16	45½ 47	55⅝ 57⅝	54½ 55	52 53¾	49¾ 50	47⅜ 48⅜	26 26⅛	Sunday.	31⅜ 32¼	54⅛ 55½	47 47	49½ 49¾
17	46⅞ 47¼	58¼ 59	54⅝ 55¼	53¼ 53¾	Sunday.	45½ 45¾	25¾ 26	25⅝ 25¾	32¼ 32½	49½ 50	47⅞ 48½	50⅛ 50⅛
18	Sunday.	61 61½	53½ 55	51¼ 52⅞	49¾ 50	43⅞ 43¾	25 25¼	25⅝ 26	33 33¾	Sunday.	49½ 50	51⅝ 52⅛
19	47⅞ 48¼	61½ 64	54⅞ 55⅞	Sunday.	48⅛ 49½	43 43⅞	Sunday.	25 25⅜	33¾ 34	51¼ 51½	51 52¾	51⅛ 52
20	47½ 48	63½ 63⅞	54½ 55	48¾ 50¾	48⅝ 49	43½ 43¾	**23**½ 25⅜	24⅞ 25	Sunday.	49⅝ 49¾	52½ 53¼	Sunday.
21	47¾ 48¼	62½ 62¾	53⅛ 54⅞	46 47	48⅝ 50	Sunday.	26 27⅜	25¼ 25⅜	39½ 40	43¾ 46	53½ **54**	52⅛ 52½
22	47½ 48	Sunday.	Sunday.	45¾ 47¾	48½ 49⅜	43¾ 43⅞	24½ 25⅜	24¾ 24⅞	37½ 38½	42¾ 44½	Sunday.	52⅛ 52½
23	47½ 48	64¾ 64⅞	51 53⅝	48⅛ 50	48½ 49½	43⅝ 43½	25¾ 26⅛	Sunday.	37½ 38¼	45¾ 46½	53 54	52 52½
24	48¾ 49¾	68 71¾	45½ 49	51½ 52	Sunday.	43½ 44	26⅛ 26¼	24 24½	36¾ 37	46¾ 47	50½ 52	51⅝ 51¾
25	Sunday.	71½ **72**¾	41¼ 43	52 54	44¾ 46¼	44¾ 45¾	25¾ 25⅛	22½ 23⅛	38 38⅛	Sunday.	48¾ 49	Holiday.
26	48⅞ 51½	69½ 71¾	**39** 40¼	Sunday.	43½ 45	44¼ 45	Sunday.	**22**½ 23½	39 39¼	49½ 49¾	Holiday.	51½ 51¾
27	53 54¼	69⅜ 71	40 40⅞	50 53⅞	43⅝ 44⅝	43⅛ 45⅛	27½ 27½	24½ 24⅞	Sunday.	46 47¼	**43** 45½	Sunday.
28	53 54½	71½ 72	42½ 43⅛	49⅝ 50⅝	**43**½ 43⅞	Sunday.	27¼ 27⅜	24½ 24¾	42½ 43⅛	45¾ 46½	44½ 44⅜	51⅜ 52⅜
29	53 54⅝	... ...	Sunday.	50 50⅝	44⅜ 45⅛	46½ 47½	27⅛ 27¾	24¾ 24⅝	42½ **43**¼	47 48	Sunday.	52⅝ **52**¾
30	56 57¼	... ...	44½ 47¼	Fast Day.	44⅞ 45¼	46⅛ 46¾	27⅜ 27¾	Sunday.	41¼ 42	46 46⅜	48⅜ 49	51¾ 52¼
31	59½ **60**	... ...	48½ 50	... ...	Sunday.	... ...	28½ 29	28 28¼	... ...	45⅜ 46¼	... ...	51⅛ 52½

THE DAILY PREMIUM ON GOLD AT NEW YORK IN THE YEAR 1864.

Those quotations in full-face type indicate the lowest and highest rates of each month.

	Jan. 1864.	Feb. 1864.	Mar. 1864.	April, 1864.	May, 1864.	June, 1864.
1	Holiday.	**57¼** a 57¾	**59** a 60	**66½** a 68½	Sunday.	**87½** a 89¼
2	51⅞ a 52¼	57¼ 57⅜	59⅝ 60⅛	66½ 66¾	76 a 77¾	89⅞ 91
3	Sunday.	57¾ 58	60½ 61	Sunday.	77 79¾	90¾ 92½
4	**51½** 51⅞	57¼ 58¼	60¼ 61½	66¼ 66⅝	78¾ 79¼	90¾ 91
5	51⅝ 51⅞	57¼ 58¼	61⅜ 61⅞	67½ 67¾	77¼ 77¾	Sunday.
6	51½ 51⅞	57⅛ 59	Sunday.	68¾ 70⅛	74 6¾	93½ 94½
7	51⅝ 52⅛	Sunday.	61¾ 61¾	70¼ 71	72¾ 72⅞	92 94
8	51¾ 52¼	58¾ 59¼	62⅜ 63¼	69½ 70	Sunday.	93 93½
9	51⅞ 52⅛	59⅜ 59¼	67 67¼	69½ 71½	69¾ 71	95 98½
10	Sunday.	59 59¼	63¾ 64¼	Sunday.	**68** 68½	98½ 98¾
11	52⅜ 52½	59⅜ 59¼	64⅜ 64¾	71 72¼	74¼ 76¼	94½ 98
12	53⅜ 54⅛	59 59¼	60½ 62	73⅜ 75	73 74½	Sunday.
13	53¼ 53⅞	59½ 59½	Sunday.	75⅛ 75¾	70 73⅛	95¾ 96½
14	54⅜ 54⅞	Sunday.	60½ 60¾	76 77½	72 72¼	96½ 98
15	55⅛ 55⅝	59⅞ 60⅜	62¼ 62¾	73½ 73¾	Sunday.	96¾ 97¾
16	55½ 56½	60¼ **61**	61⅜ 62	71 73¼	73½ 73¾	97 97½
17	Sunday	59¼ 60	61⅛ 61½	Sunday.	77 78	96⅝ 96½
18	59½ [illegible]	59⅞ 60¼	62 63	70½ 71¼	81 81¼	95¼ 95½
19	59¼ **59¾**	58 58¾	61⅝ 62½	67 68	81½ 81¾	Sunday.
20	58⅛ 58⅝	59¼ 59¼	Sunday.	67 67½	81 81½	98 98¼
21	56¼ 57	Sunday.	61¾ 63½	66⅞ 67½	81½ 83¼	99 108
22	56¾ 57⅝	58½ 59½	63¼ 63¾	73⅛ 74	Sunday.	110 130
23	56 56⅞	57¼ 57½	64⅛ 65½	74½ 77½	82 82⅝	105 123
24	Sunday.	57¼ 57½	66 66½	Sunday.	82½ 86	113 117
25	57⅜ 57⅞	58½ 58¾	Good Frid.	79 **82½**	84¾ 84½	114 120
26	58 58⅛	57½ 58¾	69½ **69¾**	81¼ 84	83 83½	Sunday.
27	57 58⅛	57½ 58½	Sunday.	81 81½	86 86½	121 140
28	57⅛ 57¼	Sunday.	64½ 66½	77⅞ 80	86 88	134 140
29	56⅜ 57¼	... ...	65 66	78 81½	Sunday.	135 **150**
30	56¼ 57⅛	... ...	63⅛ 64¼	79½ 80	88 **91¾**	145 150
31	Sunday.	... ...	64 55	... ...	80 90½	... ...

	July, 1864.	Aug. 1864.	Sept. 1864.	Oct. 1864.	Nov. 1864.	Dec. 1864.
1	**122** a 150	151 a 159	143 a 148½	90 a 93¾	130 a 141½	125¼ a 129
2	130 150	156 158½	148½ **154½**	Sunday.	129½ 146	130¼ 133¾
3	Sunday.	156½ 158½	136 143½	**89** 91¾	127¼ 136¾	128¼ 131
4	Holiday.	Fast-day.	Sunday.	90 92¼	131⅜ 138⅝	Sunday.
5	135 149	157½ 161½	135 143½	89½ 91¼	135½ 144¾	127 129¾
6	148 161½	159¼ **161¾**	140½ 142	92¼ 97	Sunday.	130 134⅜
7	162 173	Sunday.	140⅞ 142¾	98 104	138½ 145⅞	138½ 143
8	166¾ 176½	156¾ 159½	135¾ 141	96¾ 103¼	145½ 149½	139 **142¾**
9	160 175	152¼ 155½	134⅛ 136	Sunday.	146 **160**	139½ 142⅜
10	Sunday.	154½ 155¼	118 128½	96 99	143 153	134½ 139¼
11	176 **185**	153¾ 156¾	Sunday.	98⅜ 103⅜	136⅞ 144½	Sunday.
12	171 182	155⅛ 157⅛	113½ 125	102¼ 104¾	142½ 145	132½ 137½
13	168¾ 173	154⅝ 156¼	117½ 128	103⅛ 109¾	Sunday.	133¼ 135½
14	158 168	Sunday.	123¼ 128	108 117¼	143 146⅝	133⅜ 135½
15	144 156	155¾ 156⅞	128⅛ 129½	113¼ 120	128⅝ 144	134½ 137⅜
16	148½ 161¼	155½ 156¾	124⅛ 128	Sunday.	128½ 140	133¾ 134¾
17	Sunday.	155¾ 157	120⅞ 128⅝	118½ 122½	118¼ 126¾	125⅛ 130⅜
18	154½ 161½	157 158	Sunday.	106½ 115	**110** 119	Sunday.
19	158½ 168¾	157 157⅞	123⅞ 126¾	107¼ 111½	116 125½	112¾ 117½
20	161 163¾	156½ 157⅛	123 126¾	106¼ 111¼	Sunday.	120½ 127
21	156½ 160	Sunday.	120 122	107½ 109	117½ 121½	122¼ 126
22	150½ 157¾	156⅞ 157¼	116 121¼	109½ 113½	124 129	121 124½
23	153¾ 156	157⅛ 158¼	111 117	Sunday.	120½ 123½	120½ 122¾
24	Sunday.	154⅛ 157	100 112	112¼ 116⅞	Thanks.	120⅜ 122
25	155½ 158¾	154½ 155¾	Sunday.	114¾ 118⅛	116¾ 121¼	Christmas.
26	157¾ 159½	153⅝ 156	95 98⅛	112¾ 117	119½ 124⅜	Holiday.
27	154 157¼	145 153	92¼ 95	114¼ 116	Sunday.	**116** 118
28	144 152	Sunday.	95 105	115¼ 117¼	126½ 133¾	116¼ 124
29	150 153½	135½ 145	94¼ 102	117¾ 121¼	132 136¼	122 125½
30	153 158	**131½** 136	**91** 94⅛	Sunday.	127¼ 133	126 129½
31	Sunday.	134 143	... ...	121½ **127¾**	... ...	124¼ 127⅞

THE DAILY PREMIUM ON **GOLD** AT NEW YORK IN THE YEAR **1865.**

Those quotations in full-face type indicate the lowest and highest rates of each month.

	Jan. 1865.	Feb. 1865.	Mar. 1865.	April, 1865.	May, 1865.	June, 1865.	July, 1865.	Aug. 1865.	Sept. 1865.	Oct. 1865.	Nov. 1865.	Dec. 1865.
1	Sunday.	102½ a 106	99½ a **101**	51 a 52⅞	42¼ a **45⅞**	Holiday.	39⅝ a 41	44 a 44⅞	44¼ a **45**	Sunday.	**45½** a 46	47⅞ a 48⅛
2	Holiday.	103⅛ 105¾	97 98⅞	Sunday.	41⅛ 42¼	37⅜ a 38¾	Sunday.	45 **45⅞**	44¼ 44⅝	**44¼** a 44⅞	46 46¾	47½ 48¼
3	126 **130**	105⅝ 109½	98 99	45¾ 48¾	41¼ 41⅞	36⅞ 37	**38** 41½	44⅛ 44¾	Sunday.	44⅜ 44¾	46⅝ 47	Sunday.
4	131⅝ 134¼	109 114⅞	Holiday.	46⅛ 48¼	42 43⅜	Sunday.	Holiday.	44⅜ 44½	43¾ 44¼	44¾ 46⅝	46¾ 47¼	47⅞ 48⅛
5	127¼ 129½	Sunday.	Sunday.	48 **53⅛**	42¾ 43⅞	**35⅞** 36½	39⅛ 40⅛	43⅜ 43⅝	44⅛ 44⅝	46⅜ 47	Sunday.	48⅛ **48½**
6	126¼ 128¼	112½ 114	98 99	50 52	42⅝ 43⅛	36¼ 37⅛	38¾ 39⅞	Sunday.	44½ 45	46½ **49**	46⅞ 47½	46¾ 48
7	126⅜ 127⅜	112¾ **116½**	97⅛ 99	47½ 51¼	Sunday.	36½ 37½	39⅛ 39¾	43½ 44	44½ 44⅞	46 46¾	46½ 47⅜	Holiday.
8	Sunday.	110⅝ 113½	96½ 97½	48⅝ 50¼	39¾ 43¼	37¾ 38	39⅞ 40⅛	44⅜ 45⅛	44½ 44¾	Sunday.	46½ 47⅜	45¾ 46½
9	126¾ 127	111⅞ 113⅛	93⅝ 96⅛	Sunday.	35¼ 37⅝	37½ 38	Sunday.	43¾ 44⅜	44½ 44¾	45¾ 46¾	46⅛ 46⅜	44⅝ 45⅛
10	122½ 124½	110⅝ 111½	87⅜ 91	**44** 45½	31⅛ 35¼	37½ 37¾	39¼ 40½	42¾ 43⅝	Sunday.	44¾ 45⅛	46⅜ 46¾	Sunday.
11	119¼ 124	105¼ 109	89 91¾	46½ 47	28¾ 31⅛	Sunday.	39½ 40⅛	**40⅛** 42	44½ 44⅝	44½ 45⅛	46½ 46⅞	**44⅛** 45⅜
12	117 120⅞	Sunday.	Sunday.	45½ 46	30⅝ 33⅝	38½ 40⅞	40⅞ 42	40⅛ 42	43¾ 44⅛	45 45⅝	Sunday.	44⅝ 45⅛
13	118⅜ 122	105¼ 107	85⅞ 91	46½ 46¾	**29¼** 30¼	40¾ 42¾	41⅞ 42½	Sunday.	43⅜ 43¾	44⅝ 45	46¾ 47½	44⅞ 45¾
14	117¾ 120¾	107½ 108¾	78 85	45⅜ 46¼	Sunday.	40⅛ 42⅛	42⅝ 43⅞	42¼ 43⅛	43⅛ 43¼	44½ 44⅞	46½ 47⅛	45½ 46⅛
15	Sunday.	105⅛ 106½	74½ 80	* * *	29½ 30¾	43½ **47¼**	41⅛ 42½	40⅞ 41⅞	**42⅛** 43½	Sunday.	47⅛ 47⅜	46 46⅛
16	117½ 121⅜	103½ 105½	72⅜ 77	Sunday.	30⅝ 31¼	42⅝ 45⅛	Sunday.	41⅞ 42⅞	42¼ 42⅛	45 45¾	47 47⅝	45⅞ 46⅛
17	114¾ 117	103½ 104½	62½ 68½	48⅝ 53	29¾ 30¼	43⅝ 45⅞	42 43	41⅞ 42⅞	Sunday.	45¾ 46⅞	46¾ 47	Sunday.
18	115½ 117	104 105⅜	63½ 66	46½ 47½	29½ 30¼	Sunday.	43 43⅞	42⅞ 43⅝	43½ 43⅞	46 46⅞	46⅛ 47	46¼ 46⅝
19	108 114¾	Sunday.	Sunday.	No Board.	30⅝ 31⅛	40½ 43¾	42 43⅝	43½ 44¼	43⅝ 44	46⅜ 47	Sunday.	46⅛ 46⅝
20	101¾ 107½	99½ 102⅝	62⅝ 67½	" "	30½ 31⅛	37¾ 39⅞	42¾ 42¾	Sunday.	43¾ 43½	46 46¾	46⅝ 47	46 46⅞
21	99¼ 106	**96⅞** 99⅞	55⅞ 59½	47½ 49⅞	Sunday.	40 41⅞	42⅛ 42⅝	44½ 44⅝	43⅞ 44¼	45⅝ 46½	46⅝ 47	45¾ 46¼
22	Sunday.	100½ 101¼	56 58¾	49¼ 50⅛	30¾ 31⅛	41⅝ 43½	42½ 42⅞	43⅛ 43⅞	43⅝ 43⅞	Sunday.	46⅞ 47	45½ 46⅜
23	**98** 102¾	98¾ 102	51½ 57	Sunday.	31¾ 32⅜	40⅞ 42½	Sunday.	43⅛ 43⅞	43⅛ 43⅝	45⅞ 46⅛	46⅞ 47	45¼ 45¾
24	98½ 102¾	98¾ 100½	**48¾** 53	Holiday.	32½ 34⅞	41⅝ 42¾	42⅝ 43½	43⅝ 43⅝	Sunday.	46 46⅛	46¾ 47	Sunday.
25	104¼ 107½	98¼ 99⅞	53¼ 57½	Holiday.	35¾ 38⅛	Sunday.	43 43¾	43½ 44	43 44⅝	45⅜ 46½	46⅞ 47⅛	Christmas.
26	104 106½	Sunday.	Sunday.	50½ 52	35½ 38	39½ 41¾	42⅞ 43⅞	44 44⅞	43¾ 44	44¾ 45⅝	Sunday.	45⅛ 45½
27	108¾ 115⅝	99¾ 101⅝	53 55½	47⅞ 49	35⅞ 36⅞	41⅝ 42½	43⅛ 44⅞	Sunday.	43¾ 44¼	45½ 45⅞	47⅛ 47⅝	45⅛ 45⅝
28	112½ 120	101½ 103¾	53⅞ 54⅞	46¾ 47¼	Sunday.	39⅞ 41⅝	41⅞ **46**	43⅝ 44¼	43⅛ 44⅛	45⅛ 45⅝	47½ **48⅛**	45⅜ 45⅝
29	Sunday.	... ...	51 53⅛	46 46¾	36 37	38½ 39	44½ 45½	44⅛ 44⅞	44 44⅞	Sunday.	48 48⅜	45 45⅝
30	111 114⅝	... ...	49⅞ 51⅝	Sunday.	37⅛ 38⅛	39 41½	Sunday.	43⅞ 44⅞	43⅞ 44⅛	45⅛ 45¾	48 48¼	44⅝ 45⅛
31	102⅜ 111	... ...	51 52	... ...	36⅝ 37½	... ...	43¼ 43⅝	44¼ 44⅞	... ...	45⅝ 46¼	... ...	Sunday.

* * * Death of President Lincoln. No Board.

THE DAILY PREMIUM ON **GOLD** AT NEW YORK IN THE YEAR **1866.**

Those quotations in full-face type indicate the lowest and highest rates of each month.

	Jan. 1866.	Feb. 1866.	Mar. 1866.	April, 1866.	May, 1866.	June, 1866.
1	Holiday.	39⅜ *a* **41¼**	35⅝ *a* **36½**	Sunday.	**25⅛** *a* 27	No Board.
2	44¼ **44⅝**	39¼ 40½	35⅝ 36½	27¼ *a* **28½**	26⅝ 28⅜	40⅜ 41⅝
3	43¾ 44½	39¾ 40⅝	33¼ 34⅛	27⅝ 28⅛	27⅛ 28⅛	Sunday.
4	42½ 43¼	Sunday.	Sunday.	27½ 28¼	27⅛ 27½	40½ 44
5	42⅞ 42¾	39½ 40⅛	32⅝ 34¼	27⅜ 27½	27⅛ 27¾	43⅛ 46⅝
6	41½ 43	39¾ 39⅞	32¼ 33⅝	27½ 28⅛	Sunday.	44¾ 45⅛
7	Sunday.	39¼ 39¾	33 33½	27 27⅛	27¾ 28⅝	42⅞ 45⅛
8	39⅜ 41¼	39¾ 40½	31½ 32½	Sunday.	28⅛ 29	38¾ 41¾
9	**36** 39½	39¼ 40¾	30½ 31⅝	**25** 27½	28½ 29¾	39¼ 40
10	38½ 39¾	38½ 39½	29⅝ 31⅛	25½ 26¼	28⅛ 29⅝	Sunday.
11	38¼ 39½	Sunday.	Sunday.	26⅛ 27½	28⅛ 29½	**37**½ 39½
12	38½ 39½	38¼ 39	30⅜ 32⅜	27 27⅞	28¾ 29¼	41½ 43¼
13	39 39½	38⅝ 38⅞	29½ 30⅜	26⅛ 27	Sunday.	42½ 45½
14	Sunday.	37½ 38⅝	30⅜ 31¼	25¾ 26½	30¼ 30⅞	45⅜ 47⅛
15	38⅜ 39¾	37½ 37⅛	30⅛ 31⅜	Sunday.	29⅝ 30⅞	47⅛ 49⅜
16	39 39½	37½ 37⅛	30¼ 31	25⅜ 26	30 30¼	54⅜ 60
17	39⅝ 40¼	37⅛ 37¼	29½ 30¾	25⅛ 26⅜	29⅝ 30⅛	Sunday.
18	38¾ 40	Sunday.	Sunday.	26⅜ 27⅜	29⅞ 30⅛	55¾ **67¾**
19	37½ 38¾	36⅝ 37½	27⅜ 29½	26¾ 27¾	30 30⅛	49½ 54¾
20	38½ 39½	36¾ 37¼	27½ 28⅜	26⅛ 27¼	Sunday.	51⅛ 53¾
21	Sunday.	36⅝ 37¼	28½ 28⅞	26½ 27	30½ 30⅛	48½ 50¼
22	38¾ 39¾	Holiday.	27⅜ 28⅜	Sunday.	30⅝ 34¼	48½ 49⅞
23	38¾ 39½	36⅞ 37⅝	27½ 28	26⅛ 26⅞	33⅜ 38⅛	51⅜ 53¾
24	39¾ 39½	**35½** 37	**25** 26⅜	26⅝ 26⅞	37¾ 39⅜	Sunday.
25	39¼ 39½	Sunday.	Sunday.	26⅜ 27⅛	39⅜ **41¼**	52 53¾
26	39½ 40	36¾ 37¼	25¼ 26	27⅛ 28	38 39¾	54½ 57
27	39⅜ 39⅞	36⅝ 37	26½ 28¼	28⅜ 29⅜	Sunday.	54½ 56
28	Sunday.	36⅝ 37	27½ 28¾	28⅛ **29½**	37 37⅛	51⅜ 54½
29	39⅞ 40½	... ...	27½ 28¼	Sunday.	37½ 38⅛	53⅜ 55
30	40½ 41⅛	... ...	Holiday.	25⅞ 27⅜	38 38⅝	52¾ 54
31	39½ 41¼	... ...	27¾ 28¼	... ...	38¾ 40	

	July, 1866.	Aug. 1866.	Sept. 1866.	Oct. 1866.	Nov. 1866.	Dec. 1866.
1	Sunday	48⅜ *a* 49¼	45½ *a* 47⅛	45⅜ *a* 46⅞	46¼ *a* 47¾	40⅝ *a* **41¾**
2	53⅜ *a* **55¾**	47½ 48⅛	Sunday.	47½ 48⅛	46¾ 47½	Sunday.
3	52⅞ 53¼	47¼ 48⅝	44¾ 45¾	47⅛ 48¼	47½ 48½	40½ 41¾
4	Holiday.	46¼ 48	45⅝ 46¾	48⅛ 48¾	Sunday.	40⅝ 41¾
5	52¼ 53⅜	Sunday.	46¼ 47⅛	48⅜ 49½	47⅝ *a* **48**	38⅝ 40⅝
6	53¾ 54⅛	47⅛ 48	45¾ 46½	48⅛ 49¾	47⅜ 48⅜	38⅛ 39¾
7	53⅜ 54½	47⅜ 47⅞	45⅜ 46	Sunday.	47 48	38⅛ 39
8	Sunday.	48 49	46¼ **47⅛**	48⅝ 49⅝	46 46⅝	37⅞ 38⅛
9	51⅜ 53⅛	48½ 48⅞	Sunday.	48¼ 49⅝	46 46⅝	Sunday.
10	48¼ 49¾	48¼ 48⅝	46¼ 46¾	49⅛ 51⅜	44¾ 46⅛	37 37¾
11	49⅜ 50⅜	48½ 49	45¼ 46¼	51 53⅜	Sunday.	36⅞ 37⅛
12	49⅛ 51¼	Sunday.	45½ 46¼	50⅛ 53⅛	43½ 44⅝	37⅜ 38⅛
13	52¼ 53¼	49¼ 49½	45¾ 46⅛	52⅜ **54⅛**	44⅝ 45⅝	37⅜ 37⅞
14	52 52¾	49⅛ 50⅛	44¼ 45½	Sunday.	44½ 45¼	37⅛ 38⅛
15	Sunday.	50⅛ **52¼**	44¼ 45	50¾ 53⅜	43½ 45¼	37⅜ 37⅛
16	48⅝ 49¾	51⅛ 52⅛	Sunday.	47⅜ 50⅛	42⅜ 43⅜	Sunday.
17	49 51¼	50⅛ 51¾	44¾ 45½	47½ 48⅞	41 42½	37¾ 38⅛
18	49 50½	48⅝ 51	44½ 45⅜	48 48⅞	Sunday.	37⅛ 38⅜
19	50⅛ 50¾	Sunday.	45 45½	47 49⅛	40 41¾	36⅝ 37⅜
20	49¾ 50⅝	48½ 48¾	44⅛ 45⅜	45⅞ 49	40⅞ 41⅜	34⅜ 36⅜
21	49 50⅝	47½ 48⅛	43¼ 44	Sunday.	39⅜ 41	33⅜ 34⅞
22	Sunday.	47⅜ 49⅜	**43¼** 43⅞	45½ 46⅞	**37½** 38⅞	32¾ 33¾
23	50⅜ 51⅛	49⅜ 51	Sunday.	**45⅜** 47½	38⅛ 39½	Sunday.
24	50 50⅝	48⅛ 50¾	43½ 45⅞	47 48¼	38⅜ 39½	33½ 33½
25	49½ 50⅛	46⅞ 48	44¼ 44⅞	46¼ 48	Sunday.	Christmas.
26	49½ 50	Sunday.	44½ 45¼	47 48⅛	38⅝ 41⅜	**31½** 33½
27	49⅞ 50⅜	**46½** 48¼	44¾ 45⅛	45⅝ 46¾	40¾ 44	31½ 32⅜
28	50 50⅜	48⅛ 49⅜	44⅝ 45½	Sunday.	40¾ 43¼	33 33⅜
29	Sunday.	48⅛ 48⅞	45⅝ 46½	45¾ 46¾	Holiday.	33 34
30	**47** 48	47⅜ 48⅛	Sunday.	46 46⅝	40⅜ 41¾	Sunday.
31	48⅜ 49¼	47⅜ 48	... ...	45⅞ 46⅝	... ...	33 34

THE DAILY PREMIUM ON **GOLD** AT NEW YORK IN THE YEAR **1867.**

Those quotations in full-face type indicate the lowest and highest rates of each month.

	Jan. 1867.	Feb. 1867.	Mar. 1867.	April, 1867.	May, 1867.	June, 1867.	July, 1867.	Aug. 1867.	Sept. 1867.	Oct. 1867.	Nov. 1867.	Dec. 1867.
1	Holiday.	**35¼** a 35⅞	38½ a **40⅜**	33⅝ a 34¼	**34⅞** a 36⅛	**36⅜** a 36⅝	**38** a 38¼	**39⅞** a 40⅛	Sunday.	43¼ a 43½	40½ a 41⅛	Sunday.
2	32⅞ a 33	35⅛ 36⅛	38½ 39⅛	34½ 34⅜	35⅛ 35¾	Sunday.	38 38½	39⅞ 40⅛	**41** a 41⅜	43½ 44⅛	40¾ 40½	36½ a 37⅜
3	**32** 35⅛	Sunday.	Sunday.	33¾ 34½	35¾ 36½	36⅜ 37⅛	38⅜ 38¾	40⅛ 40½	41 41½	44½ **45⅜**	Sunday.	36⅝ 37⅛
4	32⅛ 34⅜	36⅜ 37¾	38⅛ 39	33¼ 33⅞	35⅛ 36¾	36¼ 37⅛	Holiday.	Sunday.	41½ 42⅛	44¾ 45¼	39¾ **41⅜**	37 **37⅜**
5	33⅛ 35⅛	37 38⅛	36¾ 38⅜	32¾ 33⅝	Sunday.	36½ 36⅛	38¾ 39⅛	40 40⅛	42 42½	44⅜ 45	39½ 40⅛	36⅞ 37⅛
6	Sunday.	36⅛ 37⅞	35¼ 36½	32⅞ 33⅝	35¾ 37¾	36⅜ 36¾	38¾ 38⅝	40 40⅜	42¼ 42¾	Sunday.	38⅞ 39⅛	37½ 37⅛
7	35⅛ 35⅝	37¾ 39	33⅞ 35	Sunday.	37¼ 38⅛	36½ 36⅝	Sunday.	40 40⅜	42¼ 42¾	44⅞ 45¼	38⅛ 39⅛	36⅝ 37⅛
8	33¾ 34⅛	37⅛ 38⅛	**33½** 34⅞	33⅛ 36	37¾ 38¼	36¾ 37	38⅛ 39⅛	40⅛ 40⅛	Sunday.	44¾ 45⅛	38¾ 39⅛	Sunday.
9	33⅞ 34¼	36⅞ 37½	34 35⅛	34¼ 36	36¼ 38¼	Sunday.	38⅞ 38⅞	40 40⅛	42¾ 44¼	43 44¾	**38½** 39¼	36½ 37¼
10	32¾ 33¾	Sunday.	Sunday.	34⅛ 38	36⅛ 37⅛	36⅞ 37¼	38⅝ 38¾	40 40⅛	43½ 44¼	43¼ 44	Sunday.	35¼ 36¼
11	32¼ 34¼	36⅛ 36¾	34¾ 35½	36¼ 37⅝	35½ 36⅞	37⅛ 37⅛	38⅛ 39¼	Sunday.	44½ 45⅜	43⅝ 43⅞	38¾ 39	34⅞ 35¼
12	33⅞ 34½	36¾ 37¼	33⅞ 34¼	36⅜ 37⅝	Sunday.	37⅛ 37⅛	39 39¼	40⅛ 40¾	45⅜ **46⅜**	44⅛ 44⅝	39 39⅜	**33** 34¾
13	Sunday.	36¾ 37⅛	33⅞ 34¼	35½ 36	35⅛ 35¾	37 37⅛	39 39⅜	40⅝ 41	44⅞ 46	Sunday.	39½ 40⅛	33⅛ 34
14	34¼ 35	36¾ 37⅛	34⅛ 34½	Sunday.	35⅞ 37⅛	37 37⅛	Sunday.	40⅝ 40⅝	44½ 43⅞	43¾ 44⅞	39⅞ 40⅛	33¼ 34⅛
15	34¾ 35¼	36⅞ 36⅞	33⅞ 34½	34½ 35⅜	36½ 37⅛	37 37¼	39⅛ 39⅝	40⅞ 40⅞	Sunday.	43½ 44⅜	40⅛ 41⅛	Sunday.
16	35¼ 37	36½ 37	34 34½	34 34⅞	37 37⅛	Sunday.	39¾ 40⅛	40⅛ 40⅜	44 44⅝	43 43⅞	39¾ " ⅛	33⅝ 34⅝
17	35¼ 37	Sunday.	Sunday.	34⅝ 35⅛	36⅝ 37⅛	37¼ 37⅝	39⅜ 40⅜	40⅞ 40⅛	41½ 44⅝	43 44⅛	Sunday.	33¾ 35
18	36⅛ **37½**	36⅞ 36¾	34 34⅝	35¼ 37⅛	36¾ 37⅛	37⅜ 38	39½ 40	Sunday.	44½ 45⅛	44 44¾	39⅞ 40⅛	33½ 34¼
19	36 37	36⅛ 37	33¾ 34⅛	**33** 34⅞	Sunday.	37¼ 38⅜	39⅝ 40⅛	41 41⅜	44 45¼	43¾ 44⅛	39½ 39⅞	33¼ 34⅛
20	Sunday.	36⅜ 37¼	34¼ 34⅛	37¾ 39⅛	36⅞ 37⅛	37⅝ 38	39⅛ 39¾	41⅛ 41⅜	42¾ 43⅞	Sunday.	39⅝ 40	33¾ 34¼
21	36⅛ 37	37½ 38⅜	34⅜ 34½	Sunday.	37 37⅛	37⅜ 38½	Sunday.	40¾ 41¼	42½ 43¼	43⅝ 44	39⅛ 39½	33¼ 33⅝
22	35⅞ 36¾	Holiday.	34¼ 34½	37½ 38⅞	37⅞ 38⅛	38 38⅛	39⅝ 40⅛	40¾ 41⅛	Sunday.	43¼ 43⅜	38⅞ 39⅛	Sunday.
23	34½ 35¼	38¼ 38¾	34⅛ 34½	38 38¾	38⅛ **38½**	Sunday.	39¾ 40	40⅝ 41⅛	42⅞ 43⅝	43⅜ 43⅝	39⅛ 40⅛	33 33¼
24	34⅛ 34⅝	Sunday.	Sunday.	38½ **41¼**	37½ 38⅛	38 38⅛	39¾ 39¾	40½ 41	42¾ 43	42⅝ 43⅜	Sunday.	33⅜ 33⅛
25	33⅞ 34¼	37⅝ 38⅝	33¾ 34¼	39⅛ 41⅝	36⅞ 37½	38¼ 38¾	39⅛ 39¾	Sunday.	43¼ 44	41⅝ 42⅝	39¾ 40⅞	Christmas.
26	34⅜ 34¾	38¼ 39⅜	33¼ 34½	38 39¾	Sunday.	38 **38¾**	39⅛ 39¾	40½ 41⅛	43 43¾	**41⅜** 42¼	39¼ 40	33¾ 34¼
27	Sunday.	39¼ **40¼**	34¼ 34½	36⅞ 37⅛	36½ 37¼	37¾ 38⅛	39¾ 40⅜	41 41⅛	43¼ 43⅝	Sunday.	39¼ 39¾	33¾ 34⅛
28	34⅞ 34⅝	39⅞ 40¼	34⅛ 34½	Sunday.	36¾ 37⅛	37¾ 38⅛	Sunday.	41⅝ **42¾**	43 43½	42 42¾	Holiday.	33⅞ 33¾
29	34 34⅝	... ...	34⅛ 34¼	34½ 36¼	37 38	38¼ 38½	40 **40¾**	41⅝ 42	Sunday.	41⅞ 42¼	38⅞ 39⅛	Sunday.
30	34⅝ 36⅛	... ...	33½ 34⅛	35 36⅝	37¼ 37⅞	Sunday.	40 40¾	41¾ 42⅛	43 43½	40⅝ 41⅜	37⅞ 38¾	33¼ 34
31	34⅝ 35¾	... ...	Sunday.	... ...	36¾ 37⅛	... ...	39¾ 40⅝	41½ 41¾	... ...	40¼ 40¾	... ...	33⅛ 33¾

THE DAILY PREMIUM ON GOLD AT NEW YORK IN TH EAR 1868.

Those quotations in full-face type indicate the lowest and highest rates of each month.

	Jan. 1868.		Feb. 1868.		Mar. 1868.		April, 1868.		May, 1868.		June, 1868.	
1	Holiday.		40½ a	40⅝	Sunday.		38⅛ a	38¾	39¼ a	39½	**39**⅜ a	39⅞
2	**33**¼	33⅝	Sunday.		40⅞ a	**41**⅜	37¾	38⅛	39⅜	39⅝	39⅞	40⅛
3	33½	34	40⅞	41½	40½	41⅜	**37**¾	38⅛	Sunday.		39⅞	40¼
4	33⅞	34½	41⅛	41¾	40¾	41¼	38⅛	38½	**39**⅛	39½	40	40⅜
5	Sunday.		40⅞	41⅛	41	41¼	Sunday.		39⅛	39⅜	39¾	40
6	34¾	35¼	41½	42	41⅛	41⅛	37¾	38¼	39⅛	39½	39¼	39¾
7	35¼	37¼	41¾	42½	40⅝	41⅛	37¾	38⅜	39⅛	39¾	Sunday.	
8	36¼	37¾	42	42⅛	Sunday.		38⅛	38¾	39⅛	39⅝	39½	39¾
9	35¾	36½	Sunday.		39⅝	40½	38½	38¾	39⅞	40¼	39¾	39⅞
10	37	37½	42¾	**43**¼	39¾	40¼	Good Frid.		Sunday.		39¾	39⅞
11	37⅞	38	41¾	42½	39	39¾	38⅛	38½	39¾	40½	39⅞	40
12	Sunday.		41	41	39½	40¼	Sunday.		39⅛	39¾	39⅞	40⅛
13	38¼	40½	40⅞	42¼	39⅛	40	38⅛	39	39½	39⅝	39⅞	40
14	40½	**42**	**39**½	40¾	38½	39¾	38½	38⅞	39¾	**40**¼	Sunday.	
15	38¼	40½	40⅞	41½	Sunday.		38¼	38½	39⅝	39⅞	40	40⅛
16	39½	40	Sunday.		39¼	39½	38	38½	39⅝	39⅞	40⅛	40⅝
17	38½	39½	40⅞	41⅜	39	39½	38⅛	38⅝	Sunday.		40⅝	**41**⅛
18	38½	38¾	40⅜	41⅛	38½	38⅞	38½	38¾	39¼	39½	40⅛	40½
19	Sunday.		40¼	40⅞	38¼	38¾	Sunday.		39¼	39¾	40⅛	40¾
20	37⅞	39⅜	40	40½	38½	38¾	38⅝	39	39⅝	39⅞	40⅛	40⅜
21	38¾	39½	40½	40⅞	38⅝	39¼	38¾	39¼	39⅝	39⅞	Sunday	
22	39	39½	Holiday.		Sunday.		39⅝	40⅛	39¾	40	40⅛	40⅜
23	39⅜	40½	Sunday.		38⅝	39½	39½	**40**⅜	39⅛	39⅜	40	40⅝
24	40	40¾	42¼	44	**37**⅞	38¾	39⅛	39⅞	Sunday.		40¼	40⅝
25	39¾	40½	42	42½	38¼	38¾	38¾	39⅛	39⅞	40	40⅛	40½
26	Sunday.		41	41½	38¼	38½	Sunday.		39½	40⅛	40	40⅜
27	40⅜	41⅛	40⅝	41¼	38¼	38⅝	38¾	39⅛	39⅝	40⅛	40	40⅝
28	41	41⅞	41⅛	41½	38⅜	38⅝	39	39⅛	39⅝	39⅞	Sunday.	
29	41⅜	41¾	...	...	Sunday.		39	39⅜	39⅛	39½	40	40⅜
30	40½	41	...	...	38¾	39½	39	39½	39½	39¾	40¼	40½
31	40⅛	40¾	...	...	38⅛	38¾	...	...	Sunday.		...	...

	July, 1868.		Aug. 1868.		Sept. 1868.		Oct. 1868.		Nov. 1868.		Dec. 1868.	
1	**40**⅛ a	40⅜	44¾ a	45⅜	44⅝ a	45	39½ a	40⅛	Sunday.		35 a	35⅛
2	40⅜	40½	Sunday.		44¾	**45**⅛	39¼	40⅛	33 a	33⅜	34⅞	35⅛
3	40¼	40½	45	45⅛	43⅞	44⅜	39⅝	**40**½	33¼	33⅝	34⅞	35⅛
4	Holiday.		45⅝	46½	43¾	44⅛	Sunday.		33	33¾	35⅛	35¾
5	Sunday.		47	48⅜	44¼	44¾	39⅞	40⅜	32⅞	32⅝	35⅜	**36**¾
6	40½	40¾	48½	**50**	Sunday.		39¾	40¼	**32**⅛	33	Sunday.	
7	40½	41	47½	48⅛	44⅝	45	39⅛	40¼	33¾	34½	35⅝	36⅛
8	40⅞	41	46¾	47⅞	44⅛	44⅛	38⅞	39½	Sunday.		35⅛	36⅛
9	40⅞	..	Sunday.		44⅛	44⅛	38¾	39½	34⅛	34¾	35¾	35⅞
10	40⅞	40⅞	46½	47⅜	44⅛	44⅜	38⅝	38⅞	34⅜	35¼	35⅞	36⅛
11	40⅞	41¼	45⅞	46⅜	43⅞	44⅛	Sunday.		33⅞	34½	35⅛	36⅛
12	Sunday.		46⅛	46⅝	44	44⅛	37⅞	38¼	33⅞	34½	35⅛	35¾
13	41⅛	41⅞	47⅛	47¾	Sunday.		37½	38	33⅞	34	Sunday.	
14	41½	42⅛	46¾	48	43⅝	44⅛	36¾	37⅞	34¼	35	35⅛	35⅝
15	41⅞	42⅜	46⅛	46¾	43¾	44⅛	37⅜	38½	Sunday.		35⅛	35⅝
16	42¼	42⅝	Sunday.		43¾	44⅛	37½	37¾	35¼	**37**	35⅛	35⅝
17	42½	43⅛	46½	47¼	44⅛	44½	36½	37⅞	34⅛	36⅝	**34**⅞	34⅞
18	43¼	44	45½	46⅝	44⅛	44⅜	Sunday.		33⅞	35⅛	34⅞	35⅛
19	Sunday.		44½	45⅛	44⅛	44⅜	36⅝	37⅛	34⅛	35	35	35¾
20	42⅞	43⅜	43½	44⅛	Sunday.		36⅛	37⅜	34⅛	35	Sunday.	
21	42⅝	43⅛	43½	44⅜	43¾	43⅞	36⅝	36⅞	34⅝	34¾	34⅞	35⅜
22	43	43⅛	43½	44⅛	42⅞	43⅛	35½	35⅞	Sunday.		34⅞	35⅛
23	43⅛	43⅝	Sunday.		42⅞	43⅛	35	36	34	34⅞	34¾	35
24	43⅛	43¼	44½	45½	41⅞	42⅞	34⅞	35	34⅛	34⅞	34⅛	35
25	43⅛	43⅜	44½	46	41⅞	42⅛	Sunday.		34½	35⅛	Holiday.	
26	Sunday.		**44**	45	42	42⅛	33¾	34⅜	Holiday.		34¾	35
27	43¼	44⅛	44¾	45⅛	Sunday.		34⅛	34⅞	35	35⅞	Sunday.	
28	43¾	44⅛	44⅝	45⅛	41½	42⅛	33⅞	34⅜	34¾	35⅜	34¾	35
29	44	44⅛	44¾	45	**41**⅛	41⅝	34¼	34⅜	Sunday.		34¾	35
30	44⅜	**45**⅛	Sunday.		41⅜	41⅝	34	34½	35⅛	35¾	34⅞	34⅞
31	44⅜	45⅛	44⅜	45	.	. .	**33**¾	34	...	...	34⅞	35

THE DAILY PREMIUM ON **GOLD** AT NEW YORK IN THE YEAR **1869.**

Those quotations in full-face type indicate the lowest and highest rates of each month.

	Jan. 1869.	Feb. 1869.	Mar. 1869.	April, 1869.	May, 1869.	June, 1869.
1	Holiday.	35⅝ a **36⅜**	31 a 32¼	31⅜ a 31¾	**34⅝** a 35	38⅞ a 39¼
2	34¾ a 35½	35½ 35¾	31¾ **32½**	31½ 32	Sunday.	38½ 39¼
3	Sunday.	35⅛ 35¾	31⅞ **32½**	**31¼** 31½	35 36	38 38½
4	35 35½	35⅛ 35½	31⅞ 32	Sunday.	35¾ 36¼	37¾ 38⅛
5	**34⅝** 35½	35 35¼	31 31¾	31⅜ 31¾	35½ 35⅞	38⅛ 38⅞
6	34⅞ 35½	35 35¼	**30¼** 31½	31⅛ 31½	35⅝ 36⅜	Sunday.
7	35⅛ 35⅜	Sunday.	Sunday.	31½ 31⅞	36⅝ 39⅛	38½ 39
8	34⅞ 35¼	35⅛ 35½	31⅜ 32	31½ 32¼	37⅝ 39⅝	38¾ 39
9	35⅛ 35⅜	34⅞ 35⅛	30⅞ 31½	32¼ 33⅛	Sunday.	38⅞ 39¼
10	Sunday.	34⅞ 35	31⅛ 32	32⅞ 33¼	37 37⅞	38⅜ 39⅛
11	35⅛ 35¾	35⅛ 35¼	31⅜ 31⅞	Sunday.	37⅞ 38¾	38⅛ **39¾**
12	35¼ 35⅝	35 35¼	31 31⅞	32½ 33⅛	38⅛ 38⅞	39⅛ 39½
13	35½ 35⅞	34⅞ 35¼	31⅛ 31⅜	32⅝ 32⅞	37½ 38⅝	Sunday.
14	36⅛ 36½	Sunday.	Sunday.	32⅞ 33¼	38⅛ 38⅝	39⅛ 39⅜
15	36⅛ 36½	35 35¼	30⅞ 31⅜	32⅛ 32¾	39⅛ 39⅝	38⅛ 38⅞
16	36⅛ 36⅝	35 35⅛	31⅝ 31⅞	32⅝ 33⅛	Sunday.	37⅛ 37⅞
17	Sunday.	34⅞ 35⅛	31⅝ 31⅞	33 33⅛	40½ 42	37⅜ 38¼
18	35⅞ 36⅛	34⅛ 34⅞	30⅞ 31¼	Sunday.	41⅝ 42½	37⅝ 38
19	35¾ 35⅞	33½ 34	30½ 31⅜	33¼ 33⅞	41⅞ 43⅝	**36⅞** 37
20	35½ 35⅞	33½ 33¾	30¾ 31⅛	33⅞ 34¼	43⅛ **44⅛**	Sunday.
21	35⅝ 3[illegible]	Sunday.	Sunday.	34⅛ 34⅜	41⅝ 43¼	36⅛ 37⅛
22	35½ 35⅞	Holiday.	31 31⅜	34 **34⅜**	40½ 41¾	37¾ 38⅛
23	35⅞ 36⅛	32½ 33½	31 31¼	33½ 33¾	Sunday.	36⅛ 37¼
24	Sunday.	32¼ 32⅞	31¼ 31½	33¼ 33½	41¾ 42½	36⅝ 37¼
25	36⅛ 36½	32⅝ 33½	31 31¼	Sunday.	40¾ 41½	37 37½
26	36⅛ **36⅞**	31½ 32½	Good Frid.	33⅜ 33⅝	39⅛ 40½	37⅜ 37⅞
27	36⅛ 36⅝	**30⅞** 32½	31 31¼	33⅝ 34	38¾ 39⅝	Sunday.
28	36½ 36⅝	Sunday.	Sunday.	33⅛ 33⅝	39⅛ 39¾	37¼ 37⅝
29	36⅜ 36⅝	... ...	31⅛ 31¼	33⅝ 34⅜	39¾ 40⅛	37⅛ 37½
30	36 36¼	... ...	31⅜ 31⅝	34 34½	Sunday.	36⅞ 37¼
31	Sunday.	... ...	31¼ 31⅜	... ...	38⅜ 38⅞	... ...

	July, 1869.	Aug. 1869.	Sept. 1869.	Oct. 1869.	Nov. 1869.	Dec. 1869.
1	37⅛ a 37¾	Sunday.	33⅛ a 33⅝	30 a 30⅝	28⅛ a **28⅜**	21½ a 22⅛
2	36⅝ 37⅛	36⅛ a **36⅝**	33¼ 34⅜	30⅛ 30½	27¼ 28	22⅛ 22⅝
3	36¾ 37¼	35⅞ 36⅛	35⅛ 36	Sunday.	27⅛ 27⅜	22⅛ 22⅞
4	Sunday.	35¾ 36	35½ 37⅜	29 29⅞	26⅞ 27⅛	22¼ 23⅛
5	Holiday.	35⅞ 36⅛	Sunday.	28⅞ 30⅜	26¼ 27⅛	Sunday.
6	35⅝ 37	36 36⅛	36 37¾	29½ 30¾	26½ 27¼	23¾ 23⅝
7	**34** 35¼	36⅛ 36⅜	36⅛ 37	31⅛ **32**	Sunday.	22¾ 23¼
8	35⅛ 35⅞	Sunday.	34⅝ 36⅛	30⅝ 31⅝	26⅝ 26⅞	23⅛ **24**
9	35¾ 36¼	36 36⅜	35⅛ 35⅞	30⅛ 30⅞	26¾ 27⅜	23⅛ 23⅞
10	35¾ 36	35⅛ 35⅞	35 35⅞	Sunday.	26⅞ 27⅛	22⅞ 23⅛
11	Sunday.	35⅛ 35¼	35⅜ 35⅞	30¼ 30⅞	26⅞ 27	23 23⅜
12	36¼ 36⅞	34 35⅛	Sunday.	30⅝ 30⅞	26⅞ 26⅞	Sunday.
13	36⅛ **37⅞**	34⅛ 34¾	35½ 35⅞	30⅛ 30⅞	26¾ 27	22⅜ 23
14	37 37⅝	33⅞ 34⅛	35 36⅛	30 30⅛	Sunday.	22 22⅜
15	36¾ 37⅛	Sunday.	36 36⅜	29⅞ 30⅛	26⅝ 27⅛	21½ 21⅞
16	36 36⅞	33⅞ 34½	36⅛ 36⅜	30 30⅛	27⅛ 27⅛	21⅞ 22⅛
17	35¼ 35⅞	32⅞ 33⅞	36⅛ 36¾	Sunday.	26⅞ 27⅛	21⅛ 22
18	Sunday.	32⅝ 33⅜	36½ 36¾	30 30⅜	Thanks'g.	20¼ 20⅞
19	35⅝ 36⅛	32¾ 33⅝	Sunday.	30 30⅛	26⅛ 26¾	Sunday.
20	35 35⅝	32⅝ 33	36⅝ 37⅜	30 30½	26⅜ 26⅞	20⅜ 21¼
21	34⅞ 35⅛	**31⅞** 32⅛	37⅛ 37⅝	30⅛ 31⅛	Sunday.	**19** 20½
22	35 35½	Sunday.	37⅜ 41½	30⅞ 31⅜	26⅜ 26⅝	20⅛ 20¾
23	35¼ 35¾	31⅛ 32⅛	41 44¼	30⅞ 31⅛	26½ 26⅞	20⅝ 21
24	35⅝ 36⅛	32⅜ 32⅞	33 **62½**	Sunday.	26 26⅝	20⅝ 20¾
25	Sunday.	32½ 33⅜	†No Board.	30⅞ 31¼	24⅞ 25¾	Christmas.
26	36¾ 37⅛	33 34	Sunday.	30⅛ 30⅞	24⅞ 24⅞	Sunday.
27	36⅛ 37⅝	32⅛ 34⅛	†No Board.	30 30⅛	24⅞ 25	20⅛ 20⅝
28	36⅛ 36¾	33⅝ 34⅛	†No Board.	28¾ 29⅜	Sunday.	20⅛ 20⅜
29	35⅝ 36⅜	Sunday.	**30½** 32	**28½** 28⅞	21½ 23	19¾ 20
30	36⅛ 36⅜	33⅝ 34⅛	30⅝ 32	28⅝ 29¼	**21⅛** 23	19½ 20⅛
31	36⅛ 36⅜	33⅛ 33⅞	... ...	Sunday.	... ...	19⅝ 20⅜

† Suspension of Gold Exchange Bank, Sept. 25, 1869, and no meeting of the Gold Board for four days.

THE DAILY PREMIUM ON GOLD AT NEW YORK IN THE YEAR 1870.

Those quotations in full-face type indicate the lowest and highest rates of each month.

	Jan. 1870.	Feb. 1870.	March, 1870.	April, 1870.	May, 1870.	June, 1870.	July, 1870.	Aug. 1870.	Sept. 1870.	Oct. 1870.	Nov. 1870.	Dec. 1870.
1	No Board.	21¼ a 21½	15 a 16	**11½** a 11¾	Sunday.	14¼ a 14⅝	12⅛ a 12¼	20⅞ a 21½	16⅜ a **16⅞**	13¾ a 14	11¼ a 11½	10½ a 10¾
2	Sunday.	21⅛ **21⅝**	15¼ **16¼**	11½ 11¾	14½ a 15½	14½ **14¾**	11¾ 12⅛	21⅝ 22	16 16⅝	Sunday.	10⅞ 11¼	10⅝ 11⅛
3	19½ a 20⅛	20¼ 21½	15⅛ 15⅝	Sunday.	14½ 15	14⅜ 14½	Sunday.	21¼ 21⅞	14 15⅜	13⅝ 13⅞	10½ 10⅞	11 **11⅜**
4	**19⅜** 19⅝	20⅜ 20¾	13⅞ 14	11½ 11⅞	14¼ 14⅞	14¼ 14½	Holiday.	21⅝ **22**	Sunday.	13 13⅜	**10** 10½	Sunday.
5	19⅞ 20	20½ 21	13½ 14	11⅞ 12⅛	14⅜ 14⅝	Sunday.	11⅜ 11⅞	21⅛ 21½	13¼ 14⅛	13 13¼	10¼ 10½	10⅞ 11¼
6	20¼ 20⅝	Sunday.	Sunday.	11¾ 12⅛	14⅝ 14⅞	13⅞ 14⅜	**11¼** 11¾	20¾ 21⅛	14⅛ 15	12⅞ 13	Sunday.	10⅝ 10⅞
7	21½ 21⅞	20⅝ 21⅛	12½ 13⅛	11⅞ 12⅛	14¾ 15⅛	13½ 14	11¼ 12⅛	Sunday.	14⅛ 14⅝	13 13¼	10½ 10⅞	10⅝ 10⅞
8	21½ 23	20½ 21	10⅞ 12½	12⅛ 12¼	Sunday.	13⅛ 13½	11¾ 12¼	18½ 19⅝	13⅝ 14½	13½ 13½	10½ 10¾	10⅝ 10¾
9	Sunday.	20½ 20¾	**10¼** 11½	12¼ 13⅛	14⅝ 14⅞	13⅜ 13¾	12 12¾	17½ 18⅝	13⅝ 14⅛	Sunday.	10⅜ 10⅝	10¾ 10⅞
10	22 **23¼**	20⅛ 20¾	10½ 11¼	Sunday.	14⅝ 15	13⅜ 13⅝	Sunday.	16¾ 18	13¾ 14⅛	13½ 13¾	10⅝ 10¾	10¾ 11
11	21¾ 22½	19¾ 20¼	12⅝ 13⅛	13⅝ 14⅛	14⅞ 15¼	13¼ 13⅜	13⅛ 15⅛	15⅞ 17¾	Sunday.	13⅛ 13½	10¾ 11⅛	Sunday.
12	22 22½	19⅞ 20⅛	11¼ 12⅝	12⅝ 13⅜	15 **15½**	Sunday.	13 14⅛	17⅛ 18	13⅝ 13⅞	13⅛ 13⅜	11 11⅜	**10½** 10¾
13	21½ 21⅝	Sunday.	Sunday.	12¾ 12¾	14¾ 15⅛	12¾ 13⅛	12 12¾	17½ 17⅝	13⅝ 14	13⅝ **14⅛**	Sunday.	10½ 10⅝
14	21½ 21⅞	19½ 19⅞	11⅞ 12¾	12⅝ 13	14⅝ 14⅞	12¾ 13	12⅞ 13⅞	Sunday.	14 14⅜	13¼ 13¾	11¾ 12¾	10⅝ 11⅛
15	21¼ 21⅝	19½ 20	11⅝ 12⅛	Good Frid.	Sunday.	12⅞ 13⅜	14 15½	16½ 17¾	13⅞ 14⅛	13 13⅜	10⅞ 11½	11 11¼
16	Sunday.	19⅝ 20	11¾ 12¼	13¼ 13¾	14⅜ 14¾	13⅛ 13⅜	16½ 16¾	16¾ 17¼	14 14⅛	Sunday.	11¾ 12½	10⅝ 10⅞
17	21¼ 21½	19⅜ 19⅝	12 12¼	Sunday.	14¾ 15	12¾ 13⅛	Sunday.	17¼ 17¾	13⅞ 14⅛	13 13¼	12⅜ **13¼**	10½ 10⅞
18	21⅜ 21⅞	19 19⅜	11⅞ 12¼	13¼ 13¾	14¾ 15	12¾ 13⅛	17¾ **22½**	16⅞ 17	Sunday.	12½ 13½	12½ 13¼	Sunday.
19	21½ 21⅝	18⅞ 19⅛	12 12⅝	13¼ 13¾	14½ 14⅞	Sunday.	20½ 22½	16 16¼	13⅝ 14	12¾ 12⅞	12⅛ 12¾	10⅝ 10¾
20	21 21½	Sunday.	Sunday.	13¼ 13⅝	14½ 14¾	12⅝ 12⅞	21⅝ 22⅛	**14¾** 15⅜	13¾ 13⅞	12⅞ 13¼	Sunday.	10⅝ 10¾
21	20½ 21	18¾ 19⅛	12¼ 12¾	13 13½	14⅝ 14⅞	12¾ 12⅞	20½ 21½	Sunday.	13⅝ 13⅞	12½ 12⅞	11½ 11¾	10⅝ 10¾
22	20½ 20⅞	Holiday.	12¼ 12½	12¾ 13¼	Sunday.	12⅝ 12⅞	18¾ 20⅛	15⅛ 15¾	13¾ 13⅞	12⅝ 13	11⅝ 12	10½ 10¾
23	Sunday.	17¾ 18⅝	12¼ 12⅞	13⅛ 13½	13⅞ 14⅜	11⅜ 11⅞	19½ 20⅛	15¾ 16½	13 13¾	Sunday.	11⅝ 12⅛	10½ 10⅝
24	20⅞ 21⅜	16⅞ 17⅝	12¼ 12⅝	Sunday.	**13¾** 14⅛	11⅛ 11¾	Sunday.	16⅞ 17¾	**12¾** 13⅛	11⅞ 12¼	Holiday.	10½ 10⅝
25	21 21½	16⅞ 17¼	11¾ 12⅜	13½ 13⅞	14¼ 14⅝	11 11¼	20⅛ 21¼	16½ 18	Sunday.	11½ 11⅞	11¾ 12⅛	Sunday.
26	21½ 22	15⅞ 17⅛	11⅜ 11¾	13½ 13¾	14¼ 14⅜	Sunday.	20⅞ 21½	16½ 16⅝	13⅛ 13½	11¾ 12⅛	11¾ 12	Holiday.
27	21½ 22¼	Sunday.	Sunday.	13⅞ 14¾	14⅝ 15⅛	**10⅞** 11¼	21 22	16⅝ 16⅞	13¼ 13¾	11⅞ 12⅛	Sunday.	10⅝ 10⅞
28	21⅜ 21¾	**15** 16⅝	11⅜ 11¾	14⅝ 15½	14½ 14⅞	10⅞ 11½	21½ 22	Sunday.	13⅜ 14	11¼ 11⅝	11¼ 11½	10¾ 11
29	21⅛ 21½	... ...	11⅝ 12	14¾ **15⅝**	Sunday.	11¼ 11⅝	20½ 21¾	16⅛ 16⅜	13⅝ 14	11⅜ 11⅝	11 11⅜	10⅝ 10¾
30	Sunday.	... ...	11¾ 12⅛	14½ 15¼	14⅜ 14½	11½ 11⅞	20½ 21	16 16½	No Board.	Sunday.	10¾ 11	10⅝ 10⅞
31	21⅛ 21⅜	... ...	11⅝ 12¼	... ...	14¼ 14⅝	... ...	Sunday.	16⅛ 17⅛	... ...	**11⅛** 11½	... ...	10¾ 10⅞

WORKS ON GEMS, COINS, MEDALS,
&c.

BILLING (A). The Science of Gems, Jewels, Coins, and Medals, Ancient and Modern. 1 handsome vol. 8vo, full of fine photographic illustrations. Extra cloth, gilt sides and edges, $15.75.

THE BRITISH Foreign and Colonial Trade-Marks Directory, to which is added an International Guide, and an Appendix of General Commercial Information; with Translations into French, German, Spanish, Italian, Portuguese, Dutch, Swedish, Russian, Chinese, etc. Imperial 4to, $5.00.

EMMANUEL (Harry). Diamonds and Precious Stones; their History, Value, and Distinguishing Characteristics. With simple tests for their identification. Second and cheaper edition. With a new table of the present value of Diamonds. 1 vol. quarto, large paper, antique morocco, $25, or 1 vol. 12mo, $4.

DOYNE (W.). Tokens issued in the Seventeenth Century in England, Wales, and Ireland, by Corporations, Merchants, Tradesmen, etc. With 42 plates. 1 large vol. 8vo, $12.50.

DACTYLIOTHECA Smithiana. Gemmarum ectypa, et A. F. Gorii enarrationes complectens. 2 vols. folio, full of engravings of gems, fine copy, in full russia extra, very rare, 1767, $20.

HUMPHREY's Coin Collector's Manual; a Popular Introduction to the Study of Coins, Ancient and Modern; numerous highly-finished engravings on wood and steel. 2 vols. 12mo, $5.

KING (C. W.). The Natural History of Precious Stones, and of the Precious Metals. 1 vol. small 8vo, cloth, $5.25.

KING (C. W.). The Natural History of Gems or Decorative Stones. 1 vol. small 8vo, cloth, $5.25.

KING (C. W.). Antique Gems; their Origin, Uses, and Value as Interpreters of Ancient History, and as Illustrative of Ancient Art. With Hints to Gem Collectors. 1 handsome vol. 8vo, finely illustrated, full polished calf, $16. Or, in cloth, $10.50.

KING (C. W.). Hand-Book of Engraved Gems. With numerous illustrations. 1 handsome vol. small 8vo, vellum, cloth, $6.

KING (C. W.). Natural History, Ancient and Modern, of Precious Stones and Gems, and of the Precious Metals. With numerous Illustrations. 1 handsome vol. royal 8vo, $10.50.

MARTIN & TRUBNER. The Current Gold and Silver Coins of all Countries; their Weight and fineness, and their Intrinsic Value in English Money. With Fac-similes of the Coins. 1 very large vol. 8vo, extra cloth, $25.

MADDEN (F. W.). History of Jewish Coinage, and of Money in the Old and New Testaments. 1 vol. 4to, large paper, half morocco, $31.50.

PINKERTON (J.). Essay on Coins and Medals, especially those of Greece, Rome, and Britain. 2 vols. 8vo, calf, very scarce, $6.50.

SEALY (H. N.). Treatise on Coins, Currency, and Banking. 2 large vols. 8vo, $9.

SNOWDEN (J. R.). Manual of Coins of the United States. Quarto, $10.

Mineralogy, Metallurgy, and Mining.

BAINBRIDGE (W.). Treatise on the Law of Mines and Minerals. Third edition. 1 vol. large 8vo, $15.

BAUERMANN (H.). Treatise on the Metallurgy of Iron, containing Outlines of the History of Iron Manufacture, Methods of Assay and Analysis of Iron Ore, Process of Manufacture of Iron and Steel. 1 vol. small 8vo, 1868, $6.

BRISTOW (H. W.). Glossary of Mineralogy. 1 vol. 12mo, $3.

BUDGE (J.). Practical Miner's Guide. Together with a collection of Essential Tables, Rules, and Illustrations applicable to Mining Business. 1 vol. 8vo, cloth, third edition, enlarged, $6.

CROOKE's & ROHRIG's Practical Treatise on Metallurgy, elaborated after the last German edition of Kerl's Metallurgy for use in Great Britain and the English Colonies. 2 vols. 8vo, 1868. (Preparing.)

HALL (T. M.). The Mineralogist's Directory; or, a Guide to the Principal Mineral Localities in the United Kingdom of Great Britain and Ireland. 1 vol. small 8vo, $3.

HUNT (R.). Mineral Statistics of the United Kingdom of Great Britain and Ireland, for the year 1866. Large 8vo, paper, $4.

JEVONS (W. S.). The Coal Question. Second edition, revised, 8vo, $5.25.

JARVIS (W. P.). The Mineral Resources of Central Italy. Including Geological, Historical, and Commercial Notices of the Mines and Marble Quarries; with a Supplement, containing an account of the Mineral Springs, accompanied by the most reliable analysis. 1 vol. 8vo, paper, $2.50.

JONES (W.). The Treasures of the Earth; or, Mines, Minerals, and Metals. With original illustrations. 12mo, $1.75.

LAMBORN (Dr. R. H.). The Metallurgy of Silver and Lead. 1 vol. 12mo, limp cloth, $1.

LAMBORN (Dr. R. H.). The Metallurgy of Copper. 1 vol. 12mo, limp cloth, $1.

LAWRENCE (P. H.). Lithology; or, Classification of Rocks, with their English, French, and German Names, and the most important Minerals. 4to, paper covers, $2.50.

MINING. The Last Thirty Years in a Mining District; or, Scotching and the Candle versus Lamp and Trades-Unions. 1 vol. small 8vo, $1.75.

MAKINS (G. H.). Manual of Metallurgy, more particularly of the Precious Metals, including the Methods of Assaying them. 1 vol. crown 8vo, $6.

MITCHELL (J.). Manual of Practical Assaying, for the Use of Metallurgists, Captains of Mines, and Assayers in general; with copious Tables for ascertaining in Assays of Gold and Silver the Precise Amount in Ounces, Pennyweights, and Grains of Noble Metal contained in One Ton of Ore from a given quantity. Second edition, revised and enlarged, 1854, 580 pp., with 360 woodcuts, 8vo, $10.50.

PHILLIPS (J. A.). The Mining and Metallurgy of Gold and Silver. 1 large vol. royal 8vo, numerous engravings, $15.75.

PHILLIPS (W.). Elementary Introduction to Mineralogy, revised and enlarged by Brooke & Miller. 1 thick vol. small 8vo, $5.

THE METALLURGY of Lead, Silver, Gold, Platinum, Tin, Nickel, Cobalt, Antimony, Bismuth, Arsenic, and other Metals, by John Percy, M. D., F. R. S. With illustrations. 8vo. Also, a new and revised edition of vol. 1 of Percy's Metallurgy. (In preparation.)

RAMSAY (A.). Rudiments of Mineralogy; a Concise View of the General Properties of Minerals. 12mo, 1868, $1.50.

RICKARD (W.). Miner's Manual of Arithmetic and Surveying. With a Compendium of Mensuration; also a Course of Mine Surveying, together with Leveling and Surveying. 1 vol. 8vo, $5.25.

ROGERS (A.). The Law Relating to Mines, Minerals, and Quarries in Great Britain and Ireland, with a Summary of the Laws of Foreign States. 1 vol. 8vo, $15.

SMYTH (W. W.). Treatise on Coal and Coal Mining. 12mo. $3.75.

TRAILL (G. W.). An Elementary Treatise on Quartz and Opal, including their varieties. With a Notice of the Principal Foreign and British Localities in which they occur. 1 vol., $2.

URE'S Dictionary of Arts, Manufactures, and Mines, containing a Clear Exposition of their Principles and Practice. Edited by Robert Hunt, F. R. S., etc. Sixth edition, carefully rewritten and greatly enlarged. 3 large vols. thick 8vo, with nearly 2,000 wood engravings. Very superior to the American reprint, $47.25, or, in half russia extra, $56.

WARD (H. G.). Mexico in 1827. 2 vols. 8vo, (the fullest work on the Mines of Mexico), and a folio Atlas of Engravings, beautiful copy, uncut, half red morocco, very scarce, $21.

WILKIE (G.). The Manufacture of Iron in Great Britain; with Remarks on the Employment of Capital in Iron-Works and Collieries. 1 vol. 8vo, $5.

FOREIGN GOLD COINS.

Statement of the weight, fineness, and value of Foreign Gold Coins at the United States Mint.

Country.	Denominations.	Weight.	Fineness.	Value.	Value after Deduction
		Oz. Dec.	*Thous.*		
Australia.....	Pound of 1852.......	0.281	916.5	$5.32.4	$5.29.7
"	Sovereign of 1855–60..	0.256.5	916	4.85.7	4.83.3
Austria	Ducat	0.112	986	2.28.3	2.27
"	Sovereign	0.363	900	6.75.4	6.72
"	New Union Coin (as'md)	0.357	900	6.64.2	6.60.9
Belgium.......	25 Francs	0.251	899	4.72	4.69.8
Bolivia........	Doubloon..........	0.867	870	15.59.3	15.51.5
Brazil.........	Twenty Milreis	0.575	917.5	10.90.6	10.85.1
Central America	Two Escudos........	0.209	853.5	3.68.8	3.66.9
"	Four Reals	0.027	875	0.48.8	0.48.6
Chili	Old Doubloon.......	0.867	870	15.59.3	15.51.5
"	Ten Pesos	0.492	900	9.15.4	9.10.8
Denmark	Ten Thalers.........	0.427	895	7.90	7.86.1
Equador	Four Escudos	0.433	844	7.55.5	7.51.7
England	Pound or Sovereign, new	0.256.7	916.5	4.86.3	4.83.9
"	" " average	0.256.2	916	4.85.1	4.82.7
France	Twenty Francs, new...	0.207.5	899	3.85.8	3.83.9
"	" " average	0.207	899	3.84.7	3.82.8
Germany, North	Ten Thalers.........	0.427	895	7.90	7.86.1
" "	" Prussian ...	0.427	903	7.97.1	7.93.1
" "	Krone (Crown).......	0.357	900	6.64.2	6.60.9
" South	Ducat.............	0.112	986	2.28.2	2.27.1
Greece	Twenty Drachms.....	0.185	900	3.44.2	3.42.5
Hindostan	Mohur	0.374	916	7.08.2	7.04.6
Italy..........	Twenty Lire........	0.207	898	3.84.3	3.82.3
Japan.........	Old Cobang........	0.362	568	4.44	4.41.8
"	"	0.289	572	3.57.6	3.55.8
Mexico........	Doubloon, average....	0.867.5	866	15.53	15.45.2
"	" new....	0.867.5	870.5	15.61.1	15.53.3
"	Twenty Pesos (Max.)...	1.086	875	19.64.3	19.54.5
"	" (Repub.).	1.090	875	19.72.0	19.62.1
Naples........	Six Ducati, new......	1.245	996	5.04.4	5.01.9
Netherlands ...	Ten Guilders	0.215	899	3.99.7	3.97.6
New Grenada..	Old Doubloon, Bogata.	0.868	870	15.61.1	15.53.3
"	" Popayan.	0.867	858	15.37.8	15.30.1
"	Ten Pesos........	0.525	891.5	9.67.5	9.62.7
Peru..........	Old Doubloon........	0.867	868	15.55.7	15.47.9
"	Twenty Sols........	1.055	898	19.21.3	19.11.7
Portugal	Gold Crown	0.308	912	5.80.7	5.77.8
Prussia	New Crown (assumed).	0.357	900	6.64.2	6.60.9
Rome	2½ Scudi (new).......	0.140	900	2.60.5	2.59.2
Russia	Five Rubles	0.210	916	3.97.6	3.95.7
Spain	100 Reals	0.268	896	4.96.4	4.93.9
"	80 "	0.215	869.5	3.86.4	3.84.5
Sweden	Ducat.............	0.111	875	2.23.7	2.22.6
"	Carolin, 10 frs........	0.104	900	1.93.5	1.91.5
Tunis	25 Piastres	0.161	900	2.99.5	2.98.1
Turkey........	100 "	0.231	915	4.36.9	4.34.8
Tuscany.......	Sequin	0.112	999	2.31.3	2.30.1

FOREIGN SILVER COINS.

Statement of the weight, fineness, and value of Foreign Silver Coins at the United States Mint.

Country.	Denominations.	Weight.	Fineness.	Value.
		Oz. Dec.	*Thous.*	
Austria	Old Rix Dollar	0.902	833	$1 02.3
"	Old Scudo	0.836	902	1.02.6
"	Florin before 1858	0.451	833	51.1
"	New Florin	0.397	900	48.6
"	New Union Dollar	0.596	900	73.1
"	Maria Theresa Dollar 1780	0.895	838	1.02.1
Belgium	Five Francs	0.803	897	98
Bolivia	New Dollar	0.801	900	98.1
Brazil	Double Milreis	0.820	918.5	1.02.5
Canada	Twenty Cents	0.150	925	18.9
"	Twenty-five Cents	0.187.5	925	23.6
Central America	Dollar	0.866	850	1 00.2
Chili	Old Dollar	0.864	908	1.06.8
"	New Dollar	0.801	900.5	98.2
China	Dollar (English), assumed	0.866	901	1.06.2
"	Ten Cents	0.087	901	10.6
Denmark	Two Rigsdaler	0.927	877	1 10.7
England	Shilling, new	0.182.5	924.5	23
"	" average	0.178	925	22.4
France	Five Francs, average	0.800	900	98
"	Two Francs	0.320	835	36.4
Germany, North	Thaler before 1857	0.712	750	72.7
" "	New Thaler	0.595	900	72.9
" South	Florin before 1857	0.340	900	41.7
" "	New Florin (assumed)	0.340	900	41.7
Greece	Five Drachms	0.719	900	88 1
Hindostan	Rupee	0.374	916	46 6
Japan	Itzbu	0.279	991	37.6
"	New Itzbu	0.279	890	33.8
Mexico	Dollar, new	0.867.5	903	1.06.6
"	Dollar, average	0.866	901	1.06.2
"	Peso of Maximilian	0.861	902.5	1.05.5
Naples	Scudo	0 844	830	95.3
Netherlands	2½ Guilders	0.804	944	1.03.3
Norway	Specie Daler	0.927	877	1.10.7
New Grenada	Dollar of 1857	0 803	896	98
Peru	Old Dollar	0.866	901	1.06.2
"	Dollar of 1858	0.766	909	94.8
"	Half Dollar 1835 and 1838	0.433	650	38.3
"	Sol	0.802	900	98.2
Prussia	Thaler before 1857	0.712	750	72.7
"	New Thaler	0.595	900	72.9
Rome	Scudo	0.865	900	1.05.8
Russia	Ruble	0.667	875	79.4
Sardinia	Five Lire	0.800	900	98
Spain	New Pistareen	0.166	899	20.3
Sweden	Rix Dollar	1.092	750	1.11.5
Switzerland	Two Francs	0.323	899	39.5
Tunis	Five Piastres	0.511	898.5	62.5
Turkey	Twenty Piastres	0.770	830	87
Tuscany	Florin	0.220	925	27.6

THE ORIGIN OF NOTED COINS.

Quotations from the Encyclopedia Britannica are denoted E. B. Those from the Numismatic Chronicle are from a recent periodical issued in the City of London. Those from Chambers' Cyclopedia are denoted C. C.

ANGEL. A gold coin, first used in FRANCE, and introduced into ENGLAND in the reign of EDWARD IV., (1461–1483). It varied in value from that period till the time of CHARLES I., from 6s. 8d. to 10 shillings. It was impressed with ST. MICHAEL and the DRAGON ; whence the name. — *E. B.*

The Angel was discontinued in the seventeenth century. The Angel was well known in the days of SHAKSPEARE, who uses the term in various plays, viz. :

"*He hath a legion of angels.*" ....M. WIVES, I. 3.
"*I had myself twenty angels given me this morning.*" .... "   "   II. 2.
"*Rich she shall be, that's certain ; noble, or not I for an angel.*" . MUCH ADO. II. 3.
"*They have in England a coin that bears the figure of an angel stamped in gold.*" ....M. VENICE. II. 7.
"*Here are the angels that you sent for to deliver you.*" .....C. OF ERRORS. IV. 3.

In the year 1548 (HENRY VI.) the value of the Angel was fixed by proclamation at 8s. 8d. ; the Riall, 14s. 6d. ; the new Sovereign, 20s. ; the Crown, 5s. In the time of MARY, (1553–1558), the Angel was ordered to be current at 10s. The pound of gold was, in 1582–'3, coined into seventy-two Angels at 10s. each, with halves and quarters in proportion. In the year 1617–1618 (James I.) the Angel was coined of the value of 15s., having a lion crowned. The Angel of 10s. had a stamp of an angel striking a serpent.

AS. A ROMAN coin of different weight and material in different ages of the Commonwealth. Under NUMA POMPILIUS, according to EUSEBIUS, the Roman money was either of wood, leather or shells. In the time of TULLUS HOSTILIUS it was of brass, and called *As Libra, Libella* or *Pondo,* because actually weighing a pound or twelve ounces. The first PUNIC war, 420 years later, having exhausted the treasury, the *As* was reduced to two ounces. In the second PUNIC war, it was again, to half its weight, viz.: to one ounce. And, lastly, by the PAPIRIAN law, it was reduced to half an ounce, and continued so even to the reign of VESPASIAN. Its original stamp was that of a sheep, ox or sow, but from the time of the Emperors it had on one side a JANUS with two faces, and on the reverse the rostrum or prow of a ship.—*E. B.*

ASSIGNAT. The name given to a peculiar species of paper money issued during the first FRENCH revolution.—*E. B.*

AUREUS, or AUREUS NUMMUS. The first gold coin of ROME, struck B. C. 207, value in American gold about $5.10, known in later times as *Solidus.— Prime on Coins.*

BAAL, or Melkart. A copper coin of COSSYRA, (PHŒNICIAN), about the size of a cent or half penny.—*C. C. Vol.* 1, 594.

BALAHAT. A gold coin struck during the reign of BALAN in Kashmir, about the year 400 A. D.—*Numis. Chron.*

BEARD TOKEN. A copper coin struck by PETER THE GREAT, of Russia, in 1724, to be given to those who had paid the tax of fifty roubles every year for the privilege of wearing their beards.—*Numis. Chron.*

BESANTS, or Bezants. Circular pieces of bullion, generally gold without any impression, supposed to represent the old coinage of Byzantium, brought home by the CRUSADERS, and hence of frequent occurrence as Heraldic Charges.—*C. C. Vol.* 2, 62.

BONNET PIECE. A gold coin of JAMES THE FIFTH, of SCOTLAND, so called from the King's head being decorated with a bonnet instead of a crown; coined in 1539. Weight, 72 grains. From their beauty and elegance of appearance they are among the most valued curiosities of the antiquary.—*C. C. Vol.* 2, 220.

BRITANNIA. The first example of this personification is on a Roman coin of ANTONINUS PIUS, (died 161 A. D). The figure of BRITANNIA next reappears on the copper coinage of CHARLES II. (1665). The celebrated beauty, Miss STEWART, afterward DUCHESS OF RICHMOND, is said to have served as model to the engraver, PHILIP ROETER. The Britannia that appears on the reverse of British copper coins since 1852, was the design of Mr. Wyon.—*C. C. Vol.* 2, 354.

BYZANTINE, is the term applied to coins of the BYZANTINE empire. They are of gold, silver and bronze; bear distinctions of impression from those of the earlier ROMAN coins. The commercial relations of the Eastern Empire served to distribute its coinage over all the then known world. It was current in INDIA, as well as in the North of EUROPE. The standard of the BYZANTINE coins were copied in several countries.—*C. C. Vol.* 2, p 473.

BLACK MONEY. This was copper coin, struck at Tours, and made current in Britain in the reigns of EDWARD II. and EDWARD III. In the year 1335, reign of EDWARD III, the use of this money was prohibited. Another species of Black Money called TURNEYS, was made at private mints in Ireland in the latter reign.

CAROLUS. An old English broad piece of gold, struck in the times of CHARLES I., and worth twenty shillings sterling. Also a small copper coin, mixed with a little silver, struck under CHARLES VIII. of FRANCE, and worth twelve deniers.

CAROLINE. A silver coin current at Naples, worth about four-pence sterling.

CENT. The name of a copper coin of the United States of America, equal to the hundredth part of a dollar. The Cent was authorized by Act of Congress, 2d April, 1792, to contain eleven penny-weights of copper, and half cents in proportion. The Cent was, by Act of 1857, altered to 72 grains, eighty-eight per cent. of copper, and twelve per cent. of nickel; the coinage of the half cent to cease from that time.

By the Act of 1864, April 22d, the weight of the CENT was re-duced to 48 grains, or one-tenth of an ounce troy, consisting of 95 per cent. copper and five per cent. of tin or zinc. The two cent coins were at the same time authorized, weight 96 grains. The former be-came a legal tender to the amount of ten cents; the latter to the amount of twenty cents. By the Act of 1865, the coinage of three-cent pieces was first authorized, thirty grains in weight, composed of copper and nickel; a legal tender to the extent of sixty cents; and the one and two-cent coins became each a legal tender by the same Act, to the amount of four cents only. By the Act of May, 1866, a five-cent piece was authorized, weight seventy-seven and 16-100 grains, composed of copper and nickel. This coin was made a legal tender to the amount of one dollar.

CHALLIES. A copper coin of CEYLON, sixty-four being equal to one *Rheedy.— Numis. Chron., N. Y.*

COWRIE. A small shell found at the MALDIVE Islands, used in some parts of INDIA, and the coast of AFRICA, as a coin; 3,200 are about the value of one rupee.—*E. B.*

CROWN. The Crown was in use in England for several centuries; generally of the value of five shillings. In the time of JAMES I. (1604), the Double Crown was ordered, value 10s.; the Thistle Crown, 4s.; Half Crown, 2s. 6d. The Crown was frequently quoted by SHAKSPEARE. Among these are the following:

" *Ay, and more. A French Crown more.*"......................M. for M. I. 2.
" *The payment of a hundred thousand Crowns.*"..............L. L. LOST. II. 1.
" *Bequeathed me by will but a poor thousand Crowns.*"......AS Y. LIKE IT. I. 1.
" *I have five hundred Crowns, the thrifty hire I saved*"........ " " " "II. 3.
" *I'll add three thousand Crowns to what is past already*"....ALL'S WELL. III. 7.
" *Crowns in my purse I have, and goods at home.*"..............T. SHREW. I. 2.
" *And in possession twenty thousand Crowns.*"..................   "   II. 1.
" *Hath cost me one hundred Crowns since supper time.*"........   "   V. 2.

The first Crowns issued in the reign of GEORGE III. were in the year 1817. The early Crowns coined in England were in the year 1552,

(EDWARD VI.), when the pound weight of Crown gold was made into 132 Crowns. A pound weight of silver was made into 12 Crowns or 24 Half Crowns. In the reign of HENRY VIII., (1526), a gold *Crown of the Sun* was ordered, to be current at 4s. 6d. Also the Crown of the Double Rose, value 5s., and half Crown, 2s. 6d. In the time of JAMES SECOND, (1689), Crown pieces of brass were coined, but were soon after withdrawn. A few Crowns, of the white metal, were made about the same time, year of the battle of the Boyne.

CRUSADE. A coin of Portugal, current in England in the reign of MARY. This coin, with a long cross, was valued at 6s. 8d.; the Pistolet, 6s. 2d.; the single Crusade, with a short cross, 6s. 8d. PHILIP of Spain, married to MARY in 1554, brought with him a vast number of Portuguese and Spanish coin.

DIME or Disme. A silver coin of the UNITED STATES OF AMERICA, value ten cents; first coined in the year 1796. The weight by law was 41.3-5 grains, and made 900-1000 fine. The half dime was authorized by the same act, 2d April, 1792. By the Act of 1853, the weight of the dime was reduced to one-fifth of the new half dollar, or 38.4-10 grains, and the half dime reduced accordingly; and the new silver coins were legal tender to the amount of five dollars only. The three-cent silver coin was authorized by Act of March, 1851; a legal tender to the amount of thirty cents only.

DOIT. A small copper coin current in Scotland during the reign of the STUARTS. It was a Dutch coin, (Duit), and in value 160th part of a guilder, which, estimated at 20d. sterling, would make the doit equal in value to one-eighth of a penny or half of a farthing. This coin is said to have been common in the early part of the reign of JAMES THE SIXTH of SCOTLAND—*C. C. Vol.* 3, 618.

DOLES. Sums of money or provisions given at funerals, a custom formerly carried out in ENGLAND, WALES, IRELAND, and SCOTLAND, supposed to be traced to the sin offerings of the HEBREWS—*C. C. Vol* 3, 619.

DOBRA. The half dobra of Brazil, coined of gold by PETRUS SECOND; date, 1832; value. £1 15s. 10¾d. sterling.

DOLLAR. A silver coin, the unit of the United States, taken from the old Spanish dollar or *piastre*, and is only slightly less. In 1849, when there was a great influx of gold from California, gold dollars were largely issued. The origin of the word dollar is from the GERMAN *Thaler*, Low GERMAN *Dahler*. DANISH *Daler*.—*C. C. Vol.* 3, 620.

Dollar is also the name of a silver coin of SPAIN and of the UNITED STATES, worth 100 cents, or about 4s. 2d. sterling; first struck in the United States in 1794. The Dollar, (*Thaler*), appears to have been originally a GERMAN coin, and in various parts of GERMANY there are coins of different values, so called. The dollar issued by the mint of the United States weighs 412.5 grains, and is a legal tender for any sum.

The dollar seems to have been a coin known to the scholars of the sixteenth century. It is mentioned in SHAKSPEARE'S " *Tempest;*" also in " *Measure for Measure,*" and " *Macbeth.*"

" *To three thousand dollars a year.*"* .... M. FOR M. I. 2.
" *Till he disbursed, at Saint Colmes' Inch,*
    Ten thousand dollars to our general use." .... MACBETH. I. 2.

Dollars of 412 grains were coined in the reign of CHARLES II. for Scotch circulation.

The silver dollar was first authorized by Act of Congress 2d April, 1792, to contain 416 grains of standard silver; the half dollar to contain 208 grains, and the quarter dollar to contain 104 grains. By the Act of 1837, January 18th, the weight of the silver dollar was fixed at 412½ grains; the half dollar, 206¼ grains; the quarter dollar, 103¼ grains; and legal tender for any sum. The gold dollar was authorized by act of Congress in March, 1849, the same year in which California gold was first coined at the mint. The gold dollar was not found a convenient coin for circulation, and is now used for specimens only. Three dollar gold pieces were authorized in the year 1853.

By the Act of Congress of 21 February, 1853, the weight of the half dollar was reduced to 192 grains, (instead of 206½,) and became a legal tender for sums of five dollars or less. The weight of the quarter dollar, dime and half dime, was reduced in the same proportion. By the Act of 3d March, 1865, was authorized the legend, "In God We Trust," upon all coins issued thereafter.

DARIC. A very pure gold piece; value about £1 1s. 10d.; supposed to have been first coined by DARIUS, the son of HYSTASPES, during his stay at BABYLON. Specimens of this coin, in the British Museum, weigh 128.4 grains, and 128.6 grains. They are stamped on the one side with the figure of a kneeling archer, clothed in a long robe, with a spiked crown on his head, holding a bow in his left hand, and an arrow in his right; and on the other side with a sort of quadrata incusa, or deep cleft. In those parts of the Scripture written after the Babylonish captivity, they are called *Adarkonim*, and by the TALMUDISTS, *Darkonoth*. There were also silver darics. —*E. B.*

DENARIUS. Chief silver coin amongst the ancient ROMANS, worth about 7½d. sterling. It was originally of 62 grains weight, and was considered equivalent to the *Attic Drachma*, which, however, weighed 67 grains.—*E. B.*

DENIER. A small FRENCH copper coin, of which there were twelve to a *Sol* or *Sous*. Blanc Deniers (sometimes called grosses) were current in the reign of Henry V. Deniers d'or, called also Salutes, were current in Normandy in the time of HENRY V. at 25 sols each; also Demi-Salutes, Deniers-Blancs, called Doubles, and Petit Deniers Blancs.

*By critics considered a quibble upon *dolours.*

DOUBLE. This was solely an Irish silver coin, of the reign of EDWARD IV. (1467), made of silver, having the print of a crown on one side, and a sun with a rose on the other; ten pieces to the ounce of silver, and value equal to eight Deniers.

DOUBLOON. A gold coin of SPAIN, MEXICO, and many of the SOUTH AMERICAN States; value from $14.66 to $16.—*Eckfeldt, Manual of Gold and Silver Coin.*

DOYTS. This was a copper coin of France and Holland, the importation of which was in England prohibited in the year 1685. All coins of this order might be seized and confiscated.

DRACHMA, an ancient Greek silver coin, in value about 9¾d., or equivalent to the French franc. The weight of the Attic drachma was about 66 grains; and the Eginetan was 1 2-3 of the Attic. An Alexandrian drachma weighing 126 grains has also been found. The weight called drachm, used by the modern apothecary, is equivalent to the eighth part of an ounce, or 60 grains, or 3 scruples.—*E. B.*

DUCAT. A foreign coin either of gold or silver struck in the domains of a Duke. The first *ducat* was coined by LONGINUS, Governor of ITALY, who revolted against the Emperor JUSTIN THE YOUNGER, and made himself Duke of Ravenna. His *ducat* was of very pure gold, with his own stamp, and as PROCOPIUS relates were called *Ducati (Ducats)*. According to DU CANGE, ducats were coined by ROGER, King of SICILY, in the year 1240. The *Venetian ducat* was first struck by JOHN DANDOLO in the year 1280, and inscribed with this legend: "*Sit Tibi, Christe, datus, quem tu regisiste Ducatus.*"—*E. B.*

The ducat was the prevailing gold coin of ITALY for several centuries. It is frequently mentioned by SHAKSPEARE, and in ten of his plays.

"He has three thousand ducats a year."........................12TH NIGHT. I. 3.
"Be cunning in the working this, and thy fee is a
   thousand ducats" .... MUCH ADO. II. 2.
"Three thousand ducats for three months, and Antonio bound"...... M. V. I. 3.
"Two thousand ducats by the year of fruitful land"............ T. SHREW. II. 1.
"For forty ducats is too much to lose"......................... C. ERRORS. IV. 3.
"My ten thousand ducats are yours"............................. CYM. I. 5.
"Hold, there is forty ducats, let me have a dram of poison"..... R. AND J. V. 1.
"Two thousand souls and twenty thousand ducats,
   will not debate the question of this straw."................. HAMLET. IV. 4.

DUCATEN. A gold coin of FRANCIS JOSEPH I. of AUSTRIA, dated 1855, worth £1. 17s. 7½d. sterling; the two Ducaten piece, a gold coin of the reign of JOSEPH II. of AUSTRIA, 1774, worth 1 s. 9¾d. sterling. The Hungarian Ducat, or Ducat of Kremnitz, a gold coin of FERDINAND of AUSTRIA, dated 1843, worth 9s. 5½d. sterling.

DUCATOON. A silver coin struck chiefly in ITALY, particularly at Milan, Venice, Florence, Genoa, Lucca, Mantua, and Parma; though there are also DUTCH and FLEMISH Ducatoons.

9

DUDU-MASP, *i. e.* Hook money. A pure silver coin of the reign of PARAKRAMA BAHU, who governed an ancient city called Palla-naⁱōōwa, in the Island of Ceylon, about the year 1500. The king of Kandy, (Ceylon,) allowed his subjects to fabricate a kind of money, from pure silver wire, in the shape of a fish hook ; about the same period, the value was about 5d. sterling.

EAGLE. Originally a sort of base coin which was current in IRE-LAND in the early part of the reign EDWARD I, that is, about the year 1272. There were also *Lionines, Pollards, Crocards, Scaldings, Rosades*, and many other coins of the same sort, named according to the figures with which they were impressed. The current coin of the kingdom at that time was a composition of copper and silver in deter-minate proportions ; but these were so much inferior to the standard of that time, that they were not intrinsically worth half so much as the others. They were imported from FRANCE and other countries. When EDWARD had been a few years established on the throne, he set up mints in IRELAND for coining good money, and then prohibited the use of *Eagles* and other kinds of base coin, making the penalty for violation death and confiscation of effects, or to import any more of them into the kingdom. *Eagle* is the designation of the principal gold coin of the UNITED STATES ; weight 258 grains ; 900–1000 fine. This gold coin was first authorized by Act of Congress, 2d April, 1792. The half-eagle was authorized at the same time, and the quarter eagle.

EARNEST, or Arles, as it is called in SCOTLAND, from the civil law word "Arrhoe" A small sum of money, which is given in proof of an existence of a bargain.—*C. C. Vol. 3*, 734.

EIGHT PIECE, or Piece of Eight. A name once popularly given to the SPANISH dollar, as being divided into eight reals. These coins were for a long time current in the United States at their nominal value, although reduced by wear and tear ten or twenty per cent. By the Act of Congress of 1857, they were receivable at par and were melted at the mint, and were thus taken out of circulation.—*C. C. Vol. 3*, 797.

ECCLESIASTICAL COINS. These were issued during the reign of STEPHEN, (1135–1154), and bore the name of the monarch, and of the Archbishop of CANTERBURY, of the value of a penny. (RUDING'S ANNALS.) The grants from the king to individuals to coin money, were confined to ecclesiastics ; to archbishops and bishops, and also to some abbots of the higher order.

FARTHING. A small ENGLISH copper coin amounting to one-fourth of a penny. It was anciently called *fourthing*, as being the fourth of the integer, or penny. A farthing of gold, equal in value to the fourth part of a *noble*, or 20d. in silver, is mentioned in statute 9th. HENRY V. farthings were coined in the reign of EDWARD III, and were also known to the Saxons. The first farthings legally coined were in the time of JAMES I., as farthing tokens of brass and copper, who granted the right of coinage of farthing-tokens to Lady HARRINGTON in 1614. Similar powers were granted to other ladies subsequently. The silver farthings totally ceased in the time of EDWARD VI.

FLORIN. Was the name of a gold coin first struck in FLORENCE in the thirteenth century. It was the size of a ducat, and had, on one side a lily, and on the other the head of JOHN THE BAPTIST. Some derive the name from the city, and others from the flower. These coins were soon imitated all over Europe. Florins were coined in ENGLAND as early as the reign of EDWARD III. (1327–1377).—*C. C.* The Florin of GERMANY and AUSTRIA is a silver coin, (sometimes called *Guldes*), of various values. Of LEIPSIC rate 16.90, the value was for specie Florin 54 cents; convention rate 17.53, for specie Florin 48 6–10 cents. Convention rate, 1837–1838, for Florins 39.7–10 cents. The *Florin* or *Guilder* of the NETHERLANDS, a silver coin of the government of WILLIAM V. is valued at 39½ cents; of the BATAVIAN REPUBLIC, 38 2–10 cents. The Florin coined at the royal Mint, British value, one-tenth of a pound sterling.—*Eckfeldt's Manual.*

FRANC. A FRENCH silver coin. This term was first introduced by HENRY III. in 1575, who ordered a coinage of francs, of the value of 20 sols or sous each. This coin was afterwards disused, but by the law of 1803 it was re-coined. The name was long employed in common parlance as a synonym for *livre.* Its present value is about 18¾ cents.—*Eckfelt's Manual of Coins.*

The franc which (since 1795, when it supplanted the *Livre Tarnois*), forms the unit of the FRENCH monetary system, has also been adopted by BELGIUM and SWITZERLAND, value about 9½d. sterling or 18¾ cents.—*C. C. Vol. 4, 469.*

FREDERICKS D'OR, and Christians D'Or. A DANISH gold coin, value 16s. 3d. sterling.—*Martin and Trubner's Manual.*

FWANG, of Siam. A silver coin worth about 3¾d. sterling.

GAZETTE. A Venetian coin, worth something less than ½d. sterling. The name was afterwards applied to a small newspaper, that was sold in Venice for that sum.—*C. C. Vol. 4, 653.*

GROAT. An Old English silver coin, equal to four pence. Other nations, as the DUTCH, POLES, SAXONS, BOHEMIANS, and FRENCH, have likewise their *groats, grouts, groschen, gros,* and the like. In ENGLAND, in the Saxon times, no silver coin larger than a penny was struck, nor after the conquest till the reign of EDWARD THE THIRD, who, about the year 1351, coined *grosses,* or *great pieces,* which were current for four pence each; and so the matter stood till the reign of HENRY VIII., who in 1504 first coined shillings.—*E. B.*

In the year 1227, (HENRY III.), the coinage of the English groat was ordered; also, in the year 1249 the groat of silver was ordered. The groat was a common coin in early English days. It is mentioned nine times in SHAKSPEARE:

" *Seven groats in mill sixpences.*" ....M. WIVES. I. 1.

" *As fit as ten groats is for the hand of an attorney.*" ....ALL'S WELL. II. 2.

" *A half-faced groat five hundred pound a year!*" ....K. JOHN. I. 1.

" *The cheapest of us is ten groats too dear.*" ....RICH. II. V. 5.

" *What money is in my purse? Seven groats and two pence.*" ...2 HEN. IV I. 2.

" *Hold you, there is a groat to heal your pate.*" ....HENRY V. V. 1.

" *I take thy groat, in earnest of revenge.*" .... "　　" V. 1.

" *Or any groat I hoarded to my use* " ....HEN. VI. III. 1.

" *Things created to buy and sell with groats.*" ....COR. III. 2.

Half groats were coined in the reign of EDWARD I., about the year 1279. In his time the sterling was ordained to be equal to thirty-two grains of wheat in weight. Leathern money, stamped, was in use at the same period. The groats, half groats, penny and halfpenny. coined in SCOTLAND, were in the reign of RICHARD II. (1390), declared to be current at only one-half their former values.

Among the treasonable charges against CARDINAL WOLSEY, year 1529, was that of placing the Cardinal's hat on the coin of groats, " which like deed hath not yet been seen to have been done by any subject within your realm before this time." The coin of THREE GROATS were struck at TOURNAY, FRANCE, in the same reign. At this time the harp first appeared upon the IRISH money.

GROSS. In the reign of EDWARD III. (1327-1377), the GROSS was coined of the value of four sterlings, and the HALF GROSS of the value of two sterlings. The GROSS, HALF GROSS, QUARTER GROSS, and PETIT DENIERS, were in use in the fifteenth century.

GUILDER or GULDEN. See *Florin.*

GUINEA. A gold coin formerly struck and current in BRITAIN, and so denominated because the gold of which the first specimens were struck, (TEMP. CAROLUS II.), was brought from the coast of GUINEA; and for a like reason it originally bore the impression of an elephant. The value of the guinea varied greatly at different periods, but latterly it was worth twenty-one shillings. Its weight was five pennyweights, 9.4125 grains. On the introduction of the *sovereign*— again coined in 1817—the old guinea coinage was gradually superseded in Great Britain.—*E. B.*

In the year 1718, (GEORGE I.), a new coin called a quarter guinea was made, but they attained a small circulation only. In the year 1649, in CROMWELL'S time, the parliament had under consideration a coinage made from the gold from GUINY.

HEARTH MONEY. An old tax in ENGLAND, abolished during the reign of WILLIAM AND MARY.—*C. C.* Vol. 5, 279.

HERRING SILVER. A composition in money in lieu of supplying a religious house with a certain number of herrings.—*C. C.* Vol. 347.

ICHIBA, of Japan. A silver coin; value about 1s. 5¼d. sterling.

ITZABONE. A silver coin of JAPAN; value two or three to a dollar.—*C. C. Vol.* 5, 687.

INDIAN MONEY. An English coinage, was made about the year 1601, (ELIZABETH), known as Indian money, or Portcullis money, for use by the East India Company, equal to the Spanish piastre, and the half, quarter, and half quarter.

KRONE, of FRANCIS JOSEPH I. of AUSTRIA. A gold coin dated 1859; value £1 7s. 3¼d. sterling; also half krones, date 1858; value 13s. 7¾d. sterling.

KUFIC COINS The earliest of the MAHOMEDAN coins, first struck in the year 638 A. D. (gold and silver).—*C. C. Vol.* 5, 823.

LAMB. An Egyptian weight, of the form of a lamb, used for the weighing of gold and silver many centuries before the coinage of money. It is supposed in the early pastoral ages that the value of cattle was the earliest mode of fixing the value of money; the word "pecuniary" is derived from the Latin word *pecunia*, money, and this was derived from *pecus* (a flock of sheep or cattle).

LISBONINE. A former name for the *Moidore.*—*C. C. Vol.* 6, 511

LUSSHEBOURNES. These were base coins brought into England from the continent in the reign of EDWARD III., and were prohibited by various acts of Parliament. The death penalty awaited those detected in circulating them.

MANCUS. A name given to an ancient ARABIC coin in gold and silver.

MARK. The MARK was a Scottish silver piece in the times of JAMES I. (1603–1620); value thirteen half pence. The mark was a DANISH mode of computation, and was introduced among the Saxons in the reign of AELFRED. The silver MARK was, early in the tenth century, estimated at one hundred pennies, and in the year 1194 at one hundred and sixty pennies. This valuation was continued to the present century.

MOHUR. A gold coin of HINDUSTAN. Those dated 1818 of the BENGAL PRESIDENCY were worth $8.08; of the MADRAS PRESIDENCY, $7.10; of the BOMBAY PRESIDENCY, $7.09. Those dated 1835, during the reign of WILLIAM IV., the value is $7.10.—*Eckfeldt's Manual.*

MOEDA D'OURO, of BRAZIL, a gold coin of PETRUS I.; date, 1824; value, £1 0s. 1d. sterling.

MOIDORE. A PORTUGESE gold coin, first struck in 1688; in the year 1689, under the reign of PETER II., its value was $6.45; under the same reign those struck in 1705 the value was $6.52; during the reign of JOHN V. those dating from 1714 to 1726 were valued $6.48. This coin continued to be struck until the year 1732.

MUSSAWWA, Kharaz, or Glass Beads. The currency of ABYSSINIA, about thirty strings being worth one dollar.—*Numis. Chron.,* N Y.

NANDIO-GUIN. A silver coin of JAPAN, weighs 160 grains, and worth about forty cents United States currency.

NI SHOO. Japanese Coin, partly gold and silver; value 9d. sterling.

NOBLES. These were coined in the reign of Edward III. (1327—1377); with others termed maille nobles and ferling nobles. At that time the pound weight of gold was coined into 39½ nobles, at six shillings and eight pence each—equal to £13 3s. 4d. In the year 1345, the noble was in value half a mark, six shillings, six pence half-penny.

The new nobles coined in the reign of Edward IV., coined in the year 1465, were also called Rials, a name given to a French coin because it bore the figure of the King in his royal robes. The George Noble and the Crown of the Double Rose, were first ordained about the year 1526, by Henry VIII.

OBANG of JAPAN. Gold used only for imperial presents; value £15 0s. 7½d. sterling.

PARA. A coin of copper, silver or mixed metal, though most generally of copper, in use in TURKEY and EGYPT; it is the fortieth part of a *Piastre;* value about 1·18 of a penny sterling.— *C. C. Vol. 7,* 254.

PESO, or *Piastre of eight Reals.* Silver, of CENTRAL AMERICA; value 4s. 3½d. sterling; date 1824. The Peso of gold of Central America, date 1860, value 3s. 9⅞d. sterling.

PETERS PENCE. A name given to a tribute which was collected for the Roman Pontiff, in reverence of the memory of ST. PETER; the first idea, however, of an annual tribute appears to have come from ENGLAND (A. D. 721). An effort was made since the ROMAN REVOLUTION of 1848 to revive this tribute, and with some success.— *C. C. Vol. 7,* 446.

PENNY. This coin was known to the Ancients B C. It is frequently mentioned in the Scriptures. It was known as an English coin in the seventh century, and appears in the laws of INA, King of the West Saxons, about the year 688. Its probable origin is from the word *pendu,* to weigh, and is considered the original unit of the English currency. Two hundred and forty pennies, it is supposed, were fabricated out of a pound weight of silver, giving thus 24 grains to each, and making the pound consist of 5,760 grains. Hence the term "pennyweight," equal to 24 grains, and the two hundred and fortieth part of a pound. (*See History of the Coinage, ante, p.* 8) The first coinage of gold in England was in the year 1257, in the reign of HENRY III. This was the gold penny, which weighed two sterlings, and was current for twenty pence. The gold penny was coined during the next ten years, and was raised in value from 20 to 24 pence.

The Galley Halfpence were imported into England in large quantities about the year 1414, by orders of the "*merchants of Venice,*" and were treated as fraudulent coin. The ROSE PENCE were coined in England, for circulation in Ireland, time of PHILIP and MARY (1554), but were withdrawn from use, except in Ireland, two years afterwards. The first IRISH mint was authorized in the time of CHARLES II. (1662), with the penny, two penny, and three penny pieces. The halfpenny to have a crown on one side and the harp on the other. The SCOTCH mint was at the same time authorized to coin the twenty MARK piece of gold; the four and five Mark pieces. No gold was coined in Scotland in that reign. Tin pence and half pence were coined in the reign of WILLIAM and MARY. SHAKESPEARE brought the penny into line, in various of his plays. He is led to say:

" *I will not lend thee a penny.*"..............................M. WIVES. II. 2.
" *A penny. No, I'll give you a remuneration.*"............L. L. LOST. III. 1.
" *Methinks, I have given him a penny.*"..................AS YOU LIKE IT. II. 5.
" *You beg a single penny more; come, you shall ha't*........ALL'S WELL. V. 2.
" *What penny hath Rome borne, what men provided?*"............K. JOHN. V. 2.
" *A friend i' the court is better than a penny in thy purse.*"......2 HEN. IV. V. 1.
" *Nor ever had one penny bribe from France.*"................2 HEN. VI. III. 1.
" *There, take an inventory of all I have, to the last penny.*"..HENRY VIII. III. 2.
" *No, truly, sir; not a penny.*"..............................R. & JULIET. II. 4.

PENNY-POISE. This was a coin in the reign of JOHN (1199–1216), wanting one-eighth of a penny, used as a means of detecting light weight or clipping in other pennies. Those coins detected to be of light weight or clipped were, by law, to be bored through, and the owner or possessor was liable to be attached as a thief.— *Ruding's Annals.*

PISTOLE. The Pistole was in use in various countries in the seventeenth century. A gold coinage of pistoles was made in Scotland in the reign of WILLIAM III. Also, half-pistoles, both with the king's head, but not with the numeral III attached. The SCOTCH deciding that although he was the third WILLIAM of ENGLAND, and the second of SCOTLAND, he was the first WILLIAM of GREAT BRITAIN.

QUINARIUS. A small ROMAN coin, equal to half the denarius, and consequently worth about three pence, three farthings of English money. It was called *quinarius*, because equal in value to five asses, just as the denarius was named because containing ten.— *E. B.*

RAPPEN. A small SWISS coin, made of an alloy of copper and tin, value 1–100 of a modern *Franc.*— *C. C. Vol. 8, 115.*

REAL. A SPANISH coin of two sorts; first the real of plate, value about 4 3-4d sterling; and the real of Vellon, worth about 2 1-2d. sterling.

RIDER. The Rider was a gold coin of the reign of HENRY VI, 1422, &c.; valued at 4s. At the same time the following coins were in use : the Ducat, 4s. 2d. ; the Jean, 4s. 2d. ; the Salute, 4s. 2d. ; the Crown, 3s. 4d.; the Burgoinge Noble, 6s. 8d. In IRELAND the Rider was valued at five shillings, and foreign coins became in general use—the Ducat, Leo, Crown, Crusado. A Rose-Real was coined by HENRY VII, while in France, having the arms of France in the centre of the double rose.

RIX DOLLAR OF CEYLON, silver, worth 1s. 6d. sterling, dated 1821,

RING MONEY. The precious metals, gold and silver, have been used from the times of ancient EGYPT as ornaments, and as occasion may require they have been used as a circulating medium. Thus, on some ancient tombs in EGYPT carvings have been found, of its being weighed, and in the 11th verse of the 42d chapter of JOB, it is mentioned that each of JOB's friends brought him an earing or lamb, (see *Lamb*). At the present time in EASTERN countries where there is no method of investment, the surplus coin is made up into ornaments, and when necessity requires it, there is no difficulty in or trouble of disposing of them, as the merchant takes them as readily as coin. CÆSAR describes Ring Money as having been used in ENGLAND and other parts of EUROPE. – *Prime on Coins and Medals.*

RHEEDY. A silver coin of CEYLON, value 7d. sterling.

ROUBLE. A RUSSIAN coin. A gold Rouble of date of 1779 is worth 74 9-10 cents; a silver Rouble of 1837-38, is worth 75 4-10 cents.— *Eckfeldt's Manual.*

RUPEE. A silver coin of HINDOSTAN, first struck by native princes, and called the *Sicca Rupee*; was worth about 47 cents. The rupee now coined by the BRITISH government in INDIA is worth 44 5-10 cents.— *Eckfeldt's Manual.*

SALUNG, or MIAM. A silver coin of SIAM, worth about 7½d. sterling.

SALUTE. A new coin entitled the Salute was coined by Henry V. in the year 1422, by virtue of his power as Regent of France by the treaty of Troyes. On this coin the arms of England and France were stamped.

SHILLING. The name of a money in use throughout many European States, partly as a coin, and partly as a money of account. In all probability the name as well as the thing itself is derived from the Roman Solidus, which, with the other remains of Roman institutions, was adopted by the Francs and other German nations. Others give more fanciful derivations, as from *schellen* to ring, on account of the particular ring of the coin, and from St. Killian, whose effigy was stamped on the shilling of Wurzburg. The Solidus shilling of the middle ages has suffered various degrees of diminution in the different countries. Thus the English shilling (silver) is one-twentieth of a pound sterling. The Danish copper shilling is one ninety-sixth (1-96) of a Ryks-daler, and equal to one-fourth of one penny sterling; and the Swedish shilling is one forty-eighth of a Ryks-daler, equal to one half penny sterling.

In Mecklenburg, Slesvig Holstein, Hamburg, and Lubeck, the shilling is used as a fractional money of account, the one-tenth part of a mark, and one forty-eighth of a thaler, and as small silver change, each coin being a shade less than one penny sterling.—*C. C.*

A shilling coinage was ordered in the time of ELIZABETH (1568) for the use of the Irish, equal to 9d. English, but to circulate in Ireland at 12d. This was soon withdrawn as a base coin. The Harp shilling in the times of James I. was valued at 16d. Irish, or 12d. English. The Pine tree shilling, coined " by a parcel of honest dogs " [according to CHARLES II.], in the colony of Massachusetts, in the time of CROMWELL. The five shilling pieces, or crowns, were ordered by Henry VIII. in the year 1526.

The Shilling was in numerous instances introduced in Shakspeare's plays; among others were the following:

" Two shovel boards that cost me two shilling and two pence" ..... M. WIVES I. 1.
" I had rather than forty shillings I had my book of songs." ...... " I. 1.
" I had rather than forty shillings I had such a leg." .... 12TH NIGHT. II. 3.
" Five shillings to one on't, with any man." .... MUCH ADO. III. 3.
" Every tod yields — pound and odd shillings." .... W. TALE. IV. 2.
" Thou cam'st not of the blood royal, if thou darest not stand for ten shillings." .... I. HEN. IV. I. 2.
" Eight shillings and sixpence." .... " II. 4.
" Now, as I am a true woman, holland of eight shillings an ell.... " III. 3.
" And did'st thou not kiss me, and bid me fetch thee thirty shillings?" .... 2 HEN. IV. II. 1.
" Quoit him down, Bardolph, like a shove-groat shilling." * ..... " II. 4.
" And here is four Harry ten shillings in French crowns for you." " III. 2.
" You will pay me the eight shillings I won of you at betting." ... HENRY V. II. 1.
" And one shilling to the pound, the last subsidy." .... 2 HEN. VI. IV. 7.
" I'll undertake, may see away their shilling richly in two short hours" .... HENRY VIII.

Such was the debasement of the Shilling in the times of STEPHEN, (A.D. 1135-1154·, that in ten or more shillings the value of ten pence could scarcely be found. At that period, each castle had its own mint.—*Ruding's Annals.*

SOUS MARQUES.—Foreign copper coins known as Tempes, and Sous Marques, and gold and silver Johannes and Dollars, were counterfeited in England for circulation in the British West Indies, but the coinage was quite limited.

* Shove-groat in the 33d year of Henry VIII was a new game—the term Shove-groat shilling was applied to smooth coins of shillings.

SCUDO. An ITALIAN coin; gold scudi were coined in ROME in 1799, value $32.64 6-10. Silver coins of this denomination were also coined in ROME, in the years 1799, 1800-02 and 1815, value from 98 8-10 cents, to $1.01 8-10. Scudo of *six lire*, a silver coin, of the reign of MARIA THERESA, dated Milan, 1778, value 85 1-10 cents. Scudo of the CISALPINE REPUBLIC, dated 1798, value 85 6-10 cents.—*Eckfeldt's Manual.*

SHEKEL. The name of a coin current among the ancient JEWS. The value of the silver shekel was 2s. 3½d. sterling; the golden shekel was supposed to be worth £1 16 6d. sterling.—*E. B.*

SOLIDUS. (See *Aureus.*)

SEQUIN or ZECCHINO. A ROMAN gold coin of the reign of PIUS VI, date 1775-83, value $2.25 2-10. Also a TUSCAN and VENETIAN gold coin, value $2.27 6-10 to $2.30 1-10, sometimes called *Zecchino Gigliato*, dates 1765-79 and 1824-39. There are also TURKISH gold coins, denominated *Sequin Foundook*, value $1.80 9-10, and *Sequin Zomahboub*, value $1.24, the dates of which are 1789.—*Eckfeldt's Manual.*

SKEATTAE, (or *Sceata*). A silver coin introduced by the SAXONS to ENGLAND after the departure of the Roman legions; it was probably an imitation of some Byzantine coin, value one twenty-fifth part less than one penny sterling.—*Humphrey's Manual.*

SOUVERAINS D'OR. A gold coin of Joseph Second of Austria, issued for the former Austrian Netherlands, value £1 7s. 9¾d. sterling. The English Sovereign came into use in the fifteenth century (1489), in the time of Henry VII; the half Sovereign was coined also in the reign of Henry VII, (1504). The words Dei Gratia (by the Grace of God) were first placed upon the English coins about the year 1377, (EDWARD III). In the days of Henry VIII, the Sovereign was valued at 22s., the Riall, at 11s., the Noble, at 7s. 4d. A new Sovereign was coined in July, 1817, with the image of ST. GEORGE AND THE DRAGON, and the motto, "*honi soit qui mal y pense,*" value 20s. The silver tokens previously issued were now called in and new coin given in exchange. The first gold brought to the royal Mint for coinage was in the 18th year of Edward III, consisting probably of foreign coins or bullion imported by merchants. The first gold coinage of the realm is stated to have been in the year 1257, or 41st year of Henry III. (*Ruding's Annals.*)

STYCA. An Anglo Saxon coin of Ethelred, who began to reign 946 A. D.—*Numis. Chron.*

TAO and POO Money, silver, of CHINA, struck 2205, B. C. The *Tao money* was shaped like a knife; the *Poo money* was of a form rather difficult to describe.—*Numis. Chron.*

THALER. The Kronenthaler is silver, of FRANCIS SECOND of AUSTRIA, issued for the AUSTRIAN NETHERLANDS; date 1797; value 4s. 7½d. sterling. The MARIA THERESA Thaler, or so-called *Levant*

Thaler, silver; date 1780; still issued for the Levant trade; value 4s. 2¾d. sterling. The *Convention's Thaler* (Austria) silver, of Francis first; date 1815; value 4s. 2d. Also of FERDINAND first; date 1848; same value.

TESTOONS. These were in use in the reign of Henry VIII. (1544), when the pound of gold was coined into 48 shillings; in Testoons Groats, Pence, Half-Pence, and Farthings. In April, 1548, all Testoons, (or Testons), or Twelve Pence, were called in, because grossly counterfeited.

SIR WILLIAM SHARINGTON and other officers of the Mint were about this time convicted of counterfeiting extensively. The Testoons and Groats were also entirely withdrawn from circulation, by proclamation, in the year 1561, (ELIZABETH). At this time the MILL and SCREW were used for the coinage, which succeeded the hammered coins.

TICAL, of Siam. Silver; worth about 2s. 6d. sterling; date 1861.

TOKENS. These were used largely in the fourteenth and fifteenth centuries by individuals to supply the need of small coins. In the time of Elizabeth (1574) these were become very common, and complained of loudly—made of lead, tin, latten, and leather. A license was granted to the city of BRISTOL to coin tokens of copper. The leaden tokens (*Plumbores Angliæ*), current in the times of Henry VII. and VIII., were still in use. Early in the seventeenth century lead tokens of a farthing were used; but all these were abolished by proclamation in May, 1813.

In the years 1728–9, (George II.), the scarcity of small silver coins induced traders and others in the North of England to coin copper tokens of two pence, and silver tokens of three pence. In the time of George III., immediately after the suspension of the Bank of England, the government authorized the coinage of "Bank of Ireland tokens, (of silver), six shillings;" also a large quantity of silver dollars. Also, for Ireland, the silver token of five pence and ten pence; also the Bank Dollar token, 5s. each. And in 1811 (the Bank being yet under suspension), pieces of 3s. and 1s. 6d.

TOUCH PIECE. A gold coin struck during the reigns of CHARLES SECOND and QUEEN ANNE. They were given to those whom the Sovereign had touched for King's evil.—*Book of Days.* Vol. 1, 84.

TRIENS. A gold coin of the seventh century, coined at Canterbury, (then called *Dorovernis*), Kent, England.—*Numis. Chron.*, 1840–41.

The UNIT was a coin in the times of James I, (1603–); valued at 20s., and in 1611 at 22s.

YIH SHOO, of Japan, silver; value 3⅜d. sterling—*Martin & Trübner Manual.*

ZWANZIGER (of 20 Kreutzers), AUSTRIA and TYROL silver; value 8⅜d. sterling.

ALPHABETICAL INDEX

TO SUBJECTS CONTAINED IN

THE BOOK OF COINS.

PLATE I.

GOLD COINS OF THE UNITED STATES.

I. The Eagle—Ten Dollars. 1870.

II. Double Eagle—Twenty Dollars. 1870.

III. Half-Eagle—Five Dollars. 1870.

IV. Three Dollars. 1870.

V. Quarter-Eagle—$2 50. 1870.　　　　VI. One Dollar. 1870.

Engraved for the "Merchants and Bankers' Almanac for 1871."

PLATE I.

GOLD COINS OF THE UNITED STATES.

I. THE EAGLE—TEN DOLLARS.
WEIGHT, 258 Grains.
Fineness—900-1000.

———

II. DOUBLE EAGLE—TWENTY DOLLARS.
Authorized by Act of Congress, March 3, 1849.
WEIGHT, 516 Grains.
Fineness—900-1000.

———

III. HALF-EAGLE--FIVE DOLLARS. 1870.
Authorized by Act of Congress, 1837.
WEIGHT, 129 Grains.
Fineness—900-1000.

———

IV. THREE DOLLARS. 1870.
Authorized by Act of Congress, 1853.
WEIGHT, 774 Grains.
Fineness—900-1000.

———

V. QUARTER-EAGLE. 1870.—$2 50.
Authorized by Act of Congress, January 1837.
WEIGHT, 64½ Grains.
Fineness—900-1000.

———

VI. ONE DOLLAR. 1870.—$1.
Authorized by Act of Congress, March 3, 1849.
WEIGHT, 25.8 Grains.
Fineness—900-1000.

Engraved for the "Merchants and Bankers' Almanac for 1871.

PLATE 11.

SILVER COINS OF THE UNITED STATES.

I. Half-Dollar—Fifty Cents.

II. One Dollar. 1870.

III. Twenty-Five Cents. 1870.

IV. One Dime. 1870.

V. Half-Dime.   VI. Three Cents.

Engraved for the "Merchants and Bankers' Almanac for 1871."

PLATE II.
SILVER COINS OF THE UNITED STATES.

I. HALF-DOLLAR. 1870.

Authorized by Act of Congress, 1853.

WEIGHT, 192 Grains.

Fineness—900-1000.

Legal tender not exceeding five dollars.

II. ONE DOLLAR. 1870.

Authorized by Act of Congress, 1837.

WEIGHT, 412.5 Grains.

Fineness—900-1000.

III. TWENTY-FIVE CENTS—QUARTER-DOLLAR. 1870.

Authorized by Act of Congress, 1853.

WEIGHT, 96 Grains.

Fineness—900-1000.

Legal tender not exceeding five dollars.

IV. ONE DIME—TEN CENTS. 1870.

Authorized by Act of Congress, 1853.

WEIGHT, 38.4 Grains.

Fineness—900-1000.

V. HALF-DIME—FIVE CENTS. 1870.

Authorized by Act of Congress, 1853.

WEIGHT, 19.2 Grains.

Fineness—900-1000.

Legal tender not exceeding one dollar.

VI. THREE CENTS. 1870.

Authorized by Act of Congress, March 3, 1853.

WEIGHT, 11.52 Grains.

Fineness—900-1000.

Engraved for the "Merchants and Bankers' Almanac for 1871."

PLATE III.

THE GOLD COINS OF FRANCE.

I. 50 Francs. Napoleon III.—Value £ 1 19s. 7¾d.—$ 9 58.

II. 100 Francs. Napoleon III.—£ 3 19s. 3½d.—$ 19 16.

III. 40 Francs. Napoleon I.—£ 1 11s. 8¼d.—$ 7 66.

IV. 20 Francs. Napoleon III.—15s. 10¼d.—$ 3 83.

V. 10 Francs. Napoleon III.
7s. 11½d.—$ 1 92.

VI. 5 Francs. Napoleon III.
3s. 11½d.—96 cents.

PLATE III.

THE GOLD COINS OF FRANCE.

I. 50 FRANCS.—NAPOLEON III. 1857.

WEIGHT, 248.908 Grains Troy—(16.129 Grammes).
Fineness—900–1000.
Value, £1 19s. 7¾d.—$9 58.

II. 100 FRANCS OF NAPOLEON III. 1859.

WEIGHT, 497.816 Grains Troy—(32.258 Grammes).
Fineness—900–1000.
Value, £3 19s. 3½d.—$19 16.

III. 40 FRANCS.—NAPOLEON I. 1812.

WEIGHT, 199.1235 Grains Troy—(12.903 Grammes).
Fineness—900–1000.
Value, £1 11s. 8¾d.—$7 66.

IV. 20 FRANCS.—NAPOLEON III. 1861.

WEIGHT, 99.561 Grains Troy—(6.451 Grammes).
Fineness—900–1000.
Value, 15s. 10¼d.—$3 83.

V. 10 FRANCS.—NAPOLEON III. 1859.

WEIGHT, 49.769 Grains Troy—(3.225 Grammes).
Fineness—900–1000.
Value, 7s. 11½d.—$1 92.

VI. 5 FRANCS.—NAPOLEON III. 1858.

WEIGHT, 24.876 Grains Troy—(1.612 Gramme).
Fineness—900–1000.
Value, 3s. 11½d.—96 cents.

PLATE IV.

THE SILVER COINS OF FRANCE.

I. 5 Francs. Napoleon I.—Value, 4s. 0½d.—98 cents.

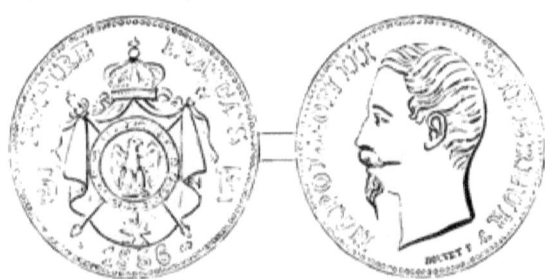

II. 5 Francs. Napoleon III.—4s. 0½d.—98 cents.

III. 2 Francs. Napoleon III.—Is. 7½d.—36.4 cents.

IV. I Franc. Napoleon III.
9½d.—18.2 cents.

V. 50 Centimes. Napoleon III.
4½d.—9.1 cents.

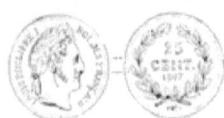

VI. 25 Centimes. Louis Philippe.
2½d.—4½ cents.

VII. 20 Centimes. Napoleon III.
2d. . . .

PLATE IV.

THE SILVER COINS OF FRANCE.

I. 5 FRANCS.—NAPOLEON I. 1812.
WEIGHT, 385.808 Grains Troy—(25 Grammes).
Fineness—900–1000.
Value, 4s. 0½d.—98 cents.

II. 5 FRANCS.—NAPOLEON III. 1856.
WEIGHT, 385.808 Grains Troy—(25 Grammes).
Fineness—900–1000.
Value, 4s. 0½d.—98 cents.

III. 2 FRANCS.—NAPOLEON III. 1853.
WEIGHT, 154.323 Grains Troy—(10 Grammes).
Fineness—900–1000.
Value, 1s. 7¾d.—36.4 cents.

IV. 1 FRANC.—NAPOLEON III. 1860.
WEIGHT, 77.161 Grains Troy—(5 Grammes).
Fineness—900–1000.
Value, 9¾d.—18.2 cents.

V. 50 CENTIMES.—NAPOLEON III. 1858.
WEIGHT, 38.580 Grains Troy—(2.50 Grammes).
Fineness—900–1000.
Value, 4¾d.—9.1 cents.

VI. 25 CENTIMES.—LOUIS PHILIPPE. 1847.
WEIGHT, 19.29 Grains Troy—(1.25 Gramme).
Fineness—900–1000.
Value, 2½d.—4½ cents.

VII. 20 CENTIMES.—NAPOLEON III. 1860.
WEIGHT, 15.432 Grains Troy—(1 Gramme).
Fineness—900–1000.
Value, 2d.

PLATE V.

ENGLISH GOLD COINS.

I. 5 Guineas. George II.—$ 25 50.

II. Guinea. George III.—$ 5 12.

III. 1-2 Guinea. George III.—$ 2 56.

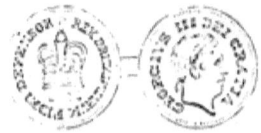

IV. 1-3 Guinea. Geo. III.—$ 1 71.   V. 1-4 Guinea. Geo. III.—$ 1 28.

VI. 2 Guineas. Charles II.—$ 10 25.

PLATE V.

ENGLISH GOLD COINS.

I. FIVE GUINEAS.—GEORGE II 1729.

WEIGHT, 647.191 Grains Troy—(41.937 Grammes).
Fineness—22 Carats—916.66–1000.
Value, £5 5s. 0d.

II. GUINEA.—GEORGE III. 1798.

WEIGHT, 129.4382 Grains Troy—(8.3874 Grammes).
Value, £1 1s. 0d.

III. HALF GUINEA —GEORGE III. 1810.

WEIGHT, 64.7191 Grains Troy —(4.1937 Grammes).
Value, £0 10s. 6d.

IV. 1-3 GUINEA.—GEORGE III. 1810.

WEIGHT, 43.146 Grains Troy—(2.7958 Grammes).
Value, £0 7s. . . .

V. 1-4 GUINEA.—GEORGE III. 1762.

WEIGHT, 32.3595 Grains Troy—(2.0968 Grammes).
Value, £0 5s. 3d.

VI TWO GUINEAS.—CHARLES II. 1684.

WEIGHT, 258.876 Grains Troy—(16.7748 Grammes).
Value, £2 2s. 0d.

PLATE VI.

COINS OF GREAT BRITAIN.

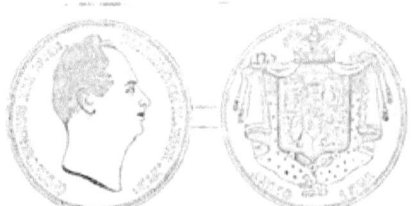

I. Two Sovereigns.—William IV. 1831.—Value, £2 $9 72.

II. Five Sovereigns.—Queen Victoria. 1839.—Value, £5—$24 30.

III. Two Sovereigns. — George IV.—Value, £2—$9 72.

IV. Sovereign.—Victoria. 1861.—Value, £1—$4 86.

V. Half Sovereign.—Victoria. 1850.—Value. 10s.—$2 43.

Engraved for the "Merchants and Bankers' Almanac for 1871."

PLATE VI.
COINS OF GREAT BRITAIN.

I. TWO SOVEREIGNS.— WILLIAM IV. 1831.
WEIGHT, 246.548 Grains Troy—(15.976 Grammes).
Fineness—916.66–1000.
Value, £2.—$9 72.

II. FIVE SOVEREIGNS.—VICTORIA.
WEIGHT, 616.372 Grains Troy—(39.9401 Grammes).
Fineness, 916.66–1000.
Value, £5—$24 10.

III. TWO SOVEREIGNS.—GEORGE IV. 1823.
WEIGHT, 246.548 Grains Troy—(15.976 Grammes).
Fineness, 916.66–1000.
Value, £2—$9 72.

IV. SOVEREIGN.—VICTORIA. 1861.
WEIGHT, 123.274 Grains Troy--(7.988 Grammes).
Fineness—916.66–1000.
Value, £1—$4 86.

V. HALF SOVEREIGN.—VICTORIA.
WEIGHT, 61.6372 Grains Troy—(3.994 Grammes).
Fineness—916.66–1000.
Value, 10s.—$2 43.

PLATE VII.

SILVER COINS OF GREAT BRITAIN.

I. Four Pence.—Victoria. 1848.

II. Three Pence.—Victoria. 1861.

III. Crown.—Victoria. 1857. 5s.

IV. Two Pence.—George III. 1818.

V. Three Half-Pence.—Victoria. 1845.

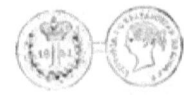

VI. Penny.—Victoria. 1851.

Engraved for the " Merchants and Bankers' Almanac for 1871."

PLATE VII.

COINS OF GREAT BRITAIN.

I. FOUR PENCE.—VICTORIA.

WEIGHT, 29.0969 Grains Troy—(1.88505 Gramme).
Fineness—925–1000.

II. THREE PENCE.—VICTORIA.

WEIGHT, 21.8181 Grains Troy—(1.4138 Gramme).
Fineness—925–1000.

III. CROWN.—VICTORIA. 1857.

WEIGHT, 436.3636 Grains Troy—(28.276 Grammes).
Fineness—925–1000.
Value, 5s.

IV. TWO PENCE.—GEO. III. 1818.

WEIGHT, 14.545 Grains Troy—(6.9425 Gramme).
Fineness—925–1000.

V. THREE HALF-PENCE.—VICTORIA. 1845.

So called MAUNDY MONEY.

WEIGHT, 10.909 Grains Troy—(0.707 Gramme).

VI. PENNY MAUNDY MONEY.—VICTORIA. 1851.

WEIGHT, 7.2725 Grains Troy—(0.47125 Gramme).

Engraved for the " Merchants and Bankers' Almanac for 1871."

PLATE VIII.

SILVER COINS OF GREAT BRITAIN.

I. Half-Crown.—Victoria. 1845.
Value, 2s. 6d.

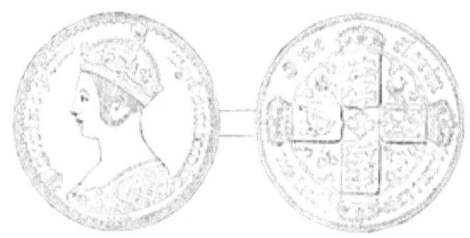

II. Florin.—Victoria. 1852.
Value, 2s.

III. Shilling.—Victoria. 1856.
Value, 1s.

IV. Sixpence.—Victoria. 1859.
Value, 6d.

Engraved for the "Merchants' and Bankers' Almanac for 1871."

PLATE VIII.

SILVER COINS OF GREAT BRITAIN.

I. HALF-CROWN.—VICTORIA. 1845.

WEIGHT, 218.1818 Grains Troy—(14.138 Grammes).

Fineness—925–1000.

Value, 2s. 6d.

———

II. FLORIN.—VICTORIA. 1852.

WEIGHT, 174.5454 Grains Troy—(11.3163 Grammes).

Fineness—925–1000.

Value, 2s.

———

III. SHILLING.—VICTORIA. 1856.

WEIGHT, 87.2727 Grains Troy—(5.655 Grammes).

Fineness—925–1000.

Value, 1s.

———

IV. SIXPENCE.—VICTORIA. 1859.

WEIGHT, 43.6363 Grains Troy—(2.828 Grammes .)

Fineness—925–1000.

Value, 6d.

PLATE IX.

ix

MEXICAN GOLD COINS.

1. Doblon or Doubloon.—Value $ 15 53.

II. 1-4 Doubloon.—$ 3 88.

III. 1-8th Doubloon.—$ 1 94.

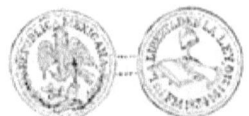

IV. 1-16th Doubloon.—97 cents.

V. 1-2 Doubloon.—$ 7 76.

Engraved for the " Merchants and Bankers' Almanac for 1871."

PLATE IX.

MEXICAN GOLD COINS.

I. DOBLOON or DOUBLOON —Onza De Oro. 1850

Weight, 417.707 Grains Troy—(27.067 Grammes).

Fineness, 875-1000.

Value, £3 4s. 8¼d.—$15 53 to $15 61.

—

II. QUARTER DOBLON.—1-4 Onza de Oro of 2 Escudos.
Year 1825.

Weight, 104.430 Grains Troy—(6.767 Grammes).

Value, £0 16s. 2d.—$3 88 to $3 90.

III. EIGHTH DOBLON.—1-8 Onza de Oro
or Escudo of two Pesos. 1850.

Weight, 52.207 Grains Troy—(3.382 Grammes).

Value, £0 8s. 1d.—$1 94 to $1 95.

IV. ONE-SIXTEENTH ONZA DE ORO. 1834.

Weight, 26.111 Grains Troy—(1.692 Gramme).

Value, £0 4s. 0½d. — 97 to 98 cts.

V. HALF DOBLON.—1-2 Onza de Oro of 4 Escudos.

Weight, 208.845 Grains Troy—(13.533 Grammes).

Fineness, 875-1000.

Value, £1 12s. 4¼d.—$7 76 to $7 80.

PLATE X.

THE COINS OF MEXICO.

I. 4 Reales de Plata—Half-Dollar. 1842.—Value, £0 2s. 2¼d.

II. Piaster of 8 Reales. 1856.—Value, £0 4s. 4½d.

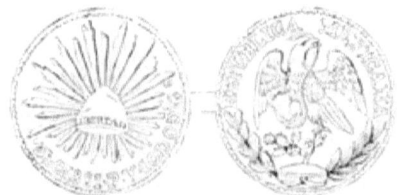

III. 2 Reales de Plata—¼ Dollar. 1861.—Value, £0 1s. 1½d.

IV. Real de Plata—⅛ Dollar. 1832.—Value, 6½d.

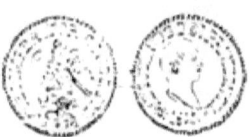

V. ½ Real de Plata.—Augustin. 1822.—Value, 3¼d.

Engraved for the "Merchants and Bankers' Almanac for 1871."

PLATE X.

THE SILVER COINS OF MEXICO.

I. 4 REALES DE PLATA—1-2 Dollar. 1842.

WEIGHT, 208.845 Grains Troy—(13.533 Grammes).

Fineness—902.778–1000.

Value, £0 2s. 2¼d.—53 cts.

———

II. PESO, or PIASTER of 8 REALES DE PLATA. 1856.

WEIGHT, 417.707 Grains Troy—(27.067 Grammes).

Fineness—902.778–1000.

Value, £0 4s. 4¾d.—$1 06.

———

III. 2 REALES DE PLATA—1-4 Dollar. 1861.

WEIGHT, 104.430 Grains Troy—(6.767 Grammes).

Fineness—902.778–1000.

Value, £0 1s. 1¼d.—$0 26 cts.

———

IV. REAL DE PLATA—1-8 Dollar. 1832.

WEIGHT, 52.207 Grains Troy—(3.383 Grammes).

Fineness—902.778–1000.

Value, 6½d.—13 cts.

———

V. 1-2 REAL DE PLATA.—AUGUSTIN. 1822.

WEIGHT, 26.111 Grains Troy—(1.692 Gramme).

Fineness—902.778–1000.

Value, 3¼d.—6½ cts.

Engraved for the " Merchants and Bankers' Almanac for 1874."

PLATE XI.

xi

THE GOLD COINS OF PRUSSIA.

I.   Krone (Crown).—Friedrich Wm. IV.   1859.—Value. £1 7s. 3¾d.

II.   2 Friedrichs d'or.—Friedrich Wm. IV.   1848.—Value. £1 12s. 11½d.

III.   Friedrichs d'or.—Friedrich Wilhelm III.   1831.—Value, £0 16s. 5¾d.

IV.   1-2 Krone.—Friedrich Wm. IV.   1858.   Value. £0 13s. 7¾d.

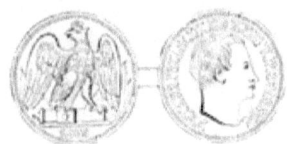

V.   1-2 Friedrichs d'or.—Friedrich Wm. III.   1839.—Value. £0 8s. 2¾d.

Engraved for the "Merchants and Bankers' Almanac for 1871."

PLATE XI.
GOLD COINS OF PRUSSIA.

I. KRONE (CROWN) OF FRIEDRICH WILHELM IV. 1859
WEIGHT, 171.467 Grains Troy—(11.111 Grammes.)
Fineness—900-1000.
Value, £1 7s. 3¾d.

———

II. 2 FRIEDRICHS D'OR.—FRIEDRICH WILHELM IV 1848.
WEIGHT, 206.221 Grains Troy—(13.363 Grammes).
Fineness—902.778-1000.
Value, £1 12s. 11½d.

———

III. FRIEDRICHS D'OR.—FRIEDRICH WILHELM III. 1831.
WEIGHT, 103.110 Grains Troy—(6.682 Grammes).
Fineness—902.778-1000.
Value, £0 16s. 5¾d.

———

IV. 1-2 KRONE. OF FRIEDRICH WILHELM IV 1858.
WEIGHT, 85.733 Grains Troy—(5.556 Grammes).
Fineness—900-1000.
Value, £0 13s. 7¼d.

———

V. 1-2 FRIEDRICHS D'OR.—FRIEDRICH WILHELM III 1839
WEIGHT, 51.55 Grains Troy—(3.341 Grammes).
Fineness—902.778-1000.
Value, £0 8s. 2¾d.

Engraved for the "Merchants and Bankers' Almanac for 1871."

PLATE XII.

THE COINS OF PRUSSIA.

I. Vereins-Thaler of Wilhelm. 1859.—Value, £0 2s. 11½d.

II. Two Vereins-Thaler of Wilhelm. 1861.—Value, £0 6s.

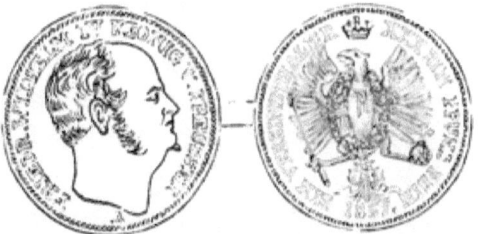

III. Vereins-Thaler of Friedrich Wilhelm IV. 1857.—Value, £0 2s. 11½d.

IV. 1-6 Thaler.—Value, 6d.

V. 2½ Silbergroschen.—Value, 2½d.

VI. Silbergroschen.—Value, 1d.

VII. Half Silbergroschen.—½d.

PLATE XII.

SILVER COINS OF PRUSSIA.

I. VEREINS-THALER OF WILHELM. 1859.

WEIGHT, 285.784 Grains Troy—(18.5185 Grammes).
Fineness—900–1000.
Value, £0 2s. 11¾d.

II. 2 VEREINS-THALER OF WILHELM. 1861.

WEIGHT, 571.568 Grains Troy—(37.0370 Grammes).
Fineness—900–1000.
Value, £0 6s. 0d.

III. VEREINS-THALER OF FRIEDRICH WILHELM IV. 1857.

WEIGHT, 285.784 Grains Troy—(18.5185 Grammes).
Fineness—900–1000.
Value, £0 2s. 11¾d.

IV. 1-6TH THALER OF WILHELM. 1862.

WEIGHT, 82.438 Grains Troy—(5.342 Grammes).
Fineness—520–1000.
Value, £0 0s. 6d.

V. 2 1-2 SILBERGROSCHEN—WILHELM. 1862.

WEIGHT, 49.708 Grains Troy—(3.221 Grammes).
Fineness—375–1000.
Value, £0 0s. 2¾d.

VI. 1 SILBERGROSCHEN.—WILHELM. 1861.

WEIGHT, 33.873 Grains Troy—(2.195 Grammes).
Fineness—220–1000.
Value, £0 0s. 1d.

VII. 1-2 SILBERGROSCHEN OF FRIEDRICH WILHELM IV. 1856.

WEIGHT, 16.913 Grains Troy—(1.096 Gramme).
Fineness—222.222–1000.
Value, £0 0s. ½d.

Engraved for the " Merchants and Bankers' Almanac for 1871."

PLATE XIII.

xiii

THE COINS OF RUSSIA.

I. 1-2 Imperial—5 Rubles Gold.

There is only one other Russian gold coin, the Ducat.

Value, £ 0 16s. 4½d.

PLATINA COINS.

II. Six Rubles—Platina.

Value, £ 0 19s. 4½d.

III. Ducat of Platina.

Value, £ 0 9s. 8¼d.

Engraved for the "Merchants and Bankers' Almanac for 1871"

PLATE XIII.
THE COINS OF RUSSIA.

I. HALF-IMPERIAL—5 RUBLES. 1860.

WEIGHT, 101 Grains Troy—(6.544 Grammes).

Fineness—Standard—916.667–1000.

Value, £ 0 16s. 4⅜d.

II. 6 RUBLES, or DOUBLE PLATINA DUCAT. 1838.

WEIGHT, 319.551 Grains Troy--(20.7066 Grammes).

Fineness—without alloy.

Value, about £ 0 19s. 4½d.

III. 3 RUBLES, or PLATINA DUCAT 1842.

WEIGHT, 159.775 Grains Troy—(10.3533 Grammes).

Fineness—no alloy.

Value, about £ 0 9s. 8¼d.

Engraved for the " Merchants and Bankers' Almanac for 1871

PLATE XIV.

THE COINS OF RUSSIA.

I. Ruble of 1849.—Value, £0 3s. 2¾d.

II. Poltina, or 50 Copecks.—Value. £0 1s. 7½d.

III. 25 Copecks. 1860.— Value, £0 0s. 9¾d.

IV. 20 Copecks. 1860.—Value, 7½d.   V. 15 Copecks.—Value, 5½d.

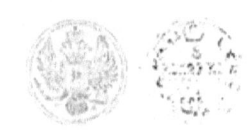

VI. 10 Copecks.—Value. 3½d.   VII. 5 Copecks. 1849.—Value. 2d

Engraved for the "Merchants and Bankers' Almanac for 1871."

PLATE XIV.

THE COINS OF RUSSIA.

I. RUBLE OF 1849
WEIGHT, 319.928 Grains Troy—(20.731 Grammes).
Fineness—868.056-1000.
Value, £0 3s. 2⅝d.

II. POLTINA, or 50 COPECKS 1859.
WEIGHT, 159.972 Grains Troy—(10.366 Grammes).
Fineness—868.056-1000.
Value. £0 1s. 7½d.

III. 25 COPECKS. 1860.
WEIGHT, 79.986 Grains Troy—(5.183 Grammes).
Fineness—same.
Value, £0 0s. 9¾d.

IV. 20 COPECKS. 1860.
WEIGHT, 63.983 Grains Troy—(4.146 Grammes).
Fineness—same.
Value, £0 0s. 7¾d.

V. 15 COPECKS. 1860.
WEIGHT, 48 Grains Troy—(3.110 Grammes).
Fineness—same.
Value, £0 0s. 5⅝d.

VI. GRIWNA, or 10 COPECKS. 1861.
WEIGHT, 31.992 Grains Troy—(2.073 Grammes).
Fineness—same.
Value, £0 0s. 3½d.

VII. 5 COPECKS. 1849.
WEIGHT, 15.991 Grains Troy—(1.036 Gramme).
Fineness—same.
Value, £0 0s. 2d.

Engraved for the " Merchants' and Bankers' Almanac for 1871."

PLATE XV.   XV

THE GOLD COINS OF SPAIN.

I. Half-Onza d'Oro—4 Escudos or 8 Piasters.—Value, £1 12s. 4½d.

II. Onza de Oro—Doubloon. Carolus IV. 1794.—Value, £3 4s. 8½d.

III. 1-4 Onza de Oro.—Carolus IV. 1801.—Value, £0 16s. 2d.

 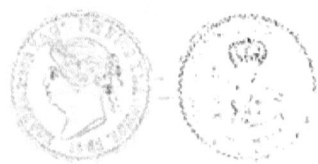

IV. 1-8 Onza de Oro—Escudo.   V. Four Piasters.—Isabella II. 1861.
Carolus III. 1788. £0 8s. 1d.   Value, £0 16s. 6d.

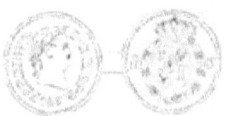

VI. 1-2 Escudo or Piaster.—Ferdinand VII. 1817.—Value, £0 4s. ½d.

Engraved for the "Merchants and Bankers' Almanac for 1871."

PLATE XV.

THE GOLD COINS OF SPAIN.

I. 1-2 ONZA D'ORO—4 ESCUDOS OR 8 PIASTERS.
CAROLUS III. 1787.

Weight, 208.845 Grains Troy—(13.533 Grammes).

Fineness—875-1000.

Value, £ 1 12s. 4½d.

II. ONZA DE ORO, OR CUADRUPLO (DOUBLOON) OF
CAROLUS IV. 1794.

Weight, 417.707 Grains Troy—(27.067 Grammes).

Fineness—875-1000.

Value, £ 3 4s. 8¼d.

III. 1-4 ONZA DE ORO OF CAROLUS IV. 1801.

Weight, 104.430 Grains Troy—(6.767 Grammes).

Fineness—875-1000.

Value, £ 0 16s. 2d.

IV. 1-8 ONZA DE ORO, or ESCUDO,—CAROLUS III. 1788.

Weight, 52.207 Grains Troy—(3.383 Grammes).

Fineness—875-1000.

Value, £ 0 8s. 1d.

V FOUR PIASTERS.—ISABELLA II. 1861.

Issued for the Philippine Islands.

Weight, 103.535 Grains Troy—(6.709 Grammes).

Fineness—900-1000.

Value, £ 0 16s. 6d.

VI 1-2 ESCUDO, or PIASTER OF FERDINAND VII. 1817.

Weight, 26.111 Grains Troy—(1.692 Gramme).

Fineness—875-1000.

Value, £ 0 4s. 0½d.

Engraved for the " Merchants and Bankers' Almanac for 1871."

THE GOLD COINS OF SPAIN.

I.　100 Reales.—Doblon.—Isabella II. 1860.—Value, £ 1 0s. 7¼d.

II.　1-2 Onza de Oro—160 Reales.—Ferdinand VII. 1822.—£ 1 12s. 4½d.

III. 80 Reales.—Isabella II. 1835.— Value, £ 0 16s. 2d.

IV.　40 Reales.—Isabella II. 1861.—Value, £ 0 8s. 3d.

V.　2 Piasters.—Isabella II.　1861.—Value, £ 0 8s. 3d.

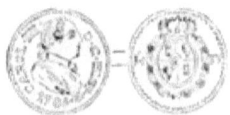

VI. Piaster.—Carolus III.　1786.— Value, £ 0 4s. 0½d.

Engraved for the "Merchants and Bankers' Almanac for 1871."

PLATE XVI.

THE GOLD COINS OF SPAIN.

I. 100 REALES—DOBLON or CENTEN. ISABELLA II. 1860.
WEIGHT, 129.430 Grains Troy—(8.387 Grammes).
Fineness—900–1000.
Value, £1 0s. 7½d.

II. 1-2 ONZA DE ORO (160 REALES).—FERDINAND VII. 1822.
WEIGHT, 208.845 Grains Troy—(13.533 Grammes).
Fineness—875–1000.
Value, £1 12s. 4⅛d.

III. 80 REALES.—ISABELLA II. 1835.
WEIGHT, 104.430 Grains Troy—(6.767 Grammes).
Fineness—875–1000.
Value, £0 16s. 2d.

IV. 40 REALES—ISABELLA II. 1861
WEIGHT, 51.76 Grains Troy—(3.354 Grammes).
Fineness—900–1000.
Value, £0 8s. 3d.

V. 2 PIASTERS.—ISABELLA II. 1861.
Issued for the Philippine Islands.
WEIGHT, 51.76 Grains Troy—(3.354 Grammes).
Fineness—900–1000.
Value, £0 8s. 3d.

VI. PIASTER.—CAROLUS III. 1786.
WEIGHT, 26.111 Grains Troy—(1.692 Gramme).
Fineness—875–1000.
Value, £0 4s. 0½d.

Engraved for the " Merchants and Bankers' Almanac for 1871."

PLATE XVII.

NEW COINS OF THE WORLD.

GREAT BRITAIN.
I. The Sovereign—1872.

Weight, .256.6.   Fineness, 916.5.   Value, $4.86.

II. The St. George Sovereign.

Weight, .256.6.   Fineness, 916.5.   Value, $4.86.

III. CANADA.   Fifty Cents.

Weight, .375.   Fineness, 925.   Value, $0.47.2.

SWEDEN.   Four Riksdaler.

or Specie Daler of Sweden.
Weight, 1.092.   Fineness. 750.   Value, $1.11.5.

PLATE XVIII.

NEW COINS OF THE WORLD.

GERMAN EMPIRE.

I. Ten Marks. William, Kaiser. Gold, 1871.

Weight, .128. Fineness, 900. Value, $2.38.

II. Twenty Marks. William. Gold. 1872.

Weight. .256. Fineness, 900. Value, $4.76.

WURTEMBERG. Double Thaler of Karl, Koenig.* Silver, 1869.

Weight, 1.190. Fineness, 900. Value, $1.46.

MEXICO. Peso (or Dollar) of the Republic, Silver. 1869.

Weight, .867.5. Fineness, 903. Value, $1.06.5.

* This Kingdom and others having been lately absorbed into the Empire of Germany, their distinctive coinage has ceased. This piece is inserted for its rare beauty, and as a memento of the past condition of these States.

PLATE XIX.

NEW COINS OF THE WORLD.

FRANCE.
I. Two Francs of the Republic, Silver, 1872.

Weight, .320.   Fineness, 835.   Value, $0.36.4.

II. Five Francs of the Republic, Silver, 1871.

Weight, .800.   Fineness, 900.   Value, $0.98.

III. Franc of the Republic, Silver, 1872.

Weight, .160.   Fineness, 835.   Value, $0.18.2.

IV. Half Franc, Silver, 1871.

Weight, .80.   Fineness, 835.   Value, $0.9.1.

PLATE XX.

NEW COINS OF THE WORLD.

AUSTRIA.
Four Ducats of Austria. Francis Joseph. Gold, 1871.

Weight, .448. Fineness, 986. Value, $9.13.

II. Union-Thaler of Austria. Francis Joseph. Silver, 1871.

Weight, .596. Fineness, 900. Value, $0.73.

III. Florin of Austria (Hungary). Silver, 1869.

Weight, .397. Fineness, 900. Value, $0.48.5.

RUSSIA. Twenty Copecks. Silver, 1870.

Weight, .11.2. Fineness, 875. Value, $0.13.3.

PLATE XXI.

NEW COINS OF THE WORLD.

SPAIN.
I. Five Pesetas of Amadeo I. Silver, 1871.

Weight, .800. Fineness, 900. Value, $0.98.

II. Five Pesetas of the Republic of Spain.

Weight, .800. Fineness, 900. Value, $0.98.

PORTUGAL.
I. Gold Coröa or 5000 Reis, 1871.

Weight, .308. Fineness, 912. Value, $5.80.5.

II. 500 Reis of Portugal. Silver, 1871.

Weight, .400. Fineness, 912. Value, $0.49.6.

PLATE XXII.

NEW COINS OF THE WORLD.

KINGDOM OF ITALY. Five Lire. Victor Emmanuel. Silver, 1869.

Weight, .800. Fineness, 900. $0.98.

Two Lire of Pope Pius IX, Silver, 1869.

Weight, .320. Fineness, 835. Value, $0.36.4.

(The Papal Coinage ceased in the year 1869.)

DENMARK. Two Rigsdaler of Christian IX, Silver, 1868.

Weight, .927. Fineness, 877. Value, $1.10.7.

NETHERLANDS. Two and a half Guilders. William III. Silver, 1869.

Weight, .804. Fineness, 944. Value, $1.03.

PLATE XXIV.

NEW COINS OF THE WORLD.

V. Five Sen, 1872.

Weight, 40.2.   Fineness, 800.   Value. $0.05.

JAPAN.   GOLD COINS.
I. Twenty Yen.

Weight, 1.072.   Fineness, 900.   Value. $19.94.

II. Five Yen, 1872.

Weight, 268.   Fineness, 900.   Value. $4.98½.

III. Two Yen. 1872.

Weight, 107.   Fineness, 900.   Value. $1.99.4.

IV. One Yen. 1872.

Weight. 53.5.   Fineness. 900.   Value. $0.99.5.

www.ingramcontent.com/pod-product-compliance
Lightning Source LLC
Chambersburg PA
CBHW030110030726

47498CB00007B/2319